RURAL POVERTY
AND THE
URBAN CRISIS

*A Strategy
for Regional
Development*

Rural Poverty

and the Urban Crisis

A Strategy for
Regional Development

NILES M. HANSEN

INDIANA UNIVERSITY PRESS

Bloomington / London

SECOND PRINTING 1971

Published in Canada by Fitzhenry & Whiteside Limited, Don Mills, Ontario

Library of Congress catalog card number: 72–108207

ISBN: 253–19002–0

Manufactured in the United States of America

To Jo

ACKNOWLEDGMENT

This report was prepared for the Manpower Administration, U.S. Department of Labor, under research contract (Project Number 81–19–68–17) authorized by the Manpower Development and Training Act. Since contractors performing research under Government sponsorship are encouraged to express their own judgment freely, the report does not necessarily represent the Department's official opinion or policy. Moreover, the contractor is solely responsible for the factual accuracy of all material developed in the report.

Contents

vii

Contents

List of Tables

List of Figures

Preface

This volume is the result of a proposal made in the fall of 1967 to the Office of Manpower Policy, Evaluation, and Research of the Department of Labor for a study of federal aid programs for Appalachian development and of alternative programs that might be undertaken to help the people of the region. In response, it was suggested that a more general critical study be made of regional development programs in the United States, since regional and urban problems and programs had never been integrated into a comprehensive and coherent frame of reference for public policy purposes. The author had recently completed a study, since published, of French regional planning which developed a policy model for dealing with opportunity costs in terms of both different types of investment and different categories of regions. That model, which is outlined in Chapter 1, is implicit throughout the present study. However, in contrast to dealing with the French situation, which is based on integrated regional planning for the entire nation, any approach to American problems related to spatial resource allocation had to begin by confronting a bifurcated and un-coordinated group of policies and institutions.

In a work of this scope the author has necessarily drawn on the published studies of numerous other persons, though extensive use has been made of unpublished materials and the author's own investigations. Also, if some of the many evaluations and suggestions set forth here are similar to those of other writers, the author has sought, with the aim of furthering rational resource allocation, to supply the comprehensiveness and consistency whose lack occasioned the request for this study. It is hoped that students, scholars, and policy makers will be able to make positive use of the proposals that are developed, and that they will be prompted to improve on any deficiencies.

Part of Chapter 6 appeared in *The Quarterly Review of Economics and Business,* VIII (Summer, 1968). A portion of chapter 9 was published in *The Journal of Human Resources,* IV (Spring, 1969). Parts of Chapter 10 appeared in *Labor Law Journal,* XX (August, 1969) and the *Papers and Proceedings of the Southeastern Regional Science Association.* Chapters 8 and 11 were published in abridged form in the *Economic and Business Bulletin,* XXII (Fall, 1969) and XX (Winter, 1970), respectively.

Final preparation of this study was aided in part by a grant from the Office of Economic Research, Economic Development Administration, under Project Number 99-7-00142. The author is indebted to numerous persons for their assistance during the preparation of this study. Organizational affiliations pertain to the period when assistance was obtained and are given only for purposes of identification. The following individuals in the Department of Labor were particularly helpful: Paul Corbin, Louis Earl, Joe Epstein, Anna-Stina Ericson, Al Fortune, Audrey Freedman, Harold Goldstein, Gregory Gross, William Haltigan, and Howard Rosen. Valuable help was received from many persons in the Economic Development Administration, including John Cosgrove, J. D. DeForest, Gerald Duskin, Tom Herrick, John Kaler, Margaret Olsen, Ray Tanner, Mary Toborg, and John White. Thanks are also due to Joe Gothier, George Hubley, Jr., and Walter Knodel, of the Bureau of Indian Affairs in Washington, to B. I. A. officials Howard Mackey, Roswell, N.M. and Joe Baker, Shiprock, N.M., and to

Rod Starkey, Project Director of the Roswell Employment Training Center. Within the Department of Agriculture the author is indebted to Fred Grover and Robert Raisch, and within the Office of Business Economics, to Lowell Ashby and David Hirschberg. Other individuals who made significant contributions are Joe Otero, Four Corners Regional Commission; David North, Interagency Committee on Mexican American Affairs; François Poulin, Conseil d'Orientation Economique du Québec; Peter M. Stern, Tennessee Valley Authority; Harold Townsend, Texas Employment Commission; Kenneth DeMott, Ling-Temco-Vought, Grand Prairie, Texas; Sidney Sonnenblum, National Planning Association; Robert T. Miki, U.S. Department of Commerce; Sidney Jeffers, Ozarks Regional Commission; Harold C. Jordahl, Jr., Upper Great Lakes Regional Commission; Richard E. Wright, New England Regional Commission; F. L. Parnell, Coastal Plains Regional Commission; Eli March and Ralph Widner, Appalachian Regional Commission; Freeman Hudson, New England Regional Commission; and Harold Rosenthal, Office of Economic Opportunity. My academic colleagues Vernon Briggs, James Brown, William Gunther, Walter Graham, Benjamin Higgins, Edgar Hoover, Sar Levitan, Ray Marshall, Kenneth McClennan, and David Ruesink were particularly helpful. Finally, I would like to express my appreciation for the fine editorial assistance rendered by Mrs. Mary B. Price and for the very able secretarial work of Carole Gibson, Candy Profitt, and Jackie Wallace.

N.M.H.

RURAL POVERTY
AND THE
URBAN CRISIS

*A Strategy
for Regional
Development*

Chapter **1**

A Preliminary Overview

Increasing urbanization and revolutionary changes in agricultural technology have made it difficult to close the gap between the poverty of lagging rural areas such as Appalachia and the South and the more economically advanced parts of the country. Moreover, the evidence from American and foreign experience shows that attempts to force-feed the growth of large lagging areas are too often not only inefficient but also ineffective. The funds available to development agencies are simply not sufficient to overcome the relative disadvantages of most poor areas.

In contrast, greater investment in human resources and expanded manpower programs—including relocation programs with comprehensive supporting services—in lagging regions would be reasonable on a national scale. The human resource development needs of the people of Appalachia and the South, of Mexican American migrants and Indians, are great, while the facilities to meet their needs are relatively meager. Obviously there are personal and social problems involved in migration from lagging regions to urban areas, but there is a great deal of evidence indicating that workers are more willing to migrate than is commonly assumed, at least if they are given skills that are in demand in receiving areas and adequate sup-

3

porting services—counseling for the worker and his family before and after moving, aid in finding housing, and financial assistance during the transition period. The attachment of poor people to their native soil has been overemphasized by many conservatives and by many liberals, for reasons ranging from the cynical to the romantic. While the values and traditions of our regional subcultures are worthy of respect, the glaring underinvestment in the human resources of many of them too often means that attachment to the area really only reflects a lack of choice.

The degree of influence that governments exercise on aggregate economic activity has become so great since the 1930's that fears of another deep and lengthy depression have all but ceased to exist. Though macroeconomics still faces important problems, particularly those pertaining to inflation, the relative success of this branch of economics has led to increased interest in problems of a structural nature. Economists who take the structural approach argue that the fundamental reason for the persistence of unemployment must be sought primarily in a mismatch of labor demand and supply. They emphasize the importance of education and training programs, better job vacancy information, area redevelopment, and relocation of workers. Their perspective contrasts with that of economists who emphasize the manipulation of effective demand by means of monetary and fiscal policies.

The present volume is essentially structuralist in nature, but this by no means implies any quarrel with the aggregative explanation for problems of unemployment and underemployment. The employment situation in local areas is influenced by general economic conditions, and the degree of success of structuralist policies is directly related to the degree of effectiveness of macroeconomic policy. On the other hand, few economists associated with the aggregative approach would deny that there are structural problems. After all, it was Walter Heller who, as Chairman of the Council of Economic Advisers, urged that "More intensive measures to attack structural unemployment are necessary to reduce the unemployment rate not merely to 4 per cent, but beyond."[1] In general, then, it is commonly agreed that the problems which are the principal concern of this study are important; at the same time, it is assumed here that the success of the policy implications which follow from the present analysis requires aggregative policies aimed at the maintenance of full employment.

Despite the high degree of interest that government officials, economists, and other social scientists have shown in recent years in both manpower problems and problems of rural to urban transition, there has not been any real attempt to integrate these concerns into a comprehensive and coherent framework of analysis, grounded on the notion of the opportunity costs of alternative programs. (To the economist, the cost of any decision is the value of the best foregone alternative, or opportunity. This approach compels the decision maker to make not only a "good" choice, but the best choice.) There is widespread and growing recognition that problems of metropolitan ghettos are linked to migration from poor rural areas, and that the future of our lagging areas is dependent on the feasibility of developing their employment base.

Over a decade ago, John Friedmann wrote that "Two different professions, two different vocabularies have grown up. Communication between them has become exceedingly difficult and on the level of practical action there appears to be little coordination between schemes of regional and urban development."[2] Unfortunately, there is still too great a tendency for urban and regional specialists to work independently of one another. Students of urban problems tend to concentrate on relations between central cities and suburbs and on the many difficulties that arise as a consequence of urban congestion, while frequently ignoring the areas which are the source of migrants who are ill-prepared for the social and economic demands of the city. On the other hand, students of lagging regions tend to concentrate on ways and means to promote economic development in their areas of concern, while too often ignoring the forces of urbanization that are making many small towns and rural areas relatively unattractive to industry, or at least to those branches that are rapidly growing and paying average or better wages in relation to national patterns. Furthermore, both groups neglect the inter-mediate areas which are neither lagging nor parts of large urban agglomerations.

Too many proposals for treating the ills of large metropolitan areas concentrate on central city solutions. Measures such as more welfare, urban renewal and public housing, and inducements to at-tract industry to the ghettos fall into this category. However, policies which assume the continuance of the ghetto, no matter how refur-bished, are not likely to resolve the basic difficulties of the cities. Since new industrial jobs continue to be located primarily in the suburbs, it is essential that ghetto residents be given greater access to them. This implies the dispersal of the ghetto. In the short run, better transportation facilities will be needed to link central city populations to suburban jobs; transportation subsidies should also be given to ghetto residents. Longer-run solutions will have to con-centrate on better housing opportunities—especially for Negroes—in the suburbs, and on more and better education and training pro-grams for the poor. Before any of these largely curative measures will be successful, however, it will be necessary to reduce the pres-sures that are represented by continuing inmigration of unskilled persons from lagging regions.

The need to provide an urban alternative to residents of lagging rural areas, and the need to reduce inmigration into our large metro-politan areas implies an urban growth center strategy based on intermediate-sized cities that already have given some evidence of growth. As will be seen, the Economic Development Administration and other regional development agencies believe that they have feasible growth-center strategies. It will be argued that these strategies are too often bootstrap operations for rural areas and small towns, and that they probably will have no more success than other efforts to force-feed the growth of depressed rural areas. A relatively large number of towns and small cities have been desig-nated as centers with a potential for growth that can positively affect the economic development of the centers themselves and their rural hinterlands. However, because of the limitations imposed by relevant legislation and because of a desire to please a large number of localities, it is difficult to concentrate development funds in a relatively few focal areas with genuine growth potential. If these centers are outside of lagging areas it has been all but impossible to give them development subsidies, on the ground that rapidly growing cities outside of lagging areas have no "need" for subsidies. In the strict sense this is true. However, an essential feature of regional policy should be to link the problems of lagging areas to opportunities in rapidly growing cities with tight labor markets. This could be done by using public policy measures to accelerate the development of growth centers on the condition that the centers employ a significant number of unemployed or underemployed persons from lagging areas (as well as from within the centers in the cases—by no means rare—where high rates of growth are accompanied by high or increasing rates of unemployment).

Evidence will be examined which indicates that a growth-center policy based on the accelerated growth of intermediate-sized cities is not only efficient from an economic point of view, but also in harmony with public locational preference patterns. Such cities offer external economies[3] attractive to private investment but they have not yet reached the point where marginal external diseconomies of congestion threaten to exceed marginal external economies of agglomeration. Some students of urban economies implicitly deny the need for a growth-center strategy based on intermediate-sized cities by arguing that it is impossible to demonstrate that any city is "too big" in the sense that marginal external diseconomies have outstripped the concomitant economies. Such arguments, however, are generally based on considerations of private costs and benefits. It is probably true that an examination of the external effects that are internalized by private firms would provide scant ammunition for detractors of the big city. The difficulty with these arguments, however, is that while private firms do internalize most of the external economies, they do not internalize many of the external diseconomies, or at least not an amount sufficient to halt the growth of large metropolitan areas once the marginal net social product would be greater in an alternative location. Traffic snarls, air pollution, crowded ghettos, lack of green space and recreational areas, and other manifestations of external diseconomies do have a real impact on the residents of congested cities, even if they are by no means fully reflected in the balance sheets of private firms. Since there is no automatic mechanism to choke off the growth of large cities once they become too big in terms of the social costs and benefits of continuing expansion, public policy might limit such expansion, either by direct measures (building permits, tax and credit disincentives, etc.), or by policy measures that shift the expansion of economic activity to alternative locations. It should be emphasized that to argue against the growth of large metropolitan agglomerations is not to argue for a policy of rural industrialization, because there are generally more efficient alternatives in intermediate areas.

The themes that have been briefly stated here are summarized in Table 1, which outlines the nature of public and private investment activity in three different types of regions over three different time

TABLE 1: INVESTMENT POLICY PROPOSALS BY TYPE OF REGION
AND BY TIME PERIOD

Phase	Type of region	Nature of public and private investment activity
I.	Congested	Overexpanded public and private investment
	Intermediate	Deficient EOC
	Lagging	Deficient SOC
II.	Congested	Public policy measures to discourage further expansion
	Intermediate	Excess EOC capacity to induce private investment
	Lagging	Emphasis on expanded SOC investment
III.	Congested	Public policy measures to discourage further expansion
	Intermediate	EOC and private investment approach optimal levels
	Lagging	Continuing emphasis on SOC investment, with increased EOC and private investment

periods.[4] Congested regions are urban areas where marginal social costs of further expansion have risen in relation to marginal social benefits to a point where the marginal net social product would be greater in an alternative location. Intermediate regions, on the other hand, are those which offer significant advantages to private firms and where expanded economic activity would result in a marginal social product to cost ratio greater than that obtained in congested regions. Lagging regions present few attributes which would tend to attract new economic activity. They generally are areas characterized by small-scale agriculture or stagnant or declining industries.

Public investment is divided into two categories, economic overhead capital (EOC) and social overhead capital (SOC). The former is primarily oriented toward supporting private investment or toward the movement of economic resources. SOC projects, on the other hand, may be regarded as equivalent to investment in human resources, including programs to encourage more rational labor mobility.

Phase 1 (Table 1) indicates the situation in the absence of regional policy measures. Because private (firm) costs do not fully reflect social costs, public and private investment are overconcentrated in congested regions. A greater proportion of EOC should be flowing to intermediate regions where it can provide external economies attractive to private investment. At the same time, lagging regions are characterized by a relatively pronounced lack of SOC. In phase II regional policy measures are introduced to increase EOC investment in intermediate areas (particularly in cities with high growth potential, e.g., growth centers) and to expand SOC projects in lagging areas. The growth of congested regions is discouraged by directing public investment flows elsewhere, if not by more direct means such as tax and credit devices or land use controls. In phase III, as intermediate regions become more concentrated, the focus of public policy shifts to the balanced growth of lagging regions, or at least to those whose populations have been prepared for development opportunities by the SOC investment of phase II.

Throughout phases II and III, though especially in the former, rational migration should be encouraged (or at least not discouraged) from lagging to intermediate regions.

It should be emphasized that these proposals are not intended to exclude other policy measures. Intermediate regions, for example, will certainly need SOC investment, and lagging regions will need EOC investment. I have merely tried to emphasize the focal issues in a comprehensive regional planning program. The measures here outlined should thus be regarded as assertions or working hypotheses; their justification and their relevance will be developed in the following chapters in terms of specific regional problems and specific public programs and proposals.

The present study attempts to examine the interrelationships among lagging, intermediate, and congested regions, and to suggest what policies might be applied to each kind of region in view of the relevant opportunity costs that face decision makers responsible for the location of both public and private investment. Moreover, the respective roles of manpower and human resource development programs, infrastructure investment in the narrower sense (roads, industrial sites, power, etc.), and labor mobility programs are integrated into the analysis.

The next chapter presents a broad background survey of regional employment and income levels and growth rates as well as of the nature and consequences of rural to urban migration and the decentralization of jobs from central cities to suburbs within metropolitan areas.

Each of Chapters 3 through 8 deals with an area or group of areas characterized by relatively lagging economic conditions. Chapter 3 explores the economic and social impediments of the economic development of the South, and points up the importance of investment in human resources and of urbanization as the region's main hopes for future progress. Chapter 4 considers the difficulties confronting the people of Appalachia, particularly those in the central part of the region, and it critically examines policy measures being applied in the region. The regional commissions that have been created on the model of the Appalachian Regional Commission are discussed in Chapter 5. The Economic Development Administration, which is charged with promoting economic growth in areas characterized by high unemployment and low income, is the subject of Chapter 6. Chapter 7 examines the prospects for attracting economic activity to Indian reservations, as well as those for giving Indians employment opportunities in urban areas. Chapter 8 deals with similar considerations with respect to the Mexican Americans, and particularly those who reside in south Texas.

Chapter 9 presents a general analysis of the feasibility of attempts to industrialize rural America. The rationale for a growth center policy based on intermediate-sized cities is developed in Chapter 10. This chapter also considers measures for alleviating the problems of metropolitan ghettos. Chapter 11 presents evidence on the feasibility of relocation programs to assist workers from lagging areas in finding employment in growth centers with labor shortages. The final chapter summarizes and integrates the analyses and policy implications developed in the preceding chapters.

Chapter 2

The National Setting

Before detailed consideration is given to specific problem areas, this chapter surveys some of the broad regional trends within aggregate national economic activity. Particular attention is given to employment and income changes because these are the variables which appropriately receive most attention from persons concerned with regional development and regional policy. In addition to examining changes at the state and multistate levels, the nature and consequence of recent patterns of urban growth are considered. Accompanying the growth of large metropolitan areas there has been a redistribution of population and jobs between central cities and suburbs. The central city has increasingly become the place of employment for office workers—mostly whites who commute from the suburbs—while unskilled and semiskilled jobs have been growing increasingly scarce in the central cities because of the movement of industry to the suburbs. However, it is also shown that while the central city-suburb dichotomy generally holds for the largest metropolitan areas and those located in the Northeast, the more numerous, if smaller, metropolitan areas of the South and West tend to have similar problems in the central cities and the suburbs. The final section of this chapter introduces some of the more prominent problems confronting rural America. Because of technological advances in agriculture, labor requirements have rapidly declined and pressures for geographic and occupational mobility have increased. Unfortunately, the opportunities that are available to farm people for training and preparation for nonfarm work and ways of life are not yet commensurate with the need for such assistance.

Employment Growth

The data in Table 2 on nonfarm payroll by region for selected periods from 1947 to 1966 show that during the period from 1947 to 1961, when the national growth rate was 1.6 percent, average yearly increases ranged from 0.6 percent for the Middle Atlantic States to 3.6 percent for the Mountain region. The mean deviation

TABLE 2: NONFARM PAYROLL EMPLOYMENT BY REGION,
SELECTED PERIODS, 1947–66

Region[a]	Number (thousands)		Percent distribution		Average annual growth rate		
	1947	1966[b]	1947	1966[b]	1947–61	1961–65	1965–66
Sum of regions	43,443	63,070	100.0	100.0	—	—	—
New England	3,333	4,156	7.7	6.6	0.8	1.9	3.6
Middle Atlantic	10,813	13,015	24.9	20.6	0.6	1.8	2.6
East North Central	10,067	13,381	23.2	21.2	0.9	3.1	4.2
West North Central	3,414	4,780	7.9	7.6	1.5	2.4	4.0
South Atlantic	5,269	8,941	12.1	14.2	2.3	4.1	4.8
East South Central	2,148	3,392	4.9	5.4	1.8	4.0	5.0
West South Central	3,059	5,131	7.0	8.1	2.4	3.5	4.4
Mountain	1,170	2,265	2.7	3.6	3.6	3.0	4.3
Pacific	4,170	8,009	9.6	12.7	3.3	3.6	5.9
Average growth rate[c]	—	—	—	—	1.6	2.9	4.2
Mean deviation	—	—	—	—	1.0	0.7	0.7
As percent of average	—	—	—	—	62.5	24.1	16.7

[a] See appendix A–1 for states comprising regions.

[b] Preliminary (11–month) average.

[c] Based on average (mean) increase of regions, weighted by size of employment change.

Note: Detail may not add to totals due to rounding.

Source: Manpower Report of the President, 1967, p. 26.

was 62.5 percent of the average national growth rate. In the period from 1961–65 the average national annual growth rate was 2.9 percent, but the mean deviation declined to 0.7, or 24.1 percent of the average growth rate; from 1965 to 1966 these three values were, respectively, 4.2, 0.7, and 16.7. Thus, slow national growth was accompanied by considerable variation in regional growth, but as the aggregate growth rate rose and remained relatively high, the growth rates of the regions became more uniform.

This convergence of employment growth rates is no doubt more related to the "competitive" element in an area's employment change (that is, the growth rate of the area in its particular industries compared with the growth rate of other areas in these same industries) than to the industry mix of an area. Lowell Ashby has shown that the importance of industry mix effects is declining relative to competitive effects largely because the industrial employment structure of regions, states, and even local areas is becoming more homogeneous. The principal reason for this is continuing migration from rural to urban areas, and the concomitant movement out of agricultural employment into nonagricultural jobs. In the process the entire national mix has been moving closer to that of the industrialized states.[1] Similarly, Borts and Stein have demonstrated that "Interstate differences in growth rates of manufacturing production worker employment do *not* arise because states have different compositions of industries. These differences arise because, in the industries they contain, states grow at rates different from the national average in those same industries."[2] On the other hand, the unfavorable industry mix of some areas, e.g., the South and Appalachia, is a major factor in explaining why they have a disproportionate share of their employment in labor-intensive, low-wage sectors, as well as per capita income levels below that of the nation as a whole.[3]

Income Growth

Per capita personal income in the United States in 1967 averaged $3,137, but there were large differences among the states. Average state per capita income ranged from $1,895 in Mississippi to $3,865 in Connecticut. New York, Illinois, Delaware, California, Alaska, Nevada, and New Jersey all had values over $3,600. On the other hand, the southern and border states generally ranked below the rest of the nation (see figure 1).

Between 1948 and 1965 the largest gains in personal income occurred in the western and southern parts of the United States, while the smallest gains were found in the northeastern and north

TABLE 3: PER CAPITA PERSONAL INCOME, BY STATES
AND REGIONS, 1948-67

State and Region	1948	1953	1958	1963	1967[a]
United States	1,430	1,804	2,068	2,455	3,137
New England	1,494	1,921	2,258	2,710	3,436
Maine	1,235	1,422	1,742	1,961	2,620
New Hampshire	1,285	1,616	1,957	2,347	3,019
Vermont	1,134	1,375	1,650	2,013	2,775
Massachusetts	1,500	1,910	2,287	2,770	3,488
Rhode Island	1,493	1,879	2,042	2,507	3,238
Connecticut	1,713	2,346	2,642	3,118	3,865
Mideast	1,648	2,068	2,387	2,807	3,534
New York	1,797	2,139	2,518	2,979	3,726
New Jersey	1,689	2,247	2,516	2,965	3,624
Pennsylvania	1,431	1,870	2,130	2,441	3,149
Delaware	1,721	2,379	2,610	3,013	3,700
Maryland	1,467	1,964	2,205	2,675	3,434
District of Columbia	1,957	2,363	2,818	3,370	4,268
Great Lakes	1,603	2,062	2,203	2,620	3,392
Michigan	1,560	2,161	2,149	2,587	3,393
Ohio	1,558	2,028	2,148	2,509	3,212
Indiana	1,451	1,930	1,998	2,472	3,241
Illinois	1,815	2,186	2,466	2,915	3,725
Wisconsin	1,419	1,787	2,018	2,378	3,153
Plains	1,444	1,642	1,970	2,308	2,995
Minnesota	1,432	1,665	1,990	2,372	3,111
Iowa	1,589	1,598	1,921	2,303	3,093
Missouri	1,389	1,728	2,023	2,358	2,993
North Dakota	1,402	1,243	1,700	2,002	2,485
South Dakota	1,497	1,377	1,668	1,908	2,550
Nebraska	1,509	1,612	1,963	2,276	2,938
Kansas	1,334	1,722	2,073	2,352	3,009

TABLE 3—*Continued*

State and Region	1948	1953	1958	1963	1967[a]
Southeast	984	1,267	1,507	1,837	2,429
Virginia	1,130	1,488	1,684	2,095	2,776
West Virginia	1,120	1,282	1,549	1,781	2,341
Kentucky	990	1,292	1,496	1,837	2,387
Tennessee	944	1,229	1,448	1,776	2,369
North Carolina	973	1,223	1,436	1,804	2,396
South Carolina	891	1,199	1,259	1,581	2,167
Georgia	968	1,288	1,519	1,879	2,513
Florida	1,180	1,526	1,827	2,145	2,796
Alabama	866	1,124	1,404	1,673	2,166
Mississippi	789	923	1,128	1,436	1,895
Louisiana	1,032	1,346	1,613	1,843	2,445
Arkansas	875	1,035	1,279	1,627	2,090
Southwest	1,187	1,555	1,836	2,095	2,674
Oklahoma	1,144	1,467	1,762	1,992	2,623
Texas	1,199	1,583	1,851	2,105	2,704
New Mexico	1,084	1,386	1,827	2,052	2,462
Arizona	1,274	1,653	1,863	2,219	2,681
Rocky Mountain	1,419	1,699	2,001	2,324	2,859
Montana	1,616	1,779	2,059	2,266	2,759
Idaho	1,316	1,508	1,800	2,048	2,608
Wyoming	1,595	1,893	2,143	2,419	2,997
Colorado	1,433	1,767	2,115	2,483	3,086
Utah	1,240	1,578	1,831	2,215	2,617
Far West	1,715	2,144	2,433	2,910	3,588
Washington	1,600	2,001	2,231	2,622	3,481
Oregon	1,621	1,868	2,082	2,472	3,055
Nevada	1,814	2,462	2,651	3,244	3,626
California	1,752	2,204	2,511	2,997	3,660

[a] Preliminary.
Source: Survey of Current Business, April, 1968, p. 14.

central areas. From the cyclical peak in 1948 to the first quarter of 1965—the last quarter not greatly affected by the Vietnam buildup—personal income in the Far West, Southeast, and Southwest combined grew about 30 percent faster than in the rest of the country. When the 1948–65 period is broken into four timespans, each starting and ending at a cyclical peak, relative differences in regional growth trends are of about the same magnitude in each

FIGURE 1: PER CAPITA PERSONAL INCOME, 1967

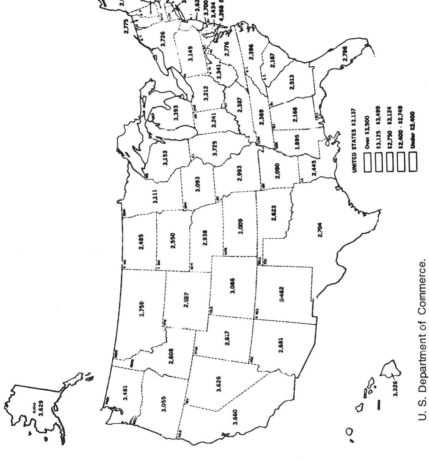

U. S. Department of Commerce.

TABLE 4: REGIONAL GROWTH RATES IN PERSONAL INCOME
FOR SELECTED PERIODS

	Growth rates (Average percent change per quarter, annual rates, compounded)						
	IV-1948 to II-1953	II-1953 to III-1957	III-1957 to I-1960	I-1960 to I-1965	I-1965 to IV-1966	IV-1966 to IV-1967	IV-1948 to I-1965
United States	6.5	4.9	4.5	5.4	8.3	6.2	5.5
Fast-growing regions	7.6	5.7	5.1	6.2	8.7	7.3	6.6
Far West	8.5	6.1	6.4	6.2	8.0	8.2	6.0
Southeast	6.8	5.0	4.8	6.6	9.0	6.5	5.9
Southwest	7.6	5.7	4.1	5.6	8.5	6.6	6.9
Slow-growing regions	6.1	4.4	3.9	4.9	8.1	5.5	5.0
Rocky Mountain	6.0	5.9	4.6	4.9	6.6	6.6	5.2
New England	6.3	4.6	4.4	5.1	8.6	5.7	4.9
Great Lakes	6.9	4.0	3.5	5.1	8.6	5.3	5.0
Mideast	6.0	4.7	4.0	4.9	7.3	6.1	4.4
Plains	3.9	4.5	3.5	5.1	8.8	5.4	5.4

	Relative differences between regional and national growth rates[a]						
	IV-1948 to II-1953	II-1953 to III-1957	III-1957 to I-1960	I-1960 to I-1965	I-1965 to IV-1966	IV-1966 to IV-1967	IV-1948 to I-1965
United States	0.0	0.0	0.0	0.0	0.0	0.0	0.0
Fast-growing regions	16.9	16.3	13.3	14.8	4.8	17.7	20.0
Far West	30.8	24.5	42.2	14.8	−3.6	32.3	9.1
Southeast	4.6	2.0	6.7	22.2	8.4	4.8	7.3
Southwest	16.9	16.3	−8.9	3.7	2.4	6.5	25.5
Slow-growing regions	−6.2	−10.2	−13.3	−9.3	−2.4	−11.3	−9.1
Rocky Mountain	−7.7	20.4	2.2	−9.3	−20.5	6.5	−5.5
New England	−3.1	−6.1	−2.2	−5.6	3.6	−8.1	−10.9
Great Lakes	6.2	−18.4	−22.2	−5.6	3.6	−14.5	−9.1
Mideast	−7.7	−4.1	−11.1	−9.3	−12.0	−1.6	−20.0
Plains	−40.0	−8.2	−22.2	−5.6	6.0	−12.9	−1.8

[a] [(Regional growth rate divided by national growth rate) less 1.00] 100.
Source: Survey of Current Business, April, 1968, p. 15.

subperiod as in the longer period (see Table 4). The consistency of growth trends in individual regions is illustrated by the fact that among the 32 observations for the eight regions in the four time periods, only three have signs that depart from the normal pattern in relation to national growth rates.

During the seven quarters of rapid expansion between the first quarter of 1965 and the fourth quarter of 1966 there was a high degree of uniformity among regional growth rates. The growth rate of the three fast-growing regions exceeded that of the five slow-growing regions by less than 10 percent, whereas the differences earlier had been 30 percent. Furthermore, the region that normally has had the fastest growth rate—the Far West—grew at a rate below average whereas income growth in three normally slow-growing regions—New England, Great Lakes, and Plains—had rates exceeding that of the nation. The main reason for the increased uniformity in regional income changes was the rapid growth in aggregate economic activity, which had resulted in similar uniformities during previous recovery and expansion phases of the business cycle. In four of the five periods of expansion since World War II, differences in regional income growth rates have been reduced.[4]

The rapid expansion of economic activity during 1965–66 was in large measure a consequence of the Vietnam buildup and the tax reduction of 1964–65. Increases in manufacturing payrolls played a key part in improving the relative growth rates of normally slow-growing regions. In 1966 manufacturing accounted for about 25 percent of total personal income in slow-growing regions but only 18 percent in those that are usually fast-growing. Generally accelerated manufacturing activity therefore had a particularly marked effect on income growth in the slow-growing regions. In addition, the annual rate of growth of factory payrolls in the slow-growing regions increased from 3½ percent during the 1960–65 period to 9 percent in 1965–66, whereas the comparable increase in fast-growing areas was from 5¾ to 10¾ percent. In other words, the rate of growth of manufacturing payrolls in slower-growing regions moved closer to that in faster-growing regions. This shift was brought about primarily by large government purchases of conventional military equipment relative to missiles and electronics purchases. Production of conventional military equipment is concentrated in slow-growing areas, so the shift in military procurement mix contributed to the large increase in manufacturing wages and salaries in these areas.[5]

During 1967 the national rate of economic growth slowed and relative regional growth rates again conformed to the long-run pattern. The West and South had relatively high income growth rates, while those in the Northeast and North Central areas were below the national average. Personal income in the three fast-growing regions rose during the year by 30 percent more than it did in the other regions; this was the same differential that prevailed during the 1948–65 period. During the first half of 1967, when overall growth was especially sluggish and durable goods output declined significantly, the rate of income growth in the usually fast-growing regions exceeded that of the slow-growing areas by 40 percent. However, when the pace of economic advance quickened during the last half of the year, regional growth rates again converged. As in the case of the economic expansion of 1965–66, the rate of growth of the fast-growing regions exceeded that for the others by only about 10 percent.[6] In general, then, although regional income differences are becoming less pronounced, the pace of convergence is slow and considerable absolute differences still remain among the states. Personal income behavior in metropolitan areas will be examined in the following section.

Urban Growth

Analysis of employment and income trends in terms of states and multistate regions is important in studying the geographic dimensions of manpower policy, but it is even more important to consider spatial economic change in terms of the dynamics of urban growth. Marion Clawson correctly maintains that "Urbanization is perhaps the dominant social, economic, and political movement in the contemporary American scene."[7] A region is most likely to grow fast when its metropolitan areas are growing fast; it is the metropolitan growth that determines regional growth rather than the converse.[8]

America's urban areas, which include large metropolitan centers and smaller urban places ranging down to 2,500 inhabitants, account for most of the country's employment and industrial activity and for the homes of nearly three-fourths of the total population. About two-thirds of the country's population live in standard metropolitan statistical areas (SMSA's), that is, in areas that contain at least one central city with at least 50,000 inhabitants, plus the county of the central city and any contiguous counties that are metropolitan in character and economically and socially integrated with the county of the central city.[9] Over three-quarters of population growth in the United States during this century has been accounted for by the growth of SMSA's. Industrial and population concentration in SMSA's is greatest in the Northeast and North Central regions, but it has been increasing more rapidly in other parts of the country. As shown in Table 5, population growth in SMSA's between 1950 and 1965 in the Northeast was 19.6 percent and in the North Central region it was 31.9 percent; in contrast, the comparable values for the South and the West were, respectively, 52.8 percent and 72.1 percent.

Although cities of all sizes are growing they are doing so at varying rates. Figure 2 shows that between 1950 and 1960 cities in the 10,000 to 100,000 population range grew more rapidly than either small or very large urban places. However, many of the cities in the middle-sized group are close to a larger city or within an urban complex, rather than being independent entities dominating their own hinterland. Indeed, the trend seems to be in favor of the growth of large urban complexes.[10]

In 1966 SMSA's had an average population of about 600,000 and per capita personal income of $3,314. The seven largest SMSA's had nearly a quarter of all income although they had only a little over one-fifth of the national population. Their average income of about $3,800 was nearly 25 percent greater than that of other SMSA's and 70 percent more than in non-SMSA's. The 25

Rural Poverty and the Urban Crisis

TABLE 5: POPULATION OF STANDARD METROPOLITAN STATISTICAL
AREAS, BY REGION, 1950 AND 1965[a]
(Numbers in thousands)

Region[b]	Population		Change, 1950–65	
	1950	*1965*	*Number*	*Percent*
Northeast	32,917	39,380	6,463	19.6
New England	7,408	8,877	1,469	19.8
Middle Atlantic	25,509	30,503	4,994	19.6
North Central	26,589	35,084	8,495	31.9
East North Central	21,093	27,801	6,708	31.8
West North Central	5,496	7,284	1,788	32.5
South	20,871	31,890	11,019	52.8
South Atlantic	9,670	15,723	6,053	62.6
East South Central	3,873	5,034	1,161	30.0
West South Central	7,329	11,133	3,804	51.9
West	14,160	24,365	10,205	72.1
Mountain	2,144	4,153	2,009	93.7
Pacific	12,016	20,212	8,196	68.2

[a] Population data for 1950 and 1965 cover 214 identical SMSA's defined by the Department of Commerce as of 1967. These include some areas that were not classified as SMSA's in 1950 or 1965, but that by 1967 had attained such status. For New England, 12 State economic areas and 2 counties were used. These include the 23 officially defined SMSA's in New England. The consolidated metropolitan areas of New York-Northeast New Jersey, Chicago-Northwest Indiana, and Los Angeles-Orange County were included as individual areas.

[b] See Appendix A-1 for states comprising region.

Note: Detail may not add to totals due to rounding.

Source: Manpower Report of the President, 1968, p. 130.

SMSA's with the highest average incomes were located in all Office of Business Economics (OBE) regions except the Southeast and Rocky Mountains. (See Appendix A-2 for the states comprising these regions). The highest ranking SMSA in the Southeast, Richmond, Virginia, ranked forty-eighth nationally, and the highest ranking Rocky Mountain SMSA, Denver, Colorado, ranked fifty-fourth. It is particularly noteworthy that only four of the 25 SMSA's with highest incomes (Midland, Texas; Las Vegas, Nevada; Salinas-Monterey and Los Angeles-Long Beach, California) were in the southern two-thirds of the country, that is, south of a line running

FIGURE 2: MIDDLE-SIZED URBAN PLACES HAD FASTEST
          POPULATION GAIN DURING THE 1950's

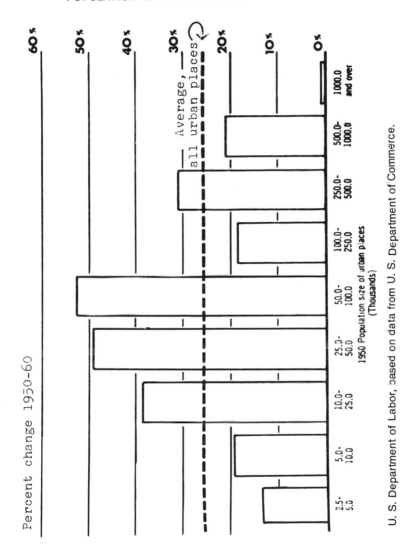

U. S. Department of Labor, based on data from U. S. Department of Commerce.

from Wilmington, Delaware, to San Francisco (see Table 6). Eight of the 25 highest-income SMSA's were found along the East Coast between New Haven, Connecticut, and Wilmington, Delaware. Ten were in a large rectangle centering on Chicago, and six were scattered along the West Coast from Seattle to Los Angeles-Long Beach. Three of Iowa's five SMSA's ranked among the thirteen highest ranking, a record unequalled by any other state.[11]

The lowest ranking SMSA's were more widely scattered than the highest ranking ones. Nevertheless, 20 of the 25 SMSA's with lowest per capita incomes were found in the two southern OBE regions.

TABLE 6: HIGHEST AND LOWEST RANKING SMSA's IN PER
            CAPITA INCOME, 1966

Highest

		Percent of national average
1. Paterson-Clifton-Passaic, N.J.	4,054	137
2. San Francisco-Oakland, Cal.	3,976	134
3. New York, N.Y.	3,962	134
4. Wilmington, Del.-N.J.-Md.	3,911	132
5. Chicago, Ill.	3,892	131
6. Reno, Nev.	3,892	131
7. Cedar Rapids, Ia.	3,875	131
8. New London-Groton-Norwich, Conn.	3,840	130
9. Des Moines, Ia.	3,824	129
10. Las Vegas, Nev.	3,816	129
11. Newark, N.J.	3,788	128
12. Los Angeles-Long Beach, Cal.	3,759	127
13. Waterloo, Ia.	3,729	126
14. Seattle-Everett, Wash.	3,723	126
15. Hartford-New Britain, Conn.	3,707	125
16. Midland, Tex.	3,698	125
17. Detroit, Mich.	3,695	125
18. Rockford, Ill.	3,685	124
19. Minneapolis-St. Paul, Minn.	3,621	122
20. Salinas-Monterey, Cal.	3,607	122
21. Milwaukee, Wisc.	3,591	121
22. New Haven-Waterbury-Meriden, Conn.	3,581	121
23. Jersey City, N.J.	3,567	120
24. Ann Arbor, Mich.	3,562	120
25. Cleveland, Ohio	3,559	120

TABLE 6—*Continued*

Lowest

		Percent of national average
1. McAllen-Pharr-Edinburg, Tex.	1,250	42
2. Laredo, Tex.	1,379	47
3. Brownsville-Harlingen-San Benito, Tex.	1,725	58
4. Tuscaloosa, Ala.	1,850	62
5. Provo-Orem, Utah	1,874	63
6. Charleston, S.C.	1,941	66
7. Fort Smith, Ark.-Okla.	1,955	66
8. Pine Bluff, Ark.	2,091	71
9. Lafayette, La.	2,133	72
10. Fayetteville, N.C.	2,148	72
11. Johnstown, Pa.	2,156	73
12. Texarkana, Tex.-Ark.	2,235	75
13. Wilmington, N.C.	2,251	76
14. Biloxi-Gulfport, Miss.	2,261	76
15. El Paso, Tex.	2,288	77
16. Monroe, La.	2,301	78
17. Gadsden, Ala.	2,305	78
18. Montgomery, Ala.	2,310	78
19. San Antonio, Tex.	2,313	78
20. Wilkes-Barre-Hazleton, Pa.	2,318	78
21. Mobile, Ala.	2,340	79
22. Durham, N.C.	2,364	80
23. Corpus Christi, Tex.	2,365	80
24. Salem, Ore.	2,382	80
25. Lewiston-Auburn, Me.	2,386	81

Source: United States Department of Commerce News (Office of Business Economics), August 26, 1968.

The low standing of the southern regions is similarly seen in the fact that only about one out of eight of the SMSA's in the Southeast and Southwest had incomes above the national average, and in most of these cases the values were only slightly above the national average.[12]

Personal income growth in SMSA's between 1959 and 1966 ranged from an annual rate of just under 3 percent in South Bend, Indiana, and Lake Charles, Louisiana, to between 10 and 12 percent in Anaheim-Santa Ana-Garden Grove, California, Huntsville, Alabama, Las Vegas, Nevada, and Augusta, Georgia. Of the 75 fastest growing SMSA's in terms of personal income, 59 were in the West and South, with 34 of these being in the Southeast. Of the 75 slowest growing, 46 were in the Northeast and North Central regions.[13]

Analysis of the regional distribution of changes in personal income shows that the SMSA's of the Southeast had the largest relative gain from 1959 to 1966. The next largest gains were in the Far West and Southwest. The Rocky Mountain rate was equal to that for the nation, while the Great Lakes, New England, Plains, and Mideast regions' SMSA's grew at rates somewhat below the national average. Thus, interregional comparisons in terms of SMSA's follow the same general pattern with regard to levels and growth of income as did comparisons in terms of states.[14] The trend toward diminishing interregional income differentials in SMSA's is also shown in the decline of the coefficient of variation of median family income in the 15 largest areas from .069 in 1950 to .057 in 1960. Wilbur Thompson interprets this decline as an indication that as SMSA's grow larger they are able to support an increasingly diversified industrial mix and that they will therefore have increasingly similar per capita incomes. This does not mean that every metropolitan area will become self-sufficient, but it does indicate that they will produce a wide variety of products, and "that even random industry mixes, if large enough, will tend to produce average performance characteristics." Moreover, a diversified mix "not only blends high and low wage rates but also mixes labor demands by sex, age, color, and education to achieve similar labor force participation rates between urban areas," so that "Boston, Baltimore and Birmingham will all come to have a similar mix of rich and poor."[15]

Central City and Suburbs

Accompanying the growth of our large metropolitan areas has been a redistribution of population and jobs within urban agglomerations. The postwar exodus of white, middle-class couples with children to the suburbs has been accompanied in many areas by population loss in the old central city. In 1960 the proportion of metropolitan area residents living in the central city was 51 percent; by 1985 this value is expected to decline to 33 percent.[16] The movement of northern whites to the suburbs is in part a quest for more space, but it is also the product of technological market forces that have pushed excess labor from southern agriculture and attracted it to what hopefully would be relatively better housing and income opportunities in the north. Too often, however, migrants to the cities have merely exchanged rural for urban slums. Nevertheless, their continuing influx has served to maintain property values in the old central cities, thereby facilitating the movement of middle class whites to the suburbs. The movement of southern Negroes, and to a lesser extent Appalachian and other "poor whites," into the central cities has added a "push" factor to the pull of suburban living.

Urban slums have been aptly characterized as areas "impacted by segregation and discrimination; blighted by derelict and dilapidated houses, non-conforming land uses, and uncollected trash; overcrowded by a shortage of low-income housing units, and gouged by too-high rents in code-violating dwellings."[17] In Newark the incidence of tuberculosis and infant mortality has been found to be 2⅔ times as great in slums as in public housing areas, and the incidence of communicable diseases among children under five years of age 2½ times as great. Studies have shown that in Louisville, Cleveland, Philadelphia, and many other metropolitan areas the juvenile delinquency rate is several times as high in bad housing areas as in other areas. The high economic cost of slum living consumes resources that might otherwise contribute to eradicating poverty. In Los Angeles, for example, the slums, in relation to other areas, cost the city 87 percent more per capita in police protection, 67 percent more in fire department services, and 125 percent more in health services—yet they yield only 38 percent as high a rate of tax revenues.[18]

To gain a clearer understanding of the problems of poverty and unemployment in urban slums, the Department of Labor and cooperating state agencies conducted a series of intensive surveys in eight U.S. cities and San Juan, Puerto Rico, in November, 1966. Comparable data for slum areas in Cleveland, Detroit, Los Angeles, and Oakland were obtained from independent studies. The results with respect to unemployment in the slums and for the metropolitan areas as a whole are presented in Table 7.

TABLE 7: UNEMPLOYMENT RATES FOR SLUM AREAS AND FOR METROPOLITAN AREAS AS A WHOLE[a]

	Unemployment rate	
Metropolitan area and slum area	Slum area, November, 1966	Metropolitan area, average for year ending August, 1966
Boston-Roxbury area	6.9	3.7
Cleveland-Hough and surrounding neighborhood	15.6	3.5
Detroit-Central Woodward area	10.1	4.3
Los Angeles-South Los Angeles	12.0	6.0
New Orleans-several contiguous areas	10.0	([b])
New York:		
Harlem	8.1 ⎫	
East Harlem	9.0 ⎬	4.6
Bedford-Stuyvesant	6.2 ⎭	
Philadelphia-North Philadelphia	11.0	4.3
Phoenix-Salt River Bed area	13.2	([b])
St. Louis-north side	12.9	4.5
San Antonio-east and west sides	8.1	([b])
San Francisco-Oakland:		
San Francisco-Mission-Fillmore	11.1 ⎱	
Oakland-Bayside	13.0 ⎰	5.2
San Juan-El Fangito	15.8	([b])

[a] Metropolitan area data are based on special tabulations of data from the Current Population Survey.
[b] Data not available from the Current Population Survey.
Source: Manpower Report of the President, 1967, p. 75.

The results of the Labor Department study indicate that about 10 percent of workers in the slums of the cities in question were unemployed. This rate was three times the national average. With the exception of San Juan, the unemployment rate was highest of all in the Hough area of Cleveland, yet the Cleveland metropolitan area had an unemployment rate below the national average.

Of course, unemployment figures are only a part of the total complex of problems related to poverty in the slums. Nearly 7 percent of the slum residents with jobs were employed only part time, though they preferred full-time work. Twenty percent of the full-time workers were earning less than enough income to reach the "poverty-line" income of about $3,000 per year for a family of four. Moreover, about two-fifths of all slum families reported annual incomes of less than $3,000. The rate of nonparticipation in the labor force, as indicated by the number of able-bodied adult men who were neither working nor seeking work, was 11 percent in slum areas, in contrast to a national rate of 7 percent. Finally, a fifth or more of the adult males who were expected to be in the slum areas were not located by the surveys (this parallels the Census "undercount" for nonwhite males). To obtain a measure of the complex of work problems in slum areas these various factors were combined in the construction of a Subemployment Index. Subemployment rates for ten slums are shown in Table 8. The average rate of subemployment for these areas was 34 percent.[19]

TABLE 8: SUBEMPLOYMENT RATES FOR SELECTED SLUM AREAS, 1966

Area	
Boston-Roxbury area	24
New Orleans-several contiguous areas	45
New York:	
Harlem	29
East Harlem	33
Bedford-Stuyvesant	28
Philadelphia-North Philadelphia	34
Phoenix-Salt River Bed area	42
St. Louis-north side	39
San Antonio-east and west sides	47
San Francisco-Mission-Fillmore	25

Source: Manpower Report of the President, 1967, p. 75.

One of the major obstacles to employment of slum residents has been the movement of business and industry away from the central city to the suburbs. Between 1947 and 1967 total employment in seven large central cities rose by 50,000, but during the same period the suburbs of these cities experienced an employment increase of 900,000. Between 1954 and 1965 about two-thirds of the value of all new industrial buildings and over half of all new stores were constructed outside of the nation's central cities. In Los Angeles, for example, 85 percent of new industrial buildings and 63 percent of the stores were located in the suburbs. Increasingly the central city is becoming the working place of office workers—mostly whites who commute from the suburbs—while there is a growing shortage of unskilled jobs in or near slum areas.[20]

The burden of getting to a suburban job is particularly great for the Negro, especially in view of housing discrimination in the suburbs. Public transportation to the suburbs is expensive and often circuitous, if it is available at all. There is considerable evidence that central city residents using public transportation spend more money and time reaching suburban jobs than do commuters in the opposite direction.[21] The Traffic Commission of New York City estimates that it would cost a worker in Harlem $40 a month to commute by public transportation to work in a Farmingdale, Long Island, aircraft plant, in a Yonkers or Portchester parts plant, or in a Staten Island chemical plant or shipyard. The cost of commuting from Bedford-Stuyvesant to work in these same places would be $50 a month. Moreover, since auto ownership rises with earnings, slum residents are the most likely persons to take public transportation to work. Most nonwhite families living in central cities do not in fact have an automobile.[22]

The difficulties of slum residents in our large metropolitan areas will be explored at greater length in subsequent chapters, particularly Chapter 10. It should be pointed out here, however, that the stereotyped dichotomy between a central city where most of the social and economic problems of a metropolitan area are found, and a healthy, happy suburbia where most problems are only a result of growing pains, is by no means universally relevant.

Marjorie Cahn Brazer has analyzed the structure of all SMSA's with populations of 100,000 or more in terms of 41 variables measuring such characteristics as nonwhite population, age, mobility, families with children under 18, unrelated individuals, education, occupation, women in the labor force, family income, unemployment, substandard housing, and commuters. She found that for only three of the 41 characteristics—race, broken families with children, and unrelated individuals—is a metropolitan dichotomy indisputable and pervasive. In addition, in many metropolitan areas of the South and West and in smaller SMSA's throughout the country, low status nonwhites make up a larger proportion of the suburban population than of the central city population. Substandard owner-occupied housing is also more prevalent in the suburbs everywhere except in the Northeast. For the country as a whole "the cities and suburbs of most metropolitan areas face similar social problems and by and large enjoy similar human and personal economic resources with which to meet these problems."[23] Nevertheless, in the largest SMSA's and those located in the Northeast, the central city-suburb dichotomy is marked and does conform to the stereotype. While these SMSA's are numerically in the minority, they account for most of the total metropolitan population. Of the 190 SMSA's analyzed by Brazer, 41 are found in the Northeast and those in the rest of the country with a population of more than one million numbered only 17. In most of the remaining SMSA's the areas as a whole share similar problems and should recognize the advantages of intrametropolitan cooperation in dealing with them.[24]

Rural America

In March, 1967, about 57 million persons lived in rural America. Of this total, 47 million were in the nonfarm population.[25] Since World War II the average number of persons engaged in agricultural production has dropped from 10 million to about 5.2 million. Of these, about three-fourths are farm operators and members of their families; the rest are hired workers.[26]

A large proportion of farms have been too small to offer full employment to farm families. Technological advance has been incorporated into the operations of many small inadequate farms while the number of large commercial farms has been increasing. As a result labor requirements have rapidly declined and pressures for migration and occupational change have increased. Farm people have been highly mobile, but the migration process has drained away the most productive age groups even though the migrants are frequently ill-prepared for alternative work. Some segments of American agriculture have also continued to depend on the services of a large population of seasonal and migratory workers whose employment opportunities are not sufficient to lift them out of poverty.[27]

The annual average number of hired farm workers in 1966 was about 1.4 million, but about 2.8 million persons did some farmwork for wages during the year. A high proportion of these workers did only a few days of work, mostly during the planting and harvesting seasons. Over half worked in the South, and most worked on large farms.[28] The difficulties faced by many rural workers are not adequately reflected in unemployment rates. For example, in 1960 their unemployment rate averaged 5.3 percent compared with 5.1 percent for urban workers. The most pervasive problem for rural workers is underemployment and low earnings rather than total absence of work. The wage differential between farm and nonfarm sectors of the economy is substantial.[29] In 1966 wage rates of farmworkers averaged $1.23 an hour, whereas workers in manufacturing earned an average of $2.71. Seasonality of employment increases the farmworkers' disadvantage. Male adult workers averaged $1,452 in income in 1965, compared with $2,988 for farm operators, $3,343 for nonfarm laborers, $4,068 for service workers, and $5,317 for operators of industrial and other equipment.[30]

It has been estimated that if the rural labor force had been utilized as efficiently as was the labor force of the country as a whole, the money income of the nation would have been increased by about $10 billion in 1965.[31] There is general agreement that the redundant supply of labor in agriculture is largely responsible for low incomes and underemployment in rural America; though the magnitude of "excess" labor in agriculture is difficult to estimate, a number of attempts have been made. For example, Tyner and Tweeten, working with man-hour requirements based on estimates of optimum resource combinations in agriculture, found that labor was in excess supply for the period from 1952 to 1961 by two-fifths.[32] Kaldor and Saupe, using a model of income-efficient agriculture in thirteen north central states in 1959, estimate that only 34 percent of the labor actually used in that year was really required.[33] In view of this situation it is evident that while good opportunities still exist in farming if there is a high capital-labor ratio, the number of farms will continue to decline rapidly. Heady suggests that an investment of $200,000 per farm may define the lower limit for successful commercial farms by 1980. His projections indicate that during the period from 1960 to 1980 the number of farms in the nation will decline from 3.2 million to 1.5 million, while farm employment will fall from 6 million persons to 3.5 million, or possibly even to as low as 2.5 million. Recent trends would seem to support the lower figure.[34]

While it is clear that millions of farm people need or will need training and preparation for nonfarm work and ways of life, their adaptation is often strained by poverty and all of its unfortunate attributes. Table 9 shows the number of persons in poverty in both rural and urban areas in March, 1965, as estimated by the President's National Advisory Commission on Rural Poverty. Here it is seen that there is proportionally more poverty among rural residents than among urban residents. In metropolitan areas one person in eight is poor; in the suburbs, one in 15. However, one out of every four rural residents is poor. About 30 percent of the national population lives in rural areas, but these areas account for about 40 percent of the nation's poor. Three out of four of the rural poor live in small towns and villages rather than on farms, and of the 14 million poor, 11 million are white. Nevertheless, a higher proportion of Negroes are poor. Three out of five rural nonwhite families are poor, and 90 percent of them are concentrated in the nation's poorest counties. Low income whites, on the other hand, are more widely scattered as well as more numerous.[35] Some have even argued that

TABLE 9: PERSONS IN POVERTY, BY RURAL AND URBAN
          RESIDENCE, MARCH, 1965

Item	Persons at all income levels		Poor persons[a]		Percent poor
	Number (millions)	Percent distribution	Number (millions)	Percent distribution	
United States	189.9	100.0	33.7	100.0	17.7
Total rural	55.3	29.1	13.8	40.9	25.0
Farm	13.3	7.0	3.9	11.6	29.3
Nonfarm	42.0	22.1	9.9	29.4	23.6
Total urban	134.6	70.9	19.9	59.1	14.8
Small cities	27.1	14.3	6.4	19.0	23.6
Metropolitan areas	107.5	56.6	13.5	40.1	12.6
Central cities	58.6	30.8	10.2	30.3	17.4
Suburbs	48.9	25.8	3.3	9.8	6.7

[a] Income data relate to 1964. Poverty statistics presented here are preliminary estimates, based on the Social Security Administration poverty
lines for urban and rural nonfarm. However, the Commission calculates
that farm families need about 85 percent as much income as comparable
families in urban areas. The Social Security Administration poverty line
used 70 percent as the farm-nonfarm ratio.

Source: President's National Advisory Commission on Rural Poverty, The
People Left Behind (Washington, D.C.: Government Printing Office, 1967),
p. 3.

recent programs to aid the poor and to develop poor areas may put
poor whites at a disadvantage, since "antipoverty, civil rights, and
related activities tend to be identified, particularly in the South, as
programs for Negroes rather than for disadvantaged people generally."[36] In addition, there is the more general problem that "Emphasis on the poor, as they are identified through an arbitrary, dis-
crete criterion such as income level, tends to increase the chances
of ignoring the very real problems of those just beyond arbitrary
poverty lines."[37] Finally, it must also be recognized that educational,
health, and medical facilities in rural areas compare unfavorably
with those in urban areas, as do social and cultural activities. Housing conditions, too, are often bad. In 1960, 27 percent of occupied
rural housing was classified as substandard, compared with 14 percent for urban areas. Of the 9.2 million substandard occupied

houses in America, 3.9 million were in rural areas. Less than one in four occupied rural farm dwellings had water piped in, and about 30 percent of all rural families still used the traditional privy.[38]

Migration in search of agricultural employment often intensifies problems of unemployment, underemployment, and low income, and it creates a host of social problems for workers and their families. Originating in Texas and Florida, two main distinctive groups of seasonal migratory agricultural workers fan out, respectively, through the central and western states, and along the Atlantic Coast and into other eastern states. Smaller groups flow from Arizona and New Mexico to jobs in California, Washington, and Oregon. However, these long distance movers represent only a minority of all domestic migratory farmworkers. In 1964, two-thirds of all migratory workers crossed county lines but remained within their own state. Most travelled less than 75 miles from their home base, while one-fifth travelled 1,000 miles or more. The average migratory farmworker was employed for only 82 days at farmwork in 1965, but about half of the workers also held nonfarm jobs at some time during the year. The average farm wage paid migrants in 1965 was $9.70 a day. Migrants who were employed only in farmwork during the year received an annual income of about $1,000; those who also worked outside of agriculture earned $1,700, of which $1,200 was from nonfarm jobs. About half the workers lived in families whose annual income was below $3,000.[39] Moreover, the migrant worker's plight is made even more difficult by the fact that none of his slack-work periods are cushioned by health and accident insurance or workmen's compensation. It is not surprising, in view of these data, that a team of Cornell rural sociologists who studied 1,700 migrant workers in 1957 found that if completely free choice of occupations were open, not more than one out of five would prefer migratory farm work.[40]

Summary and Conclusions

The United States is experiencing considerable shifts of population and economic activity. In particular, there is a pronounced movement away from the countryside to larger urban areas. Half of all counties lost population during the 1950's and many others had declines in rural population. Although aggregate figures show that rural population has remained about constant, a finer breakdown shows that gains near large urban areas balance losses in most rural areas. Moreover, a very large decrease in white farm population has been more than offset by the increase in the white population in rural nonfarm areas. Nonwhite farm population also has declined sharply, but nonwhite migrants have, for the most part, gone to urban rather than rural nonfarm areas.

Despite rapid urbanization, the older central cities of many metropolitan areas have not grown or have declined in population. The postwar flight of people and jobs to the suburbs has, particularly in northern cities, resulted in substantial segregation of people in terms of race, income, age and economic opportunity. Especially difficult problems have been created by the continuing migration of Negroes from the South seeking jobs and improved social and economic opportunities. On the other hand, while the central city-suburb dichotomy is relevant to the largest metropolitan areas, the majority of the smaller metropolitan areas of the South and West face similar problems in the central cities and suburbs.

When employment and income growth are analyzed in broadly regional terms it is evident that despite relatively rapid growth the South remains the nation's principal problem area. Per capita personal income in the Southeast rose from $984 in 1948 to $3,137 in 1967, and its proportion of the national average rose from 70 percent to 77 percent during the same period, but its absolute gap increased from $446 to $708. Moreover, it is increasingly recognized that the South's problems are not confined to itself, but are linked to those of northern cities by migration patterns. Thus, it is necessary to give particular attention to the nature and consequences of the South's special position among the nation's regions.

Chapter 3

The South: Problems and Opportunities

Economic Structure and Growth

One of the major factors retarding the economic development of the South has been its specialization in slow-growing sectors. A high proportion of employment in the South in 1940 was found in eleven sectors[1] where national employment either declined or increased at a lower rate than the national average growth rate for all sectors between 1940 and 1960. In 1940 these sectors accounted for 43 percent of national employment, but they accounted for 62 percent of all employment in the South. The high proportion of southern employment in agriculture had a particularly adverse effect on the change in the South's share of national employment. In 1940, 34 percent of southern employment was in agriculture, whereas the comparable national figure was 19 percent. In 1960, employment in agriculture in the nation was about half the 1940 level of 8.4 million, but in the South it was only 40 percent of the 1940 level of 4.2 million. In addition, the South had considerably higher proportions of its total employment than did the nation in such declining sectors as personal services, textile manufacturing, and sawmill and planing activities.[2] In no other major region was the industry mix as important in explaining comparative gains and losses in employment. "There were 34 states which experienced a downward pull on employment increases between 1940 and 1960 from their industry-mix. Of this number, 13 were in the South. . . . More importantly, over three-fourths of the industry-mix effect in these 34 states was exerted by the 13 states of the South."[3]

On the other hand, the downward pull of the South's industry mix on employment growth was substantially offset by the competitive performance of southern industries, i.e., employment expanded at faster than the national rate in most southern industries. Of the 19 sectors that had employment gains greater than the national average between 1940 and 1960, the service-producing industries (professional and related services; wholesale and retail trade; government; finance, insurance, and real estate; and business and repair services) showed the largest gain, both in the nation and in the South. Employment in the 19 sectors in the South increased by about 6 million, and the five service industries represented 58 percent of this total. When the increase in employment in the construction sector is added to that for the services industries, the comparable figure is 69 percent.[4]

Employment in all types of manufacturing increased from 23 to 27 percent of total employment in the United States from 1940 to 1960, but in the South it rose from 15 to 21 percent.[5] This growth also played an important role in stimulating increased demand in the construction, services, and other sectors. Despite increasing diversification of employment in southern manufacturing, however, slow-growth industries still predominate. For example, in 1966 only 40 percent of the Southeast's manufacturing employment was in the fast-growing durable goods industries, whereas the national proportion was 59 percent.[6] The South's declining rural population has provided the basis for the region's above-average growth in manufacturing and nonagricultural employment in general.[7] The manufacturing industries that had the greatest increases in employment in the South between 1940 and 1960 were the traditionally low-wage, labor-intensive apparel and food processing industries that use a high proportion of unskilled labor.[8] In addition, employment increases in several of the above-average-growth, capital-intensive, high-wage industries were not widely distributed among the Southern states. For example, Texas, Alabama, Florida, and Virginia accounted for over two-thirds of employment growth in the metal-fabrication sector; and Texas, Georgia, and Alabama accounted for about the same proportion of employment increase in the manufacturing of transportation equipment, chiefly automobiles and airplanes. Three-fourths of the employment increase in the chemicals and plastics sector took place in Texas, Tennessee, Louisiana, Virginia, and Kentucky.[9]

To summarize, between 1940 and 1960 the industry mix of the South was becoming more like that of the rest of the nation. Nevertheless, in 1960 the South still had a relatively high proportion of its total employment in relatively slow-growing industries. Although the South had high rates of employment growth in rapidly growing industries, it also increased its share of national employment in all relatively slow-growing sectors, with the exception of agriculture and sawmills. If its principal employment increases continue to be concentrated in the labor-intensive, low-wage sectors, then the South's relative underrepresentation in the more desirable occupations will continue and possibly even increase in the sectors outside of agriculture. Furthermore, although per capita income will continue to increase it will remain below that of the nation. As Stober has pointed out, "A continued narrowing of income differentials, therefore, as well as differentials between the regional and national employment structures, calls for competitive gains in the more capital-intensive industries with higher skill requirements. Here, the record of the Southeast has not been impressive. In view of the increasing educational requirements for employment in these industries, the prospect for competitive gains is not bright."[10] Thus, examination of industry mix and competitive shifts in the South does not in itself explain why it is a lagging region, or what must be done to close the gap between employment and income opportunity in the South and that in the rest of the nation.[11] Here attention must be turned to the development of the region's human resources.

Human Resource Investment Needs

There is widespread and increasing agreement that the inter-related economic and social problems of the South are primarily a consequence of the region's relatively low investment, in both the past and present, in its human resources. This is particularly the case with respect to education. Theodore Schultz, for example, finds that "the South has been lagging seriously in providing people the opportunities to invest in acquiring the high skills for which the demand has been increasing at so rapid a rate, predominantly because of social, political, and economic discrimination adverse to poor people."[12] Vernon Briggs argues that "the South needs educated and skilled workers to meet the needs of its expanding private businesses and burgeoning defense industries. Its one-time asset—cheap and unskilled labor—has become an albatross."[13] Joseph Spengler similarly urges that "Both average income in the South and capacity to increase it are depressed more by lack of training in the population than by any other condition, especially in the rural white population and in the non-white population, rural and urban. Consequently, range of skill, levels of aspiration, and motivation are very low."[14] Another recent study of southern manpower issues concludes that "the only logical solution to the economic development problem facing the South lies in a highly stepped-up rate of development of the region's human resources through education and training, so that the productive capacities of all southern workers may be efficiently utilized."[15]

In addition to its greater dependence on agriculture, the South has relatively low earnings for work because its labor force has a greater proportion of Negroes than the rest of the country, and in terms of education and training southern Negroes are worse off than Negroes in other regions. Moreover, a higher proportion of whites in the South have lower educational attainment than whites elsewhere. Table 10 presents data on the proportion of persons 25 years and older who have completed fewer than five years of school by region of residence in 1960. "Five years of good schooling would appear to be close to the minimum level of educational preparation needed to perform most tasks in an industrialized society. There is every indication that 5 years of education in a Southern, and particularly a Southern Negro, school represents substantially less."[16] The data show that about 24 percent of the Negroes and about 7 percent of the whites in the United States did not have five years of school. In the South these proportions rise to 32 and 10 percent, respectively. For the Deep South—those states with a relatively high proportion of Negroes—they reach 39 and 11 percent, respectively. Moreover, if the data were given by region of birth rather than region of residence, the disparities between the South and the remainder of the country would be even larger because many Negroes living in the North and West received their few years of education in the South.

TABLE 10: PERCENT OF PERSONS 25 YEARS AND OVER COMPLETING LESS THAN FIVE YEARS OF SCHOOL, BY REGION AND RACE, 1960

	White	Nonwhite	All
United States	6.7	23.5	8.3
Northeast	6.6	12.9	7.0
North Central	4.8	14.0	5.4
West	4.8	16.0	5.6
South	10.0	31.8	14.0
Deep South[a]	10.6	39.2	18.3
Appalachia[b]	11.6	29.3	14.2

[a] Includes South Carolina, Georgia, Alabama, Mississippi, Arkansas, and Louisiana.
[b] Includes Virginia, West Virginia, North Carolina, Kentucky, and Tennessee.
Source: John F. Kain and Joseph J. Persky, "The North's Stake in Southern Rural Poverty," Harvard University Program on Regional and Urban Economics, Discussion Paper No. 18, May, 1967, p. 46.

Interregional comparisons in terms of quantity of education do not take account of the lower quality of southern education. Educational efforts in the South have always lagged behind those of the rest of the country. The growth of state-supported primary and secondary public school systems before the Civil War failed to affect the South, except for North Carolina and a few large cities. Such systems were imposed on the South during Reconstruction but they were met with resistance. By 1890, 17 percent of the whites and 72 percent of the Negroes over 20 years old in the South were illiterate, whereas the comparable figures for the North were only 7 percent and 40 percent, respectively. It was only in the early part of this century that the value of public education was recognized in most parts of the South, and even then southern schools gave relatively little emphasis to science, mathematics, engineering, business administration, and other subjects related to the promotion of economic growth. Instead, the college curriculum favored languages, law, and the humanities, and primary and secondary education were geared accordingly.[17] Even today the courses offered in many southern high schools are not related to the region's new industrial needs. For example, many of the aerospace companies with operations in Texas, Florida, and Louisiana have an unfilled demand for technicians, but few technicians are trained in the South. It is easier to import scientists and engineers by making them sufficiently attractive offers.[18] Similarly, most students in southern high schools are taking essentially college preparatory courses even though less than 20 percent of them will graduate from college. And, while employment opportunities in agriculture are declining, the number of students trained in vocational agriculture is increasing.[19]

The median number of school years completed by persons 25 years and over in the United States in 1960 was 10.6 years. In the South this value ranged from 8.7 years in South Carolina to 10.9 years in Florida, the only state in the South to exceed the national median. By 1966 the national median had risen to 12.0, though individual state figures were not available. However, the median number of school years completed by persons 25 years and older was 10.8 for the eleven states included in the foregoing southern figure plus five border states and the District of Columbia. In addition, the rate of illiteracy in the South remains relatively high and the number of young men failing Selective Service preinduction and induction mental tests is above the national average.[20] Negroes in particular are adversely affected by the quality of southern education. Those Negroes who reach the twelfth grade in the metropolitan South have an average verbal ability 4.2 grades below white students in the metropolitan Northeast, while the gap for Negroes in the nonmetropolitan South is 5.2 grades. Southern whites, on the other hand, were only 0.9 years behind in the metropolitan South and 1.5 years in the nonmetropolitan South.[21]

There are two principal reasons for the inadequacies of southern school programs. First, the South's relatively low per capita income does not provide the necessary financial resources. Second, the available resources have not been used effectively because of inefficient school organization and the continuing effort to maintain many of the aspects of segregated education.

A useful measure of resources available for education is the amount of personal income per school-age child. In terms of this criterion, each of eleven southern states ranked below the national average of $10,644 in 1965. The range was from $5,559 per child in Mississippi to $9,895 in Florida.[22]

"Overdependence on State revenues by local school districts can seriously impair the quality of education in those districts. In such cases, schools are at the mercy of the political direction of the State."[23] In 1966–67 about 40 percent of all revenue income for public schools in the nation came from state sources, yet of eleven southern states only Virginia (39 percent) ranked below the national average. Alabama, North Carolina, Louisiana, South Carolina, Kentucky, Mississippi, and Tennessee each provided over half of local school district revenue. Low property tax rates help explain the small role assumed by local governments in public school financing. In 1964–65 per capita tax receipts of local governments in the nation amounted to $114, or 4.3 percent of total personal income. In contrast, the southern states ranged from Alabama, with $25 per capita (1.6 percent of personal income), to Florida, with $84 (3.6 percent). Another difficulty is the tax effort made to upgrade education. In 1966–67 the median expenditure for the nation's school districts was 1.2 percent of the property value of the district. Median expenditures in Kentucky, Tennessee, Alabama, and Mississippi, on the other hand, averaged only 0.5 percent. Financial constraints put the South at a definite disadvantage in attracting qualified teachers. The average salary of all classroom teachers in public schools in the United States in 1966–67 was $6,821, but in the South the average ranged from a low of $4,650 in Mississippi to a high of only $6,430 in Florida. The proportion of high school teachers with at least a master's degree ranged from 19 percent in Virginia to 31 percent in Alabama, whereas the national average is about 32 percent.[24]

In addition to problems of inadequate financing, southern public schools also suffer from an excessive number of inefficient small schools. Racial segregation has been a major factor in perpetuating this pattern. In 1962–63 about two-thirds of the public high schools in the South had fewer than 500 pupils, and one-third enrolled fewer than 250. Only one in ten had as many as 1,000 pupils. Although complete data are not available on the size of elementary schools, "there is sufficient support for the conclusion that elementary schools are no more efficiently organized than are high schools."[25]

If Southerners in general receive poorer education than persons in the rest of the United States, the situation of the southern Negro is still worse. This already has been indicated by the data in Table 9 and by comparisons of gaps in educational quality between the South and the Northeast. The lack of vocational training programs for Negroes is particularly glaring in view of the growing industrialization and urbanization of the South. A survey of 394 accredited southern high schools in 1963 indicated that in 312 white schools there were 66 different vocational subjects, but in 82 Negro schools there were only 37 different subjects. Typing and home economics were the only vocational subjects offered in over half of the Negro schools.[26] The combined effects of underinvestment in Negro education and training and of discrimination are clearly reflected in the South's changing manpower situation between 1950 and 1960. The

Southeast and South Central regions together added almost a million net new jobs in manufacturing, yet only a few Negro males found factory employment. According to Eli Ginzberg, "The outside figure would be 10,000, and it may have been as low as the Census suggests—only 1,000! The South has long recognized four classes of manpower—white men, white women, Negro women, and Negro men, and substantially in that order. Southern employers just do not hire Negro men if they do not have to."[27] Although the situation may be more complex than this, it is apparent that:

Enrollment in vocational education in Southern high schools is not sufficient to satisfy either the needs of people or the projected needs of the labor force of the South. High School programs are not keeping pace with the increasing numbers of young people, their concentration in urban centers, or their special difficulties in entering the labor force. The shortcomings of the occupational education program in most Southern high schools reflect generally insufficient concern for all youth and especially Negro youth.[28]

Southern leaders still must face up to the issue of how the South's Negro population will fit into an industrializing and urbanizing society. A choice must be made between tradition and progress because southern tradition contains too many elements that cannot be reconciled with the region's economic development. William Nicholls has effectively argued that these negative elements may be classified into five principal categories: (1) the persistence of agrarian values, (2) the rigidity of the region's social structure, (3) the undemocratic nature of its political structure, (4) the weakness of social responsibility on the part of the traditional sociopolitical leadership, and (5) conformity of thought and behavior.[29] Despite the persistence of these barriers to progress there are at work in the South and in the South's interrelations with the rest of the nation a number of positive forces. These include the urbanization and industrialization of the region, the increasing integration of southern economic and social life with that of the rest of the United States, the effects of population movements to and from the region, and a growing realization in the North that southern problems are in many respects national problems and should be dealt with in that perspective.

Urbanization of the South

Eli Ginzberg has pointed out that the South has approximately the same proportion of small SMSA's—cities the size of Charlotte and Savannah—as does the rest of the country. However, "if one focuses on the major metropolitan areas and disregards Florida, one finds that only 5 per cent of the South's population is concentrated in large urban centers, in contrast to a third of the population of the country as a whole."[30] There are, he continues, "only three large Southern metropolises—Dallas, Houston, and Atlanta. This means that there are few complexes with a population which has a variety of skills in depth."[31] However, this static view of the South's "retarded urbanization" masks the fact that the region is in fact urbanizing at a rapid rate.

Between 1940 and 1960 the total population of southern cities with 100,000 or more persons rose from 5.6 million to 10.3 million. This represented an increase of 83 percent, compared with 26 percent for the country as a whole and only 16 percent in all areas outside the South combined. Southern urban growth caused the proportion of the region's white population in urban areas to increase from 35 to 58 percent, and that of its Negro population in urban areas to increase from 34 to 56 percent.[32] During the decade from 1930 to 1940 SMSA's in the South accounted for 52 percent of the region's population growth; from 1940 to 1950 this figure increased to 84 percent; and from 1950 to 1960 it rose to 90 percent. This left the region with thirteen cities in the 500,000–1 million population size-class and another forty-nine in the 100,000–500,000 class, well dispersed relative to the largest cities.[33] In 1950 the South had 41 percent of the nation's rural population, but during the 1950–60 decade the annual rate of rural outmigration was 2.73 percent, compared with the national rate of 1.69 percent. In consequence, the South accounted for 60 percent of all rural outmigrants. The urban

South had a net inmigration 2.6 million persons; its inmigration rate of 1.2 percent per year was greater than the national rate of 1.07. However, urban inmigration in the South was not sufficient to offset the region's rural outmigration, so the South lost a net total of over 3 million migrants to the rest of the country. Of those who left the South it is estimated that 1.4 million were whites and 1.9 million nonwhites.[34]

The metropolitan pattern that is emerging in the South increasingly resembles the national pattern. Leonard Riessman argues that "the metropolitan conurbations in the South mean the end of the region as a homogeneous unity and the creation of a new alignment in which the older boundaries and older loyalties have less functional meaning. For most of the South this will come to mean, as it already has in some cases, the development of new chains of common interest and outlook."[35] It may be expected that this process will contribute to social, economic, and political changes since urbanization involves changes in attitudes and institutions as well as in place of residence. Thus the rural South "has become, and will increasingly become, a complex series of metropolitan conurbations, which will make out-of-date the older regional and rural conceptions of the South."[36]

The urbanization of the South is significantly changing the nature of economic development in the region. In the past the pattern of industrial growth in the South differed from that in the North in that rural areas and small towns accounted for a high proportion of manufacturing activity. Within the Deep South SMSA's contain the majority of manufacturing employment in only one state, Louisiana.[37] While it is likely that the rural South will continue to attract firms seeking low labor costs and relatively unskilled workers, a different kind of development is taking place in the region's metropolitan areas. In analyzing wage differentials in the United States, Victor Fuchs found that quality-adjusted wages for rural areas and small towns were significantly lower than for the entire South. His study also indicates that employment growth in southern metropolitan areas is much less attributable to low wages than is the case for the rural South, though quality-adjusted wages were somewhat lower in southern than in northern metropolitan areas.[38] On the basis of this evidence and of the rapid growth of southern metropolitan areas, Kain and Persky argue that where the rural South and the metropolitan North have failed to provide the rural Southerner with an opportunity "to earn a decent income in a decent environment," the metropolitan South may well be able to succeed.[39] Moreover, urban-industrial growth in the South is taking place at a time when businessmen are showing greater interest in the social responsibility doctrine, and when land use planners are offering attractive alternatives to the kind of undisciplined and wasteful growth that characterized the expansion of so many northern cities. Over thirty-five years ago Rupert Vance envisioned a pattern of urbanization for the South that still contains much promise:

> While the South develops the small city, the medium city, and a few large cities, it need not produce the metropolis. Thus, it may avoid traffic congestion, the creation of slum areas, the loss of time going to and from work, and the corrupt and inefficient municipal housekeeping almost inevitably attached to overdeveloped population centers. If such a program is possible, the South may finally attain many of the advantages of contemporary industrialization without suffering its accompanying deficiencies and maladjustments.[40]

Unfortunately, southern planners have as yet done little to take advantage of their favorable spatial situations,[41] though the rapid pace of urbanization leaves an even smaller margin of time for inaction. If the South's traditional leaders again fail to respond to the region's opportunities, then new leadership must emerge from within the South, perhaps from among the many able and well-educated inmigrants whose entry into the region has accompanied its increasing interrelations with and integration with the rest of the United States.

The South and the Nation

The great postwar growth of commercial air travel has been a potent force in increasing mutual contacts between the South and the rest of the nation. Business, professional, and educational leaders who formerly were reluctant to take up residence in the South because of the fear of being isolated can now live there and be within a few hours of cities throughout the country. The growth of air traffic and demands of the airlines have also reinforced the development of a number of southern cities—for example, Atlanta, Miami, New Orleans, Houston, and Dallas—as transportation hubs. Thus air travel has both opened up the region and emphasized the importance of its urban centers. In addition, it has broken up the primarily east-west orientation of the rail network, as well as that of the highway network that tended to parallel it. "With its greater fluidity, air transportation almost overnight has brought the South back again into a national transportation network from which it had been more or less excluded since 1869 when the first transcontinental railroad was completed."[42]

The urban South also has made considerable gains as a consequence of favorable educational selectivity in population migration patterns. As of 1960 there were 5,088,000 people living in the South who were born in the North or West. This does not include foreign-born persons or those for whom state of birth was not reported. On the other hand, there were 9,865,000 southern-born people living outside of the South. Although there were more southern-born people living outside the South than the converse, the proportion of those born "outside" (but in the United States) was greater in the South. Thus the life and culture of the South is more subject to outside influence arising from migration than the life and culture of the rest of the country is to southern influence.[43] However, the rate of outmigration of males from the South is high, especially among the youngest and best educated. Net outmigration from the South is nevertheless low because the rate of inmigration also is high. Whites have higher outmigration rates than nonwhites, but the net outmigration of whites is lower than for non-whites because nonwhite inmigration rates have been much lower than white rates. The data in Tables 11 and 12 show that whites with the least education are overrepresented while nonwhites with the least education

TABLE 11: NUMBER OF MIGRANTS (NET) AT GIVEN AGES AND LEVELS OF EDUCATION, WHITE MALES, THE SOUTHERN REGION, 1955–1960

Educational Level	Age								Total
	25–29	30–34	35–39	40–44	45–49	50–54	55–59	60–64	
5	−1548	−1196	−1089	−1063	−1015	−738	−282	+721	−6210
5–7	−3672	−991	−1013	−396	−562	+598	+1491	+2564	−1981
8	−4613	−1181	+71	+737	+1298	+2218	+3389	+5388	+7307
9–11	−6580	+755	+2698	+3282	+3221	+3205	+3524	+4006	+14111
12	−13991	+3875	+5994	+5005	+4041	+3320	+3088	+3712	+15044
13–15	−8667	+796	+1469	+1567	+1940	+1705	+1961	+2299	+3070
16+	−12868	−2819	+1226	+1149	+1182	+1482	+1493	+2046	−7109
Total	−51939	−761	+9356	+10281	+10105	+11790	+16664	+20736	+24232

Source: Rashi Fein, "Educational Patterns in Southern Migration," *Southern Economic Journal,* Vol. 32, No. 1, Part 2 (July, 1965), p. 124.

TABLE 12: NUMBER OF MIGRANTS (NET) AT GIVEN AGES AND LEVELS OF EDUCATION, NONWHITE MALES, THE SOUTHERN REGION, 1955–1960

Educational Level	Age								Total
	25–29	30–34	35–39	40–44	45–49	50–54	55–59	60–64	
5	−1125	−1311	−1022	−969	−884	−503	−509	−352	−6675
5–7	−2741	−1867	−1858	−1244	−932	−610	−274	−276	−9802
8	−2295	−1566	−899	−823	−378	−297	−226	−136	−6620
9–11	−5563	−2469	−1410	−579	−344	−268	−58	−47	−10738
12	−5261	−1380	−749	−395	−235	−118	−125	+15	−8248
13–15	−1965	−601	−306	−148	−53	−19	−81	+6	−3167
16+	−1677	−934	−375	−208	−85	−19	−10	−4	−3312
Total	−20627	−10128	−6619	−4366	−2911	−1834	−1283	−794	−48562

Source: Rashi Fein, "Educational Patterns in Southern Migration," Southern Economic Journal, Vol. 32, No. 1, Part 2 (July, 1965), p. 124.

are underrepresented in the net outmigration. Moreover, whites with the most education are overrepresented up to age 35 in outmigration, but overrepresented in inmigration above that age. Nonwhites with the most education are overrepresented in net outmigration at all ages up to 50. As a consequence of these educational selectivity patterns, the educational distribution of whites above age 30 is shifted favorably for the South, but that for nonwhites is shifted unfavorably.

Fein has analyzed the economic loss to the South of net outmigration by multiplying the net migration figure for each color, age, and educational level by the discounted (at 5 percent) value of future earnings for persons in the South with the same color, age, and education characteristics. These dollar values were then compared with the stock of human capital in the region as computed by multiplying 1955 residents by their capital value, or discounted future earnings. The net loss for the region over the 1955–60 period was about 0.34 percent of its stock of white capital and 3.3 percent of its nonwhite capital. For all persons combined the loss was 0.4 percent, or only 0.08 percent at an annual rate.[44] If differences in the quality of education of the inmigrants and outmigrants had been taken into account it is probable that this small loss would be even smaller, or possibly turned into a gain. As Fein concludes, "losses due to migration are not the big Southern problem we had presumed. The South's future may be dim, its out-migration may have social implications, but its economy is not being held back materially because of an exodus of human capital. Solutions to its problems involve more basic matters."[45]

Finally, it should be emphasized that education-selective migration has not affected the subregions of the South equally. Suval and Hamilton have shown that areas with large, growing metropolitan populations are attracting most of the well educated migrants, whereas rural areas of the South continue to lose more well educated people than they gain.[46] Thus, here again the key to the South's progress lies in its urban development. Furthermore, it is evident that discrimination results in a loss of the able Negroes who could make a contribution to even more rapid growth and give badly needed leadership to the South's Negro community.

If population migration has not had the adverse effects on the South that many people have maintained, it has worked to the relative detriment of the rest of the country. The pattern of migration of whites from the non-South to the South and the migration of non-whites from the South to the rest of the country (in relation to the educational distribution outside the South) has affected the North unfavorably. It is therefore evident that the North as well as the South has a stake in southern education. Kain and Persky maintain that:

To the extent that the metropolitan North is closely intertwined with the rural South through the forces of migration, these factors become pressing problems for that region too. To the extent that the Southern migrant, ill-prepared for urban life, becomes a problem of the metropolitan North, the improvement of the rural South is in the North's self-interest. Moreover, if Southern poverty leads to underinvestment in human capital, the consequences may well be felt to a greater extent in the more industrialized North than in the rural South.[47]

The social benefits accruing from the education of the southern migrant are by no means limited to the employers who gain trained laborers. Taxpayers in general gain through reduced costs for crime prevention, law enforcement, and welfare insofar as these are related to lack of education. If education is viewed as an investment involving future as distinct from current returns, then it also has intergenerational benefits. When today's students reach adulthood their present education will increase the likelihood that they will rear children who recognize the economic and cultural benefits of education. This implies that it is socially beneficial to educate women even if their skills and training are not directly utilized by their entry into the labor force. For all of these reasons "residents of areas of in-migration have a stake in the education of children in the areas of out-migration."[48]

The typical southern rural Negro lifetime migrant tends to move to metropolitan areas with more than a million population outside the South. Forty-eight percent of Negroes born in the South Atlantic states and now living elsewhere live in Buffalo, New York, Philadelphia, and Pittsburgh. About 40 percent of Negro lifetime migrants from the East South Central states live in Chicago, Detroit, Cleveland, and Milwaukee. Similarly, about 36 percent of this group from the West South Central states reside in Los Angeles, San Diego, San Francisco, and Seattle. Thus, Negroes have moved to northern and western cities along three major streams: one following the Eastern Seaboard, another the Mississippi Valley to Ohio and Michigan, and yet another to the West Coast.[49] White migrants follow a more diffused pattern with a tendency to move to medium-sized northern cities and metropolitan areas within the South. Between 1950 and 1960, 2.6 million southern-born whites and 2.47 million southern-born Negroes moved to cities with over a million population outside the South. In contrast, whereas 1.42 million whites went to non-southern cities in the 250,000–1,000,000 population-size class, only 420,000 Negroes followed a similar course. All SMSA's with more than 250,000 population accounted for only 60 percent of white outmigrants, compared with 89 percent for Negroes. Within the South, 2.86 million whites left their state of birth for southern SMSA's, but only 860,000 Negroes went to these cities.[50]

Kain and Persky have argued that from the viewpoint of the narrow self-interest of the North, "the economic development of the South can play a crucial role in providing leverage in the handling of metropolitan problems."[51] In addition, they argue that "gilding" programs which accept the Negro ghettos as given must be replaced by programs aimed at their dispersal. Their approach to the ghetto problem will be dealt with in greater detail in Chapter 10, but here it is necessary to examine that part of their position that relates to migration from the South:

> While ghetto job creation, like other "gilding" programs, might initially reduce Negro unemployment, it must eventually affect the system that binds the Northern ghetto to the rural and urban areas of the South. This system will react to any sudden changes in employment opportuni-

ties in Northern ghettos. If there are no offsetting improvements in the South, the result will be increased rates of migration into still restricted ghetto areas. . . . Indeed it is possible that more than one migrant would appear in the ghetto for every job created. Even at lower levels of sensitivity a strong wave of inmigration could prove extremely harmful to many other programs. The South in 1960 still accounted for about 60 per cent of the country's Negro population, more than half of which lived in nonmetropolitan areas. In particular, the number of potential migrants from the rural South has not declined greatly in recent years. The effect of guaranteed incomes or jobs available in the metropolitan ghetto can be inferred from an analysis of the patterns of migration from the South.[52]

Elsewhere Kain and Persky state with regard to rural outmigration from the South that their findings "emphasize that no sudden change in the extent of that movement is imminent. This is especially true for the Negro population."[53]

TABLE 13: NEGRO POPULATION AND ESTIMATED NET OUT-
MIGRATION OF NONWHITES FROM THE SOUTH,[a]
1940–1968 (in thousands)

	1940	1950	1960	1965	1968
Negro population in the South	9,905	10,222	11,312	11,233[b]	11,573[b]
	1940–50	1950–60	1960–65	1965–68	
Nonwhite, average annual net out-migration from the South	159.7	145.7	94.6	80.3	

[a] The South includes the States of the Old Confederacy as well as Delaware, the District of Columbia, Kentucky, Maryland, Oklahoma, and West Virginia.
[b] Excludes Armed Forces living in barracks.
Source: U. S. Department of Commerce, Bureau of the Census, Current Population Reports, Series P–23, No. 26, p. 2.

Yet, as the data in Table 13 show, there has been a recent sharp decline in the number of Negroes leaving the South. The average annual net outmigration of Negroes from the South in 1968 was only half of what it was in the 1940's, and even considerably less than it was as recently as 1965. Furthermore, between 1966 and 1968 the number of Negroes living in the central cities declined. In 1966 there were 12.1 million Negroes in these areas, but at the beginning of 1968 their number had dropped to 11.8 million.[54]

It is still too early to identify the reasons behind this sharp change in recent trends, or to know whether it signals a permanent alteration in Negro migration patterns. Part of the explanation may lie in the continuing rapid growth of the South's economy. Kain and Persky have pointed out that more rapid southern economic development could change the historic pattern of Negro migration. "Tentative research findings indicate that both manufacturing growth and urbanization reduce Southern Negro outmigration. While the holding effect of these changes is not as strong for Negroes as for whites, the difference between the two responses can be substantially narrowed."[55] The impact of the South's growth on Negro migration can only be adequately evaluated by careful study of the growth of Negro job opportunities in the South. Present trends in Negro family incomes show a rapid narrowing of the gap between median family income in central cities of the South and those of the Northeast. In 1959, the northeastern value was $4,790 (1967 dollars), or 39 percent above the $3,454 value for the South. In 1967, median Negro family income in southern central cities had risen to $5,015, only $370—or 7 percent—lower than the $5,385 median in the Northeast. Clearly, opportunities for Negroes in southern cities have been improving at a relatively rapid pace.[56]

Another reason for the loss of momentum of southern Negro migration may be the riots and violence that have taken place in the northern ghettos. They have focused national attention on the misery and lack of opportunity that characterize life in the slums. This publicity has undoubtedly not been lost on many potential Negro migrants, to whom home may now appear relatively less unattractive, especially if advances in the civil rights field kindle hope that even the South may change. Moreover, the fact that northern rioters have been preoccupied with destroying their own neighborhoods can hardly be an encouragement to potential inmigrants from the South. In any event, there is no prospect that the migration stream linking the rural South to Northern ghettos will dry up in the near future; nor will the problems of the ghettos be solved any sooner. Although slum problems will be dealt with at greater length in Chapter 10, it is clear from the discussions of this chapter that the development of the South should be one of the major elements in regional policy conceived from both southern and national points of view.

Summary and Conclusions

Although the industry mix of the South is becoming more like that of the rest of the nation, a relatively high proportion of the region's total employment is found in relatively slow-growing industries. Its main employment increases continue to be in those industries that are labor-intensive and pay relatively low wages. Thus, even though per capita income in the South will increase, it will remain below that of the country as a whole unless competitive gains can be made in attracting capital-intensive industries with relatively high skill requirements.

However, before this can happen on a large scale, there will have to be a much greater investment in the South's human resources than has heretofore been the case. Indeed, underinvestment in the South's human resources has been the greatest impediment to the region's economic progress. Moreover, this is a problem that also affects the rest of the nation, and especially the large northern cities. The pattern of migration of whites from the non-South to the South and of nonwhites from the South to the rest of the country affects the non-South adversely in relation to its existing educational distribution. For this reason it is in the self-interest of the nation as a whole to aid southern education financially. But the South should also increase its effort on behalf of education and other forms of investment in human beings. Particular efforts should be made to upgrade the health, education, and skills of those whose economic and human potential has been most neglected and oppressed by discrimination. Although many Negroes with poor education leave the South, the rest of the country is not receiving a disproportionate share of poorly educated southern Negroes relative to their total number. In other words, an even higher proportion of the Negroes remaining in the South have low levels of education.

In addition to human resource development, the key to the economic growth of the South lies in the region's urbanization. In the past the South's characteristically low-wage, low-skill manufacturing employment was located for the most part in rural areas and small towns. However, growing urbanization—southern cities with over 100,000 population grew by 83 percent between 1940 and 1960 as contrasted to 16 percent for comparable cities in the rest of the country—is providing a basis for attracting a greater share of rapidly growing and capital-intensive industries. Urban growth implies the generation of external economies attractive to business and industry. It also implies a shift away from the traditional values and attitudes that have done so much to hinder the growth of the South and its integration into the life of the nation as a whole. Moreover, with rational planning the cities of the South still have an opportunity to avoid many of the disagreeable aspects of the congested cities of the North. Thus, the concomitant development of the South's human resources and of new job opportunities in the region's expanding urban areas are objectives that merit the support of the nation as a whole.

Chapter 4

The Appalachian Region

Introduction

For 150 years the Appalachian Mountains were the official frontier between European and Indian America. In one of the first major reports on the nation's transportation needs, Albert Gallatin, Thomas Jefferson's Secretary of the Treasury, urged that four major roads be built through the mountains so that the development of the trans-mountain territories would not be impeded. Nevertheless, commerce between the seaboard and the Midwest has bypassed most of Appalachia. The only major east-west transportation routes through the mountains between the Mohawk Valley and the territory to the north of Atlanta are in Pennsylvania. The early settlers who sought isolation in the creeks and hollows of the region removed themselves from the mainstream of American life. Over the years their physical isolation became cultural isolation and then economic isolation. Indeed, there are counties in Central Appalachia that have lower per capita incomes than many of the world's underdeveloped countries. The early Scotch-Irish settlers were followed by an influx of workers—many from Central and Eastern Europe—into the region's coal mining and steel mill towns. But the miners in particular, as their farmer predecessors, were tied to the land by the nature of their work. In consequence, even though much of Appalachia has a

FIGURE 3: APPALACHIAN COUNTIES, 1967

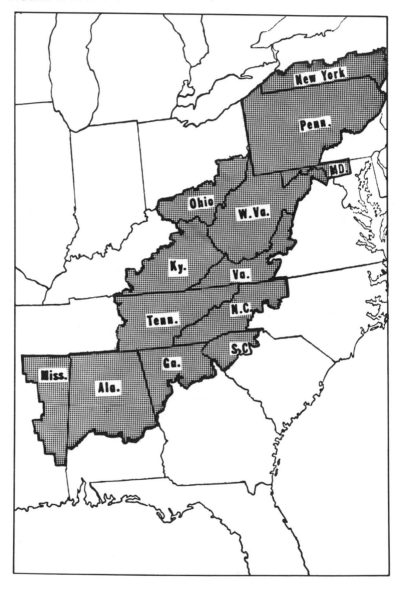

population density greater than that of the nation, there are relatively few urban centers to provide badly needed hospitals, schools, commercial activities, and jobs. In Central Appalachia only 250,000 of the area's 1.5 million inhabitants live in towns with more than 2,500 people. And the grimy towns and cities that grew up as steel and coal centers in northern Appalachia in the last century often lack the environment and facilities capable of attracting and supporting significant economic growth. Thus, Appalachia represents an unusual case among lagging regions of industrialized countries. In general, these regions are peripheral to their countries' economic heartlands. Appalachia, on the other hand, is located between two of the most highly industrialized and urbanized regions in the world —the Atlantic megalopolis and the industrial Midwest. With the rapid expansion of Atlanta to the south, Appalachia appears more and more as an island of distress in a sea of affluence.[1]

Appalachia as a Lagging Region: Some Leading Indicators

In 1966, the estimated population of the Appalachian region was 18.3 million, which represented an increase of 3.0 percent over the region's 1960 population (see Table 14). The population of the United States grew by 9.8 percent from 1960 to 1966. Net outmigration of 606,100 persons from Appalachia was largely responsible for the lower growth rate of the region. The proportion of the Appalachian population living in SMSA's or in non-SMSA counties with a total urban population over 50,000 was 49.7 percent in 1966; the corresponding national proportion was 72.4 percent. The proportion of the national population living in such areas increased by 2.2 percentage points between 1960 and 1966, but in Appalachia it declined by 0.5 percentage points.

In 1960 over 30 percent of the families living in Appalachia had an annual income of less than $$3,000, the frequently used approximate borderline between poverty and a minimally comfortable standard of living. Conversely, whereas 15 percent of all American families had an annual income in excess of $10,000, fewer than 9

TABLE 14: POPULATION AND INCOME BY LEVEL OF URBANIZATION FOR SELECTED YEARS, U.S. AND APPALACHIA

Classification of Counties by Total Urban Population 1960 Census	Population Estimate 1966 (number)	Population Change 1960–1966 (number)	Distribution of Population in 1960 (percent)	in 1966 (percent)	Share of Population Change 1960–1966 (percent)	Net Migration (number)	Per Capita Personal Income 1959 (dollars)	1966 (dollars)	Increase in Per Capita Income 1959–1966 (dollars)
UNITED STATES									
Metropolitan (SMSA)	135,289,612	15,885,832	66.7	68.8	90.5	......	2,473	3,314	814
Urban pop. over 50,000	7,019,151	683,207	3.5	3.6	3.9	......			
Urban pop. 25,000–50,000	13,256,599	951,810	6.9	6.7	5.4	......			
Urban pop. 10,000–25,000	15,143,016	249,467	8.3	7.7	1.4	......	1,573	2,236	663
Urban pop. 2,500–10,000	17,634,861	−133,264	9.9	9.0	−0.8	......			
Rural	8,311,760	−78,053	4.7	4.2	−0.4	......			
TOTAL	196,655,000	17,559,900	100.0	100.0	100.0	......	2,161	2,963	802
APPALACHIA									
Metropolitan (SMSA)	7,472,700	158,041	41.3	40.9	29.4	−295,500	2,208	2,843	635
Urban pop. over 50,000	1,612,800	28,705	8.9	8.8	5.3	−59,400	1,746	2,449	703

TABLE 14—Continued

Classification of Counties by Total Urban Population 1960 Census	Population Estimate 1966 (number)	Population Change 1960–1965 (number)	Distribution of Population in 1960 / in 1966 (percent)		Share of Population Change 1960–1966 (percent)	Net Migration [a] (number)	Per Capita Personal Income 1959 / 1966 (dollars)		Increase In Per Capita Income 1959–1966 (dollars)
			1960	1966			1959	1966	
Urban pop. 25,000–50,000	7,766,400	84,012	9.5	9.7	15.6	−23,200	1,742	2,486	744
Urban pop. 10,000–25,000	2,676,200	132,899	14.4	14.7	24.7	−42,700	1,393	2,034	641
Urban pop. 2,500–10,000	3,045,100	95,996	16.6	16.7	17.9	−125,300	1,131	1,643	512
Rural	1,691,200	38,167	9.3	9.2	7.1	−59,500	858	1,268	410
TOTAL	18,264,400	537,820	100.0	100.0	100.0	−606,100	1,661[a]	2,297[b]	636[c]

[a] The per capita income for the five nonmetropolitan groups was $1,247 in 1959.
[b] The per capita income for the five nonmetropolitan groups was $1,938 in 1966
[c] The increase in per capita income for the five groups was $691.

Source: Eli P. March, "Indicators of Appalachian Progress: Population and Income," Appalachia, Vol. 2, No. 6 (March, 1969), p. 24.

percent of Appalachian families were in this group. Savings in the region, as measured by commercial bank deposits and savings and loan association accounts, were $514 per capita in 1960, while those in the rest of the country were $920, or about 80 percent greater.[2]

The data in Table 14 show that, between 1959 and 1966, per capita personal income in Appalachia increased by 38.3 percent, from $1661 to $2297; in the United States as a whole the increase was from $2161 to $2963, or 37.1 percent. Thus, although in proportional terms the situation in Appalachia improved slightly (the Appalachian value rose from 77 to 78 percent of the national value), the absolute gap increased from $500 to $666.

The 1960 male labor force participation rate in Appalachia was 72.6 percent, compared with a 77.4 percent rate for the nation. The male unemployment rate was 7.1 percent, compared with a national rate of 5.0 percent. The unemployment situation would have been even more acute were it not for substantial outmigration during the decade of the 1950's, when the region's population increased by only 2 percent and 2.2 million persons departed; even more significant was the 5.1 percent decline in the 18–64 age group during this period. However, data for the first half of the present decade indicate definite improvement in the employment situation, no doubt as a result of vigorous expansion of aggregate economic activity in the nation. From 1962 to 1965 the regional unemployment rate dropped by 3.4 percentage points, from 8.6 to 5.2 percent. The national rate meanwhile dropped by 1.0 percentage point, from 5.5 to 4.5 percent. The gap between the regional and national rates was thus cut from 3.1 to 0.7 percentage points. However, the data for the region as a whole mask the fact that large parts of the region still are burdened "with farm market towns that no longer have any markets, mining towns ill-equipped to compete for anything but a share of the declining employment in mining, and mill towns losing their once valuable locational advantages to other markets elsewhere in the Nation without being able to compete effectively for other kinds of economic activity."[3] As will be seen shortly, the problems of Central Appalachia remain especially acute.

Urbanization and the Prospects for Economic Growth

For the United States as a whole, the most rapidly growing SMSA's are in the 500,000–1,000,000 size class, although 53 percent of the absolute growth between 1960 and 1965 was in SMSA's with over one million population. This suggests that cities that are parts of metropolitan areas will grow faster than similar-size cities elsewhere. For example, outside Appalachia urban areas which were in the 2,500–50,000 size class and which were also in metropolitan areas added 10 million to their population between 1950 and 1960. In contrast, urban areas of the same size outside metropolitan areas added only 2 million to their population. This trend has continued in the present decade. Between 1950 and 1960 the metropolitan group of Appalachian communities grew faster than their non-metropolitan counterparts in every size class. Nevertheless, with the exception of the 2,500–5,000 size class, the urban areas of Appalachia grew more slowly than their national counterparts.[4] As pointed out earlier, the population of Appalachia living in urban areas with over 50,000 inhabitants is less than half of its total population, whereas the national population living in such areas is over 70 percent. A number of the trends that characterized the Appalachian region in the 1950's seem to have been reversed during the present decade. SMSA's, which accounted for 41.3 percent of the region's population in 1960, accounted for only 29.4 percent of the total population increase between 1960 and 1966 (See Table 14). In the nation as a whole, SMSA's received over 90 percent of the population increase. The reason for this divergence is that many of Appalachia's larger SMSA's are in the northern part of the region, where many areas have experienced low rates of economic growth and considerable outmigration. On the other hand, the belated urbanization of the southern part of the region is taking place in relatively small centers. While rural areas and urban areas in the 2,500–10,000 category were losing population in the United States between 1960 and 1966, they accounted for one-fourth of the population growth in Appalachia. Another one-fourth of this growth took place in urban areas in the 10,000–25,000 category, while 15 percent took place in the 25,000–50,000 category. Income increase was about the same in the region's SMSA's as in Appalachia as a whole; in contrast, the increase was somewhat higher in each of the next three highest population size categories than in the region as a whole.

The data in Table 15 show that employment in Appalachia in the declining agriculture and mining sectors decreased at faster rates than those for the nation between 1950 and 1960. In addition, growth rates in the construction, manufacturing, and service sectors were lower for Appalachia than for the country as a whole. These patterns were reflected in rates of population change. In areas where manufacturing was the principal activity population increased by 8 percent; where agriculture was dominant the population decreased by 7 percent; and where mining was the main activity, population fell by 19 percent. For other areas the rate of gain increased (or the rate of loss decreased) with the importance of manufacturing, while the rate of population loss increased with the importance of mining.[5]

TABLE 15: EMPLOYMENT IN MAJOR INDUSTRY GROUPS IN
APPALACHIA AND THE UNITED STATES, 1960

Major Groups	Number (thousands)		Percent Distribution		Percent-Change 1950–1960	
	Region	U.S.	Region	U.S.	Region	U.S.
Agriculture	417.0	4.349.9	7.1	6.6	−51.6	−38.2
Mining	198.8	654.0	3.4	1.0	−58.2	−29.7
Construction	337.1	3,815.9	5.7	5.7	7.0	10.4
Manufacturing	1,911.6	17,513.1	32.6	26.4	17.2	19.9
Service	3,001.2	40,039.7	51.2	60.3	20.9	27.3
Total	5,865.8	66,372.6	100.0	100.0	0.0	15.5

Source: Appalachian Regional Commission.

In 1960, 60 percent of national employment was in the service sector, which grew by over 9 million between 1950 and 1960. Appalachia, on the other hand, had only 50 percent of its employment in services. In contrast, Appalachia's employment structure was relatively heavily oriented toward manufacturing; about one-third of its employment was in this sector, whereas the comparable value for the nation was only about one-fourth. Moreover, Appalachian manufacturing consisted of a relatively high proportion of relatively slow-growing, labor intensive industries. In 1954, value added per worker in manufacturing was about 10 percent below the national average; by 1963 it was more than 20 percent below. Value added per worker exceeded the national average only in West Virginia and the Appalachian part of Ohio. "The Region's competitive advantage for manufacturing has been in part its relatively lower wages and higher labor availability, advantages that will tend to diminish under the combined pressure of outmigration and increased job availability in the Region."[6]

Not only were the services underrepresented in Appalachia's employment structure, but its metropolitan areas were less service oriented than those of the rest of the nation. Proportion of employment in services exceeded the national average in only one of the region's metropolitan areas, Tuscaloosa, Alabama, because of its university. About a quarter of all service employment in Appalachia was accounted for by Pittsburgh and Birmingham, but neither of these cities had a proportion of service employment as high as similar cities outside the region. It should also be emphasized that Appalachia's underurbanization has hindered its ability to attract manufacturing industries. About three-quarters of all United States manufacturing employment is now located in metropolitan areas; by 1975 it is expected that manufacturing employment in the nation will increase by 3.3 million, and that fully 3 million of these jobs will be located in metropolitan areas.[7]

The employment estimates presented in Table 16 show that during the present decade the growth of construction, manufacturing, and tertiary activities in Appalachia compares more favorably to national patterns than was the case during the 1950's. However, the full significance of this change can only be evaluated when data on the localization of employment change are available.

TABLE 16: ESTIMATED NUMBER OF EMPLOYEES AND ANNUAL RATES OF EMPLOYMENT GROWTH, BY SECTOR, APPALACHIAN REGION, 1962-1967

| | Employment | | | | Annual Rate of Change (percent) | | | | | |
| | 1967 | 1966 | 1965 | 1962 | 1966-1967 | | 1965-1966 | | 1962-1965 | |
		Appalachian Region			App.	U.S.	App.	U.S.	App.	U.S.
TOTAL	4,314,773	4,199,129	3,859,079	3,605,669	2.8	3.9	8.8	6.3	2.3	3.2
Agricultural Services, Forestry, Fisheries	7,699	7,758	7,837	6,305	-0.8	3.1	-1.0	10.7	8.1	5.6
Mining	133,434	135,014	132,943	142,421	-1.2	-1.3	1.6	0.5	-2.2	-1.2
Contract Construction	221,181	219,086	190,295	143,542	1.0	-3.0	15.1	8.2	10.9	5.5
Manufacturing	2,014,393	1,943,410	1,833,141	1,666,132	3.7	3.5	6.0	6.7	3.3	2.4
Transportation and other Public Utilities	230,070	219,543	212,443	202,030	4.8	4.8	3.3	4.5	1.7	2.3
Wholesale Trade	214,295	202,953	197,628	181,128	5.6	3.0	2.7	4.6	3.0	2.0
Retail Trade	699,699	695,176	654,686	597,522	0.7	4.1	6.2	5.4	3.2	3.8
Finance, Insurance, and Real Estate	168,959	160,751	154,111	138,451	5.1	2.9	4.3	3.2	3.8	3.6
Services	575,695	532,128	493,479	421,907	8.2	7.4	7.8	7.9	5.7	5.5

Source: Appalachian Regional Commission, based on U.S. Bureau of the Census, *County Business Patterns,* 1962, 1965, 1966, 1967. Employees not covered by the Social Security Program are excluded. Also, data for the following types of employment covered by the Social Security Program in whole or in part are excluded from the basic tabulations in this report: government employees, self-employed persons, farm workers, and domestic workers reported separately. Also railroad employment subject to the Railroad Retirement Act and Employment Act and employment on ocean-borne vessels are not included. Employment in *County Business Patterns* amounted to approximately 68.4 percent of total United States paid civilian employment in 1967, 66.7 percent in 1966, 66.2 percent in 1965, and 63.7 percent in 1962. Details may not add to total due to disclosure rule.

The problems and prospects for the future development of Appalachia, and particularly the southern Appalachians, are frequently regarded as analogous to those of the South in general. While there are numerous points of similarity, it is apparent that there are also important differences in the two areas. Because of Appalachia's physical geography and its relatively poor transportation network, its residents have suffered from isolation. In addition, SMSA's in the South, as we have seen, are growing at a considerably faster rate than those in the nation as a whole; in contrast, Appalachia's SMSA's are growing less rapidly than their counterparts in the rest of the country, and those few that are rapidly growing tend to be on the fringe of the region, e.g., Huntsville, Winston-Salem, and Atlanta, a part of which extends into the region. Moreover, the South has avoided any significant net loss of human capital because of the inmigration of relatively well educated persons to its expanding cities; Appalachia has undoubtedly not been able to compensate in this manner for the large numbers of relatively (to the region) well educated young people who have migrated to other parts of the country. On the other hand, Appalachia is similar to the South in that its employment structure is still weighted quite heavily in favor of nationally slow-growing, low-wage industries. Heavy outmigration has also linked rural poverty to the northern metropolitan ghettos. But perhaps the most important similarity—from the perspective of the region's development as well as that of northern ghetto problems—is underinvestment in Appalachia's human resources.

Underinvestment in Human Resources

Numerous social scientists and other informed observers have, while not ignoring other problems of the region, emphasized that Appalachia's main need is to upgrade the quality of its human resources. Benjamin Chinitz, who served as Deputy Assistant Secretary of Commerce for Economic Development before becoming chairman of the Economics Department at Brown University, has remarked that "The 'ivory tower' approach of constructing an elegant model and testing it with data from published sources will serve at best only to delineate the problem" of developing Appalachia. "A strategy which operates mainly on classical location factors with the aim of making the region more competitive for industry can only be a small part of an overall strategy for growth in the latter part of this century." Instead, he maintains that "the main thrust of our efforts must be to upgrade the quality of human resources and, perhaps even more important, the social and political superstructure which we must now regard as the critical infrastructure for development."[8] William Miernyck, Director of the West Virginia University Regional Research Institute, has likewise urged that if Appalachia is to be made a more attractive region, "the primary attraction will be a greatly improved educational system."[9] Rupert Vance also points out that "few would disagree . . . that a substandard educational program is at the heart of the Region's problem."[10]

Inadequate investment in education is reflected in the fact that in 1960, 11.3 percent of Appalachian residents over 25 years of age had completed fewer than five years of schooling, in comparison with a national proportion of only 8.4 percent. Similarly, about half of the Appalachian residents over 25 years of age had not gone beyond the eighth grade, compared to less than 40 percent in the nation. For the same age group, 16.5 percent in the nation had attended college, but only 11.3 percent had in Appalachia.[11] Appalachian expenditure per pupil in 1962 was $337; the national figure was $518. Teachers' salaries in Appalachia lag considerably behind those in the nation. In 1964, the average teacher's salary for the whole country was $6,200, but in Appalachia it was only $4,200. A 1966 survey showed that in some Appalachian school districts the average was well below $4,000. These figures help to explain why Appalachian school districts have a much more rapid turnover of teachers than the rest of the nation. Since 1960 the turnover in Appalachia has been 14 percent, compared to 8 percent in the nation.[12]

Quality formal school systems and adult-training programs are seriously restricted by the depressed employment and income of

Appalachia. The improvement of school programs, the acquisition of better teachers and administrators, and the building of larger and better-equipped schools call for much greater funds, which must of necessity be provided from external sources. Especially in areas of high outmigration, local leaders cannot be expected to finance the education and training of young people whose social and economic contributions will be made in other, no doubt more affluent, areas.

A case in point is the Mayo Area Educational School in eastern Kentucky. Dr. George Ramey, the school's director, recently testified before a congressional subcommittee on education that the school has six hundred students studying eighteen trades. The students include both high-school level boys and girls and those who are getting additional vocational education. In general the students are highly motivated and anxious to gain vocational skills. For many years practically all the students have found good jobs, and it is rare that a student does not find employment in the particular trade for which he has been trained. Dr. Ramey conceded, however, that a good job often implies leaving for industrial centers outside the region. He said, "of course that's bad. But it's still better than letting them stay in the area and wind up on the dole or welfare."[13] Unfortunately, the school has a waiting list of 1,155 young people. A similar situation exists in other eastern Kentucky vocational schools. In Ashland, for example, a $1.7 million facility was opened in August, 1968, but about 300 adults and some 300 to 500 high school students still remained on the school's waiting list. Ramey pointed out that:

Many of these are high school graduates. Many of these are boys and girls who [sic] we have been telling for years that in today's world they need more than a high school education, that they should carry on for more training in a trade. I can't admit them because I don't have any place to put them. We already filled our shops for next year. We are already making excuses to explain why we can't take any more.[14]

It is significant that the attitudes of the people of Appalachia toward education for the most part do not conform to the "hillbilly" stereotype. In 1958, a well-designed survey was taken to probe the values and beliefs of the Appalachian people. In all, 1,466 completed interview schedules were obtained. Of these, 31.5 percent were from metropolitan households, 19.1 percent from other urban households, and 49.4 percent from rural households. The responses indicated that whatever may have been the force of traditional and fatalistic values a generation ago, it has been weakened considerably in recent decades.

Most of the people of the Region, according to the evidence of the survey data, have adopted the major goals and standards typical of American society. They, like other people throughout the nation, wish to have larger incomes, greater material comforts, and more prestigeful status. And if it seems unlikely that they will realize these aspirations for themselves, they would at least like to see them realized by their children.[15]

The achievement aspirations of Appalachian people were evident in their responses to questions concerning the amount of education they desired for their children. Three out of four wanted a son to finish college, and two out of three wanted the same for a daughter. Less than one percent indicated that they would be satisfied if a son or daughter had less than an eighth-grade education. Over 90 percent would prefer that a child take advantage of an opportunity to go to college rather than stay at home and help the family, and nearly all of these respondents would be willing to borrow money to help pay part of college expenses. Larger proportions of metropolitan residents expressed desires for their children to go to college, but, even so, about two-thirds of the rural residents expressed similar hopes. Moreover, over half of the lowest status and least educated respondents wanted a college education for their children. Ford states that while such aspirations are obviously unrealistic in a region where only one adult in 25 had completed four or more years of college (in 1950), they should not be dismissed "as representing nothing more than the pathetic attempts of the respondents to win the approval of their interviewers."[16] Rather, it is more likely that:

Appalachian residents view higher education in much the same way as do people in other parts of the nation, and are cognizant of its value in an industrial society. And the fact that they believe their children *should* receive a good education, whether or not they actually believe they will, is indication not only of the willingness to accept industrial society but also of the hope that an oncoming generation will be able to participate in it effectively.[17]

The development of Appalachia's human resources has been hampered not only by poor educational facilities, but also by inadequate health facilities and a severe shortage of doctors and other medical personnel. The poor health of many Appalachian residents is indicated by numerous statistics. The rate of infant mortality in Appalachia is twice that of the rest of the country, and deaths resulting from infectious diseases are one-third higher than the national average. Intestinal parasites, malnutrition, and tuberculosis, which are usually associated with the most underdeveloped countries, are still widespread in parts of the region. Hospitals that were intended for the treatment of acute illnesses are crowded with elderly persons and others who should be in institutions specializing in long-term care. In addition, Appalachia has only 92 physicians per 100,000 population, about a third less than the national figure of 140. To bring the ratio up to 100 per 100,000 population would require 2,400 more physicians in the region. In most parts of Appalachia facilities for treating mental illness and mental retardation are inadequate or nonexistent. As for dental problems, one survey in eleven southeastern Kentucky counties showed that 80 percent of the children entering school had serious tooth problems.[18]

The Appalachian Regional Development Act of 1965 permitted federal funds to be used in the construction of new hospitals, but prohibited special aid for existing facilities. The 1967 extension of the Act included existing hospitals in the health program, and a number of projects are now under way to upgrade general hospitals. Nevertheless, improving existing hospitals or building new ones still will not bring an adequate number of physicians to areas most in need of improved health care; in many areas the median age of practicing physicians is about 55,[19] so new doctors are needed just to maintain the present low physician-to-population ratios.

This writer has observed large numbers of the rural poor in town for food stamps in one of the more progressive counties in eastern Kentucky. The sheer physical debilitation of so many of these people in all age groups is unlike anything he has ever seen in rural areas or urban slums in the rest of the United States or in western Europe. Indeed, it seems almost beside the point to discuss education and training for these people without allowing for concomitant programs to improve their health substantially. Given the high incidence of chronic and acute illness among them, and their frequent neglect of even elementary sanitary measures, it is not surprising that so often they are not "motivated" to upgrade their education and training. The plight of the infants and small children who already are caught up in the culture of poverty is particularly disturbing.

Considerably greater support is needed from outside the region if Appalachia's health and educational needs are to be met. The rest of the nation is assuming more than its share of the welfare costs of Appalachia; the rest of the nation also is an importer of Appalachia's people and therefore has a stake in their quality. Thus, it is in the interest of the nation as a whole to improve Appalachia's human resources. This means not simply providing financial assistance, but also concerted programs to attract to the region teachers, doctors and nurses, and other professional personnel directly involved in developing human resources.

Initially, federal programs oriented toward Appalachian development tended to favor the construction of highways and similar infrastructure over human resource development and manpower programs. Highways accounted for over three-quarters of total outlays authorized by the Appalachian Regional Development Act of 1965. The only other specific program that received over 5 percent of total authorizations was that for demonstration health facilities (6.3 percent); only 1.5 percent was authorized for vocational education facilities.[20] Table 17 shows the amounts authorized by Congress for various Appalachian programs in the 1967 amendments to the original Appalachian Regional Development Act. Highways ac-

TABLE 17: AUTHORIZATION LEVELS BY PROGRAMS IN THE
APPALACHIAN REGIONAL DEVELOPMENT ACT
AS AMENDED IN 1967

Program	Amount (millions)
Administration	$ 1.7
Highways	715.0
Demonstration health projects	50.0
Land treatment	19.0
Timber development	2.0
Mining	30.0
Water survey	2.0
Housing	5.0
Vocational education	26.0
Sewage treatment	6.0
Supplemental grants	97.0
Local development districts and research	11.0
Authorization of appropriations[a]	170.0

[a] This item consolidates all authorizations except those for administration and highways. It is $78 million less than the sum of the individual ceilings of the relevant programs.

Source: Economic Development Acts, Part I, Public Law 90-103, Title I, Appalachian Regional Development Act Amendments of 1967, 90th Congress, 1st Session (Washington, D.C.: Government Printing Office, October, 1967).

count for $715 million and administrative costs for $1.7 million. The ceilings for the other programs, when summed, amount to $248 million, but the "authorization of appropriations" in Section 401 of the amendments places a $170 million ceiling on them for the two-fiscal-year period ending June 30, 1969. In view of this constraint, highways alone account for over 80 percent of all authorized outlays. Vocational education and health programs together amount to only about one-tenth of highway expenditures, assuming that they reached the maximum amounts authorized. Similarly, during fiscal years 1966 and 1967, the Economic Development Administration, which has placed considerable investment in Appalachia, approved a total of $564 million in projects nationally, but only $18 million went for health facilities and only $12 million went for education facilities. On the other hand, utilities (primarily water and sewage facilities) accounted for $258 million worth of projects.[21]

In fairness to the Appalachian Regional Commission it should be pointed out that actual expenditures by the Commission have been much more oriented toward human resource development than a mere consideration of authorizations would indicate. For one thing, the original highway authorization was for six years, whereas all other authorizations were for two years. After four years of authorizations, highways account for 70 percent of the total. However, spending limitations imposed by American involvement in Vietnam have sharply curtailed actual appropriations for highways. In addition, the highway program is 50 to 70 percent federally funded, whereas most of the other programs are combined as supplemental grants with other federal funds up to a maximum of 80 percent. According to the Commission's Annual Report for 1968, a total of $595 million was appropriated for all programs under the Appalachian Regional Development Act, including $370 million for highways and $225 million for all other programs.[22] The Commission's Executive Director has estimated that at this writing health and education obligations alone amount to $425 million in federal, state, and local funds; those for highways total about $400 million in federal and state funds.[23]

Despite a relative shift in emphasis on the part of the Appalachian Regional Commission toward human resource programs, there is still widespread reluctance among local political leaders in the region to give up their attachment to public works projects. In part this relates to the migration issue. Public works projects of the highway type receive relatively high political priority because (1) they are very tangible, (2) they represent a means by which, it is hoped, economic activity may be attracted *to* lagging regions; and (3) they cannot be moved to other regions as can investments embodied in human beings. Nevertheless, from the perspective of rational resource allocation in the nation as a whole, and from the viewpoint of the people rather than the place, it is essential that population migration be dealt with forthrightly.

The Problem of Outmigration

The various reports and hearings concerning the Appalachian Regional Development Act of 1965 tended to either ignore or decry the possibility of outmigration of the region's residents. However, more recent publications of the Appalachian Regional Commission suggest a more flexible position in this regard. For example, a recent Commission report states that "The primary goal of the regional development program is to provide every person in Appalachia with the health and skills he needs to compete for opportunities wherever he chooses to live."[24] This attitude has also appeared at the level of the states, where goals, priorities, and fund allocations are actually implemented through state development plans. Thus, Virginia's first State Appalachian Development Plan states that "Our general purpose will be to assist the people of Appalachian Virginia in acquiring the training, skills, and health which are necessary to participate in and contribute to the nation's economy wherever they may choose to live,"[25] as well as to improve economic opportunity in the region. It is also pertinent that the Appalachian Regional Commission has by resolution required that the curricula in vocational-technical centers be tailored to national and regional manpower requirements.

Nevertheless, while the Commission has adopted a permissive stance toward migration from Appalachia, it is still not encouraging such movement, nor is it developing comprehensive labor mobility programs linked to job opportunities in outside areas. Here the Commission is no doubt acting under legislative constraints, though one staff member has indicated to the author that it is probably legal for the Commission to spend funds outside the region so long as such spending benefits the people of Appalachia. In any case, the Commission has not chosen to test the issue.

The Commission does intend to take advantage of development opportunities pressing toward the region from such metropolitan areas as Washington, Baltimore, Atlanta, Lexington, and Cincinnati. The highway program is designed to facilitate commuting from Appalachian areas within the range of these centers. However, the highway program is still largely a device for linking jobs and workers within Appalachia, whereas links to outside areas tend to be viewed as means for opening markets to firms located in Appalachia.[26] Here again, though, no effort is being made to hinder those persons who wish to seek better opportunities outside the region.

A common objection to outmigration is that the economic gains may be outweighed by the psychic losses. This argument is generally based on the assumption that the Appalachian resident is particularly attached to family, friends, and the regional culture, and that he is likely to be a miserable "fish out of water" when he settles outside the region. We are told that when young people leave Appalachia, they "want to return because they have strong ties to cousins, to neighbors, and to a host of relatives as well as to parents. They thus stand out as psychological exceptions in a nation that has almost made a virtue of youth's rebellion and fast departure from home—often enough a final departure."[27]

No student of Appalachia can deny that the Appalachian family puts greater stress on tradition and family continuity than does the American family in general. Nevertheless, Appalachian residents have a realistic awareness of the disparities in economic opportunity that exist between their region and areas outside Appalachia. Schwarzweller, for example, asked a group of 157 young men in eastern Kentucky how they would rate their county of residence as a place to find opportunity for work. The same question was asked of a group of 150 young eastern Kentuckians who had migrated to industrialized areas of Kentucky and Ohio. Of the former (nonmigrant) group, 84 percent responded that work opportunity was "poor" or "very poor." In contrast, 71 percent of the migrants responded that their opportunities where they migrated were "very good" or "pretty good." "One can formulate a reasonable argument that the Ohio Valley—Eastern Kentucky comparison dominates the evaluation. If this assumption is made, the data reveal . . . that both migrants and nonmigrants were very much aware of regional differentials in work opportunity."[28]

Not only have national aspirations penetrated the mountains, but

Appalachian parents, as we saw earlier, desire a better future for their children. And they are willing to have them leave the region in search of a better life. In the survey discussed earlier concerning Appalachian values, beliefs and attitudes it was found that metropolitan residents favored their children's remaining by a more than two-to-one ratio; on the other hand, over half of the rural and urban area respondents stated that they would wish their children to leave. Family affection was the reason most often given by those who wanted their children to remain at home, while over three-quarters of those who said they would want their children to leave gave lack of economic opportunity at home as the reason.[29]

Similar evidence is found in a study of the first retraining program in Tennessee, involving trainees from Campbell and Claiborne counties. Campbell county is about forty miles north of Knoxville and Claiborne is adjacent and to the northeast. Kentucky borders the area on the north and Virginia borders it to the northeast. The area is typical of much of Appalachia in that the once-dominant mining and agriculture sectors have been declining and the area has in consequence experienced heavy outmigration. Of the 188 respondents in an interview sample of the area's families, more than two-thirds believed that it would take less than $4,000 a year to be as well off in Lexington, Kentucky, as in their home county. Most of the two-thirds also said they would move to Lexington or another town within 200 or 300 miles if a job in their occupation were available there and if moving costs were paid. "The fact that nearly 75 per cent of the total interview sample felt that young people should leave is a further indication of willingness to be mobile."[30]

Of course, to demonstrate the considerable attraction that economic opportunities outside of Appalachia exert on the region's young people is not to deny that family and neighborhood ties tend to discourage the potential migrant or make the new migrant uncomfortable in his new environment. Yet a study of outmigrants from eastern Kentucky by Schwarzweller indicates that of the young men residing outside of eastern Kentucky in 1960, 84 percent had never moved back after initially moving away. Moreover, about four out of five of the migrants from eastern Kentucky said that they had no intention of moving in the near future, even though many of them expressed some dissatisfaction with their present circumstances. Thus, when they realistically appraised their situations, "the pull of home and parental family ties had been relegated to a form of nostalgia."[31] It would also seem reasonable to infer that since traditional and family values are relatively strongly held in eastern Kentucky that problems involved in outmigration would be even less for most of those persons migrating from other parts of Appalachia.

Finally, it is often held that migration from the Appalachian South, as that of southerners in general and Negroes in particular, merely tends to transfer problems of rural poverty to northern ghettos. Weller, for example, believes that in the northern city:

> Opportunities for employment are limited, for the mountain man's few skills and little education enable him to get only the low-paying and insecure jobs. The inner city, too, becomes a kind of labyrinth where he gets lost in the maze of people and buildings and traffic. Here he can be cut off again from the opportunity of steady work, adequate income, health services, good education, and an environment which can be stimulating. . . . The mountaineer often simply changes place of residence when he moves to the city. The forces that mold him are much the same in either place.[32]

Kain and Persky state that the Appalachian South plays a role for white urban poverty in the North Central region similar to that which the Deep South plays in relation to metropolitan ghettos.[33] However, such comparisons can easily be overdrawn. The white Appalachian outmigrant, as the southern Negro outmigrant, tends to lower the average level of education in both the home region (because he has more schooling than those left behind) and the receiving region (because he has less schooling than the average resident). Nevertheless, the training and education of the Appalachian migrant still sets him apart from the southern Negro. In addition, though he may encounter prejudice against his "hillbilly" background, he is usually spared the humiliating discrimination that confronts the Negro. And the children of Appalachian migrants certainly have a much better chance of participating in the mainstream of American life than do those of Negro migrants.

Of particular interest is the role of the "stem family" in helping the white Appalachian migrant to adjust to the psychological, sociological and cultural stresses in finding a job and a place to live in the new community. The home, or stem, family sends out branches to northern urban-industrial areas. The stem family continues to support the "branch family" while the branch family also supports relatives who migrate from home by introducing them to the ways of city life and city people. The individual who is unhappy with his circumstances in Appalachia and wishes to advance economically and socially has an "escape mechanism" through the family structure. Thus, those who emphasize the negative aspects of the Appalachian family with regard to the mobility potential of Appalachian residents should be reminded of its positive side in supporting adjustment to new circumstances in the migration system and in helping to stabilize the migrant.[34] Indeed, one prominent student of the Appalachian migration patterns of whites told this author that he was considering examining the Appalachian ghettos in the North, but was having difficulty in obtaining relevant data. He finally came to the tentative conclusion that his inability to come to grips with the problem may be that it really is not so great as some imagine, in large part because of the branch families' success in adapting new migrants to life in urban-industrial centers. He noted that although Chicago represents an exception, most of the cities to which migrants go do not seem to have major problems with permanently "ghetto-ized" migrants. This does not deny that new migrants have difficulties in becoming integrated with their new environment, but their difficulties are often exaggerated. Most migrants who begin urban life in an Appalachian "ghetto" eventually move to more mixed neighborhoods and become integrated with the larger community; many migrants do not even begin their new life in a "ghetto."

Thus far we have been discussing outmigration from Appalachia in fairly general terms, but it is also instructive to take a closer look at some of the major migration streams. With the exception of the people who move to adjacent counties or areas, most migrants move to places outside the region or on its fringe. Migrants from eastern Kentucky tend to go to the Midwest, especially to such Ohio cities as Cincinnati, Hamilton, and Dayton, whose populations are made up of sizeable numbers of persons born in Kentucky. Western West Virginia migrants generally move to central and northeastern Ohio, to cities such as Columbus, Akron, and Cleveland. Further east in West Virginia the migrants tend to go to Pittsburgh, while still further east in the state they move to Maryland and Washington, D.C,. with some going to the Midwest. Persons leaving Alabama counties tend to go to Birmingham, while those leaving Georgia counties go to Atlanta. The latter city also draws large numbers of migrants from the Carolinas, Tennessee, and other southern states, though it does not exert much pull on Virginia, West Virginia, and Kentucky. These migratory streams are now fairly stable, yet many of them are of relatively recent origin. As recently as 1950, for example, many of the migrants from mining areas in Kentucky and West Virginia moved only short distances, nearly always to other mining areas. But by 1955–60, with sharp employment declines in mining, migrants from these areas were moving much more to areas with other industries. The proportion of persons who left the Kentucky mining areas for Ohio increased from 14 percent in 1950 to 29 percent in 1955–60; another 20 percent went to Indiana, Michigan, and Illinois in 1955–60, though few persons had gone to these states in the earlier period. Likewise, the proportion of migrants from West Virginia's mining areas who went to Ohio during this time interval rose from 8 percent to 21 percent; the comparable figures for outmigrants bound for Illinois and Michigan were 4 percent and 8 percent. Meanwhile, migration to other parts of West Virginia fell from 32 percent to 17 percent of all moves.[35]

In general, then, the "typical" Appalachian resident hardly conforms to the stereotype of the mountaineer who prefers to live his own peculiar and isolated life apart from the mainstream of American economic and social life. When economic opportunities outside the region are clearly much better than those in the region, he will leave—or at least he is quite prepared to see his children leave. Although the Appalachian family structure—which is far from being homogeneous—tends to preserve and foster traditional values, the branch family constitutes a valuable vehicle for helping migrants bridge the gap between Appalachia, on the one hand, and life and work in urban-industrial centers outside the region on the other. However, even a cursory view of the general migration streams involving Appalachian residents reinforces the point made at the outset of this chapter that Appalachia is by no means a homogeneous region. Thus, we must next consider, in at least a rough way, the nature of the Appalachian subregions, as well as the ways in which they are related to the "outside" world.

Appalachia's Subregions

The Appalachian Regional Commission distinguishes four broad subregions within Appalachia.[36] Each differs from the other in its potential for growth and in its public investment needs.

The first is Northern Appalachia, which includes some dozen counties in southern New York, most of the Allegheny Plateau area in Pennsylvania and Maryland, northern West Virginia, and southern Ohio. This subregion has a long history of urbanization and industrialization, but shifting demands and changing technology have created many problems for its economy. In particular, it is grappling with problems of converting from its dependence on coal, steel, and railroad employment to newer types of manufacturing and service employment. The area is faced with serious environmental problems, industrial blight, and community obsolescence. These in turn are a consequence of past mining and industrial activities that failed to take account of external diseconomies. These diseconomies include mine drainage pollution, mine subsidence, blight and water pollution from strip mining, mine fires and flooding, and air pollution caused by heavy industry activities. Public overhead capital in

Northern Appalachia is more developed than in much of the rest of the region, but its future growth will depend in large measure on community renewal and improvements in the quality of the environment.

Industrialization and urbanization are occurring relatively rapidly in another subregion, Southern Appalachia, though employment growth is being generated for the most part in such relatively (nationally) slow-growing, labor-intensive industries as apparel, textiles, and food processing. The states included in this area—Mississippi, Alabama, South Carolina, North Carolina, Tennessee, and Virginia—have given high priority to developing manpower skills so that their workers will be competitive with the nation as a whole. They have recognized the need to develop high school and post-high school vocational training to prepare young people for the jobs that are opening. To attract a greater share of new industries the states are also developing their higher education facilities, as well as their medical education programs. A second priority is the provision of public overhead capital for the area's growing industrial communities. The general approach, therefore, is one of balanced growth of public facilities and skilled manpower.

The third subregion, the Appalachian Highlands, extends from northern Georgia, through the Smoky Mountains of Tennessee and North Carolina, into the Blue Ridge of Virginia, and the Alleghenies, all the way to the Mohawk Valley and Catskills in New York. This highly scenic but sparsely populated strip has its greatest potential as a tourism and recreation area for the rest of Appalachia and the metropolitan populations living on either side. The Appalachian states, in cooperation with federal agencies and the Appalachian Regional Commission, are studying how this potential can be exploited through comprehensive development, conservation, and recreation complexes, often involving private capital.

The last of the four subregions, and that of greatest concern in this study, is Central Appalachia, which consists of sixty counties in eastern Kentucky, southern West Virginia, northern Tennessee, and southwestern Virginia. The data in Tables 18 and 19 show that this subregion is Appalachia's biggest problem area. Column 7 of Table 18 shows that the Appalachian parts of Kentucky, Virginia, and West Virginia each lost population between 1950 and 1960. However, the Central Appalachian portions of these states lost people at even higher rates, as shown by the figures in parentheses. The Appalachian portion of Tennessee gained 5.1 percent in population during the decade, but the Central Appalachian portion of the state lost population, the rate being −9.5 percent. The Central Appalachian portion of Kentucky was particularly hard hit, showing a −19.3 percent change.

Between 1960 and 1965 the Appalachian portions of Kentucky and West Virginia continued to show population declines, but the population in the Central Appalachian counties declined even more rapidly (Table 18, column 3). The Appalachian portion of Virginia gained population, but its Central Appalachian counties' population declined by 3.7 percent. The Central Appalachian part of Tennessee gained population, but at a lower rate than Appalachian Tennessee as a whole.

Turning to Table 19, the unemployment rate for Appalachia fell by nearly three percentage points between 1963 and 1965. In the latter year it was only 0.7 of one percentage point higher than the comparable national figure. The unemployment rates for the Appalachian portions of Kentucky (10.0) West Virginia (7.8) and Virginia (5.7) remained well above the Appalachian rate of 5.2 and the national rate of 4.5. Data on unemployment rates in the Central Appalachian area were not available for the respective states, but for Central Appalachia as a whole the rate was 11.9 percent in 1963, and it had dropped to only 10.1 by 1965.[37] Partial data for 1967 (Table 19) show that unemployment rates in the Appalachian portions of the three Central Appalachian states for which data were available were above the national rate, with Kentucky (9.1) and West Virginia (6.4) having particularly high rates. The Central Appalachian portions of these states certainly had even higher rates.

In 1960, Central Appalachia had a per capita income figure of

TABLE 18: POPULATION, RATE OF NATURAL INCREASE, AND NET MIGRATION RATE, 1950–1960, AND 1960–1965, FOR THE UNITED STATES, APPALACHIAN REGION, AND APPALACHIAN PORTIONS OF RELEVANT STATES[a]

	(1) Population 1960[b]	(2) Estimated Population 1965[b]	(3) Estimated Percent Change Population 1960–1965[b]	(4) Rate of Natural Increase 1960–1965	(5) Estimated Net Migration 1960–1965 Number
United States	179,323,175	193,795,000	+8.1	6.7	+ 2,510,500
Appalachian Region	17,726,567	18,111,015	+2.2	5.4	− 581,323
Appalachian portion of:					
Alabama	1,982,286	2,136,967	+7.8	6.8	+ 20,590
Georgia	675,024	733,900	+8.7	6.9	+ 12,619
Kentucky	922,152	908,500	−1.5	6.7	− 75,468
	(567,962)	(525,000)	(−7.6)		
Maryland	195,808	214,200	+9.4	4.9	+ 8,801
Mississippi	406,187	440,060	+8.3	7.0	− 5,369
New York	1,000,064	1,036,759	+3.7	5.4	− 16,948
North Carolina	939,740	993,443	+5.7	6.4	− 6,200
Ohio	1,119,555	1,154,159	+3.1	5.3	− 24,341
Pennsylvania	5,930,784	5,876,400	−0.9	4.2	− 300,960
South Carolina	586,523	616,500	+5.1	7.2	− 12,306
Tennessee	1,607,689	1,687,063	+4.9	6.3	− 22,507
	(300,887)	(310,376)	(+3.1)		
Virginia	500,334	506,505	+1.2	5.4	− 21,006
	(228,228)	(219,722)	(−3.7)		
West Virginia	1,860,421	1,815,000	−2.4	5.0	− 138,228
	(442,494)	(414,530)	(−6.3)		

[a] Population 1965 and net migration 1960–1965 are estimates.
[b] Values in parentheses are for the Central Appalachian parts of the states.
Source: Appalachian Regional Commission

TABLE 18—Continued

	(6) Estimated Net Migration Rate 1960–1965	(7) Percent Change Population 1950–1960[b]	(8) Net Migration Rate 1950–1960	(9) Net Migration 1950–1960 Number	(10) Population 1950
United States	*+1.4*	*+18.5*	*+ 1.8*	*2,973,000*	*150,697,361*
Appalachian Region	*−3.3*	*+ 2.0*	*−12.7*	*−2,201,899*	*17,378,110*
Appalachian portion of:					
Alabama	+1.0	+ 6.5	− 11.1	— 205,723	1,860,829
Georgia	+1.8	+ 8.9	− 10.6	— 65,722	619,766
Kentucky	−8.2	−14.0 (−19.3)	− 31.8	— 340,759	1,072,750
Maryland	+4.5	+ 3.2	− 7.8	— 14,751	189,701
Mississippi	+1.3	− 4.7	− 21.2	— 90,324	426,076
New York	−1.7	+ 9.0	− 3.8	— 35,050	917,490
North Carolina	−0.7	+ 6.6	− 9.6	— 84,691	881,560
Ohio	−2.2	+ 8.2	− 4.5	— 46,387	1,035,058
Pennsylvania	−5.1	+ 2.5	− 9.3	— 538,715	5,784,652
South Carolina	−2.1	+12.1	− 7.8	— 40,593	523,265
Tennessee	−1.4	+ 5.1 (− 9.5)	− 11.4	— 174,658	1,529,762
Virginia	−4.2	− 5.9 (−10.7)	− 22.2	— 117,815	531,649
West Virginia	−7.4	− 7.2 (−19.1)	− 22.3	— 446,711	2,005,552

b Values in parentheses are for the Central Appalachian parts of the states.
Source: Appalachian Regional Commission

TABLE 19: UNEMPLOYMENT AND PER CAPITA INCOME STATISTICS
FOR THE UNITED STATES, THE APPALACHIAN REGION,
AND THE APPALACHIAN PORTION OF RELEVANT STATES

| | Unemployment Rate | | | Per Capita Income | | |
| | | | | | | Percent change |
	1963	1965	1967	1962	1966	1962–1966
United States	5.7	4.5	3.8	$2368	$2963	25.1
Appalachian Region	8.1	5.2	—	——	——	—
Appalachian portion of:						
Alabama	5.9	4.4	4.3	1687	2169	28.6
Georgia	7.0	4.8	—	1371	1857	40.6
Kentucky	11.0	10.0	9.1	1095	1378	25.8
Maryland	8.1	5.8	5.2	2353	3137	33.3
Mississippi	6.3	5.6	4.6	1135	1589	40.0
New York	5.7	4.2	3.7	2220	2503	12.7
North Carolina	6.3	5.2	—	1712	2205	28.8
Ohio	7.4	5.6	5.2	1669	2054	23.1
Pennsylvania	8.5	4.7	4.0	2117	2683	26.7
South Carolina	5.3	3.8	—	1822	2488	36.6
Tennessee	6.8	4.2	4.3	1638	2188	33.6
Virginia	7.9	5.7	—	1229	1638	33.3
West Virginia	10.3	7.8	6.4	1726	2211	28.8

Note: A dash indicates that data were not available.
Source: Appalachian Regional Commission.

$918, compared to a national average of $1,850.[38] Though more recent data were not available for Central Appalachia, Table 19 shows per capita income values for the Appalachian portions of the relevant states. In 1966, national per capita income was $2963; the comparable value for the Appalachian portion of West Virginia was $2211; for Tennessee, $2188; for Virginia, $1638; and for Kentucky $1378. Between 1962 and 1966, per capita income in the United States increased by 25.1 percent; the increases for the four states in question here ranged from 25.8 percent for Appalachian Kentucky to 33.6 percent for Appalachian Tennessee. Nevertheless, these higher percentage increases were not sufficient to close the absolute gaps between these areas and the nation. Indeed, the absolute gap in Appalachian West Virginia increased from $642 to

$752; in Tennessee, from $730 to $775; in Virginia, from $1139 to $1325; and in Kentucky, from $1273 to $1585. It may also be inferred that the situation was even worse in the Central Appalachian portions of these states.

If it is evident that Central Appalachia poses the greatest difficulties of any Appalachian subregion, it is even more evident that eastern Kentucky poses even greater problems from an economic development point of view than does the rest of Central Appalachia. The problems of eastern Kentucky therefore invite closer examination.

Eastern Kentucky: The Toughest Problem

Kentucky is a relatively poor state, but the degree to which eastern Kentucky differs from the rest of the state is seen in a number of regression analyses using data for the state's 120 counties.[30] Analysis of the factors associated with differing levels of median family income gives the following equation:

$$(1) \quad Y_{60} = 162 + 3.76S_{58} + 18.2(P_{60}/P_{50} \times 100)$$
$$\phantom{(1) \quad Y_{60} = 162 + } (0.58) \quad (2.72)$$
$$- 22.9A_{60} + 49.4F_{60},$$
$$(2.88) \quad\quad (5.17)$$

where Y_{60} = median family income in 1960; S_{58} = service industry importance as measured by per capita dollar receipts from personal, business, and repair services in 1958; $(P_{60}/P_{50} \times 100)$ = population in 1960 as a percent of that in 1950; A_{60} = importance of agriculture as measured by the proportion of all employed persons who were farmers or farm managers; and E_{60} = educational effort, as measured by per capita expenditures from local resources for education. The values in parentheses are the standard errors of the regression coefficients. The regression coefficients are each significant at the .01 level of significance, as is the F value of 222.7. For equation (1), R = 0.89. Variation in the four independent variables is therefore quite closely associated with variation in median income. It is

particularly important to note here that the eastern Kentucky counties that are in Appalachia, as defined by the Appalachian Regional
Commission, rank very low with regard to each of the independent
variables except A_{60}, where they rank relatively high. The average
rank for the counties of eastern Kentucky for each of the four independent variables is 76, 82, 60, and 81, respectively. For the dependent variable their average rank is 86. The lowest possible average rank, considering that there are 49 counties in eastern Kentucky,
would be 95. Similarly the highest possible average rank for eastern
Kentucky counties would be 25. Low incomes in eastern Kentucky
are therefore associated with its relatively low levels of service activities and educational effort, its relative population decline, and its
relatively high proportion of employed persons in agriculture.

A broader measure of the well-being of the populations of the
counties in question is given by their socioeconomic status. This
index is derived by adding the *reversed* ranks of a county on the following variables: median family income, median value of homes,
and proportion of total employment accounted for by professional
workers. To this sum is added the rank of a county on proportions of
total employment accounted for by unskilled workers. Thus, the
larger the index, the higher is the general socioeconomic status. The
following equation is instructive in "explaining" variation in socioeconomic status:

(2) $SES = -228 + 0.047Y_{60} + 3.81B_{58} + 9.58U_{60},$
                   (.003)   (0.42)   (0.85)

where SES = Socioeconomic status; Y_{60} = median family income
in 1960; B_{58} = economic base index in 1958, as measured by adding value in manufacturing, wholesale sales, retail sales, per capita
receipts from services, and then dividing this sum by the value of
farm products sold (giving the relation between commercial and
industrial activity to agriculture); and U_{60} = urbanization as measured by the proportion of the total population that was urban in
1960.

For equation (2), $R^2 = 0.83$ and $F = 193.9$, highly significant at the .01 percent significance level. The regression coefficients are each significant at the .01 level. The significance of Y_{60} is extremely high even in view of the fact that it is in some measure being regressed upon itself. The average rank for the counties of eastern Kentucky for the three independent variables is 86, 53, and 70, respectively, while that for the dependent variable is 77, indicating the low socioeconomic level of these counties.

It was pointed out in an earlier section of this chapter that higher levels of urbanization and education are necessary if Appalachia is to capture a greater share of rapidly expanding tertiary activities. The following equation shows the influence of urbanization and education on tertiary activity in Kentucky's counties:

$$(3) \qquad C_{58} = 433 + \underset{(24.7)}{185.1 U_{60}} + \underset{(7.1)}{19.4 E_{60}},$$

where C_{58} = per capita commercial and selected services sales receipts in 1958; and U_{60} and E_{60} are as defined in equations (2) and (1), respectively. For equation (3), $R^2 = 0.51$ and $F = 60.66$. The regression coefficients and the F value are all significant at the .01 level. The average rank of the eastern Kentucky counties is again low: 70 and 82 for the respective independent variables and 74 for the dependent variable. Levels of urbanization and local educational effort therefore "explain" over half the variance in C_{58} for all counties, and the low values for these independent variables in eastern Kentucky account in large part for its low level of tertiary activities.

The low local education effort in eastern Kentucky [these counties had an average rank of 81 for F_{60} in equation (1)] is balanced in part by outside help from state and federal funds, as is shown in the following equation:

$$(4) \qquad SFE_{61} = 247 - \underset{(.0019)}{.0213 Y_{60}},$$

where SFE_{61} = state and federal educational expenditures (grades 1–12) per pupil in 1960–61; and Y_{60} = median family income in

1960. For equation (4), $R^2 = .052$; the regression coefficient is significant at the .01 level. Thus, over half the variance in SFE_{61} is "explained" by Y_{60}, the relationship being an inverse one. Since the eastern Kentucky counties had an average rank of 86 with respect to Y_{60}, it is obvious that they are relative gainers from state and federal aid.

Of course, federal aid for education has increased substantially since 1960–61, the year for which our relevant data were obtained. However, it is best to consider education within the total framework of human resource development, for, as Bowman and Haynes have remarked, "special attention to human resource development is called for on many grounds but especially because in no aspect of the mountain situation is the national as distinct from purely local interest so profoundly involved."[40] Their position is based on the argument that we have presented earlier, namely, that people are eastern Kentucky's greatest export, but they are not an export from which the mountains can derive an income. Neither can they be barred from the cities outside the region. Therefore, the nation as a whole has a stake in investing in these people who will become a part of the nation. "The cost of *not* doing so is far too great."[41]

In analyzing the federal government's implicit policy with respect to human resource development in eastern Kentucky it is useful to divide public overhead capital into two parts: economic overhead capital (EOC) and social overhead capital (SOC). Projects of the first type are primarily oriented toward supporting directly productive activities or toward the movement of economic resources, and include roads, bridges, power and water installations, and similar undertakings. SOC projects, on the other hand, are more concerned with the provision of satisfactions which have generally, at least in the past, been regarded as primarily noneconomic in nature. Although they may also increase productivity, the manner in which they do so is much less direct than is the case for EOC. Thus, SOC would include such activities as education, cultural programs, health projects, and some types of welfare. Investment in SOC may be regarded, therefore, as equivalent to investment in human resources.

It may be noted that the use of SOC here differs from that in most of the relevant literature, where it has tended to be synonymous with public overhead capital in general. However, the usefulness of disaggregating public overhead capital into SOC–EOC components has been demonstrated in a number of previously published studies by the author.[42]

An analysis of the SOC-EOC structure of federal expenditures in eastern Kentucky is presented in Table 20. The programs of three agencies were grouped together to give the SOC values. They are the Office of Economic Opportunity, the Department of Health, Education, and Welfare, and the Department of Labor. Similarly, the outlays of the Department of Commerce, the Department of Transportation, and the Small Business Administration were grouped together to give the EOC values. Of course, other agencies have SOC and EOC programs but the activities of these agencies do not fall *in toto* into either the SOC or EOC category. On the other hand, the outlays of the agencies included in Table 20 can be regarded as falling fairly clearly into either the SOC or the EOC category. The data were obtained from the Office of Economic Opportunity, which began compiling data in 1966 on federal program expenditures by state and county. On the advice of OEO officials, data for 1966 were not included in Table 20. The principal difficulty is that there were a considerable number of programs that were not reported for 1966. In contrast, these officials had reasonable confidence in the comprehensiveness and quality of their data since 1966.

The structure of EOC and SOC outlays within Kentucky is shown in columns (2) and (4). In 1967, eastern Kentucky received 46 percent of the state EOC total but it received only 28 percent of the state SOC total. Likewise, in the first half of fiscal year 1968 eastern Kentucky received about half of all the EOC expenditures in the state, but less than a third of all the SOC expenditures. Thus, even though SOC needs are relatively greater in eastern Kentucky than elsewhere, the federal programs put greater relative emphasis on EOC programs in the region relative to the rest of the state.

TABLE 20: SELECTED FEDERAL EXPENDITURES IN EASTERN KENTUCKY, FISCAL YEAR 1967 AND FIRST HALF OF FISCAL YEAR 1968, BY SOC AND EOC PROGRAMS (millions of dollars)

Period	Area	EOC[a]		SOC[b]		EOC+SOC	EOC / EOC+SOC	SOC / EOC+SOC
		(1) Amount	(2) Percent of state total	(3) Amount	(4) Percent of state total	(5) Amount	(6)	(7)
Fiscal 1967	Kentucky	152.3	100.0	685.3	100.0	837.6	18.2	81.8
	Eastern Kentucky[c]	70.4	46.2	194.7	28.4	265.1	26.6	73.4
	Rest of Kentucky	81.9	53.8	490.6	71.6	572.5	14.3	85.7
	United States	6,715.6	—	38,332.7	—	45,047.3	14.9	85.1
First half fiscal 1968	Kentucky	63.6	100.0	297.0	100.0	360.6	17.6	82.4
	Eastern Kentucky[c]	31.6	49.6	93.3	31.4	124.8	25.3	74.7
	Rest of Kentucky	32.0	50.4	203.7	68.6	235.8	13.6	86.4
	United States	4,099.0	—	19,415.2	—	23,514.2	17.4	82.6

[a] Includes expenditures of the Department of Commerce, the Department of Transportation, and the Small Business Administration.

[b] Includes expenditures of the Office of Economic Opportunity; the Department of Health, Education, and Welfare; and the Department of Labor.

[c] Includes counties in eastern Kentucky as defined by the Appalachian Regional Commission.

Note: Individual items may not always add to totals because of rounding.

Source: Office of Economic Opportunity.

The data in Table 20 may also be analyzed in terms of the EOC-SOC structure within areas. Here it is necessary to consider the values in columns 6 and 7. If the arguments presented in this and the preceding chapter concerning the relatively high priority that should be attached to SOC programs in lagging areas are correct, then Kentucky should be receiving a higher proportion of SOC than the nation as a whole. Moreover, eastern Kentucky should receive a higher proportion of SOC than the rest of Kentucky. In fact, the situation is quite different. In 1967, the proportion of the EOC-SOC total going for SOC in the United States as a whole was 85 percent. For the state of Kentucky the proportion accounted for by SOC was only 82 percent, while the comparable figure for eastern Kentucky was only 73 percent. A similar situation is indicated for the first half of fiscal year 1968. For the United States as a whole, the SOC proportion of total EOC-SOC expenditures was 83 percent, whereas for Kentucky it was 82 percent. For eastern Kentucky the SOC proportion is only 75 percent. Preliminary results from detailed analysis of the SOC-EOC expenditures of all federal agencies for all of 1967 and 1968 confirm these general relationships.

These results reflect the fact that insofar as there is a federal policy for lagging regions, it is relatively biased in favor of EOC programs. The relative neglect of programs to improve the quality of human resources in lagging areas stems in large measure, as was argued earlier, from the federal government's preoccupation with attempts to attract economic activity to lagging regions, and its concomitant failure to deal with the issue of outmigration from such areas.

Population change within Kentucky counties due to in- and outmigration is closely related to education levels. This is shown by the following equation:

$$(5) \qquad M = 47 + 1.66H_{60},$$
$$(0.12)$$

where M = population change between 1950 and 1960 resulting from in- and outmigration; and H_{60} = per cent of all persons 25 years of age and older who had at least a high school education in 1960. M is an index value where 100 indicates no gain or loss due to migration; a value over 100 indicates net immigration, while a value less than 100 indicates net outmigration. For equation (5), $R^2 = 0.63$ and the regression coefficient is significant at the .01 level. The average rank for the counties of eastern Kentucky with respect to H_{60} was 86. In general, then, even within Kentucky, counties with low education levels had relatively high outmigration, while those with relatively high education levels had the largest gains from immigration.

A survey conducted by a University of Kentucky student in the summer of 1968 and supervised by the author gives some interesting evidence concerning the locational preferences of graduating high school students in eastern Kentucky. Seniors from four schools were asked their locational preferences under differing wage rate assumptions. Eight different relative wage structures were given for three locations: the student's own community; a Kentucky city such as Lexington or Louisville (both outside of Appalachia); and a northern city (see Table 21).

If the wage rate is higher in the Appalachian community than in the other locations (case V), then over three-quarters of the respondents would stay in their home town; yet the remainder would move to another Kentucky city even if they were paid $1.00 less per hour! In case I, where wages are equal in all locations, 28 students would stay at home, but 16 would go to another Kentucky city. However, only 3 would go to a northern city.

What is striking is that in any case where the wage in another Kentucky city exceeds that of the home community, more respondents would prefer the other Kentucky city to their home. Moreover, the preference for another Kentucky city increases with the magnitude of the wage differential between the home community and the other city. For example, when the differential is only $0.25 (case II), those who would leave for another Kentucky city outnumber those who would stay home by 21 to 18. When the differential is increased to $0.50 (case III), the ratio becomes 28 to 9; to $0.75

(case IV), 28 to 6; to $1.00 (Case VII), 30 to 4; and to $2.00, 45 to 3.

TABLE 21: LOCATIONAL PREFERENCES OF EASTERN KENTUCKY
HIGH SCHOOL SENIORS UNDER DIFFERING WAGE
RATE ASSUMPTIONS

	Location	Wage Rate	Preferences Indicated
	Own town	$1.50	28
I	Kentucky city	1.50	16
	Northern city	1.50	3
	Own town	1.50	18
II	Kentucky city	1.75	21
	Northern city	2.00	8
	Own town	1.50	9
III	Kentucky city	2.00	28
	Northern city	2.50	10
	Own town	1.50	6
IV	Kentucky city	2.25	28
	Northern city	3.00	14
	Own town	3.50	36
V	Kentucky city	2.50	11
	Northern city	1.50	0
	Own town	1.50	3
VI	Kentucky city	3.50	45
	Northern city	2.50	0
	Own town	1.50	4
VII	Kentucky city	2.50	30
	Northern city	3.50	13
	Own town	1.50	2
VIII	Kentucky city	3.50	29
	Northern city	5.50	20

Note: A total of 53 responses were received to the mail questionnaire, but some respondents did not answer all of the alternatives.

Source: Mail questionnaire sent by Judith Noble to graduating seniors in Paintsville, Prestonsburg, Salyersville, and Elkhorn City high schools.

No less striking is the disposition of the respondents to avoid going to a northern city. In the two cases where the wage in another Kentucky city exceeds that of the northern city, *not a single individual* would go north. Even in case VII, where the wage in the North exceeds that in another Kentucky city by 40 percent (and both exceed the wage in the home community), the number who would go to another Kentucky city exceeds the number of those who would go north by 30 to 13. And even in case VIII, where the northern wage exceeds that in another Kentucky city by $2.00, the number who would go to the other Kentucky city exceeds the number of those who would go north by 29 to 20.

In addition to the students whose responses we have been discussing, a group of 27 students at Mullins, another eastern Kentucky high school, were interviewed and asked substantially the same questions concerning where they would choose to live and work. These responses are not included in the data in Table 21 because the students were given only five cases, and because the wage levels differed somewhat from those shown in Table 21. Nevertheless, the results were quite similar. For example, if another Kentucky city and a northern city each paid a wage of $2.40 (while the eastern Kentucky wage was $1.60), 17 students would prefer to locate in the Kentucky city; only 8 would prefer the northern city. If the Kentucky city had the highest wage, every student but one would choose to go there. The single exception would remain in his home community. (In 1969 over 600 high school seniors in the Big Sandy region were surveyed using the same wage rate assumptions shown in Table 21; Preliminary analysis corroborates the earlier results reported here.)

These findings have important implications for regional and manpower policies. First, they reinforce the position that even in the most lagging of Appalachian areas people are quite ready and willing to leave for areas with better economic opportunity. Second, it is erroneous to believe that outmigrants from lagging rural regions prefer to go to big metropolitan areas, in this case in the North. They obviously would prefer to locate in intermediate areas between the lagging rural areas and the congested cities. Policies aimed at diverting rural people from the big cities should therefore concentrate on intermediate areas, and potential migrants should be given skills and training to match the job opportunities in intermediate areas. In the present case, this would mean matching education and training programs in eastern Kentucky with the job requirements of industries in, for example, Louisville and Lexington, where labor markets are tight. Again, it is not a question of "moving out" people; in our market system it is no more possible to compel people to leave than it is possible to compel industry to move to the mountains. But it is a question of giving people viable alternatives and therefore the possibility of genuine choice.

The conclusions of Bowman and Haynes with respect to the economy of eastern Kentucky are essentially valid for Central Appalachia in general. After intensive research on all aspects of the regional economy, they found that: 142682

> Adding this all up, a few main points are absolutely clear. The Kentucky mountains will not develop a significantly expanding economy, no matter what public policies are pursued. In an area of this kind neither ARA [Area Redevelopment Administration, the forerunner of the present Economic Development Administration] nor any other program designed primarily to increase job opportunities can have any significant effect. One or two fringe locations excepted, the most that can be accomplished is to hold the line; highway and civic improvements are necessary to realize even this modest aim, but little more can be expected of them.[43]

The data presented earlier on recent economic and demographic change in eastern Kentucky and Central Appalachia in general show that time has only reinforced these findings.

Growth Centers and Appalachia's Future

Much has been made, and rightly so, in discussions of Appalachian development problems of the lack of urban centers in the region capable of providing the services, concentrated labor force, and other external economies needed to support growth. This lack is especially evident in the southern Appalachians. Many people feel that difficult adjustment problems related to migration would be less severe if the region's own cities could absorb more of the migrant population. Unfortunately, the performance of southern Appalachia's SMSA's has not been bright.

From 1940 to 1950 the SMSA's of southern Appalachia, as defined by Brown and Hillery, increased in population by 20 percent, but from 1950 to 1960 the gain was only 7 percent, while all SMSA's in the country were increasing in population by 26 percent. During the 1950–60 decade, only 30 of the 212 SMSA's in the United States had population declines or increases of less than 10 percent. Four of the six southern Appalachian SMSA's—Huntington-Ashland, Charleston, Asheville, and Knoxville—were among these. The growth rates of the other two—Chattanooga (13.3 percent) and Roanoke (18.1 percent)—were below the national median for SMSA's. Moreover, during the 1950–60 decade, the combined SMSA's of the region actually lost population related to migration, the net migration rate being −10.1 percent. Only Roanoke did not lose population due to migration and most of the other SMSA's had relatively high net outmigration rates. Thus, it is apparent that the region's SMSA's have been less attractive to migrants than other SMSA's in the country.[44] Moreover, according to Bureau of the Census projections, this pattern is going to continue. The Bureau estimates that between 1965 and 1975 the six SMSA's in question, taken together, will grow by only 3.5 percent. If Roanoke is excluded, the ten-year growth rate will be only 1.9 percent.[45] Brown and Hillery have correctly pointed out that:

As metropolitan centers have become more important in national life, the incapacity of the Appalachian Region to develop and sustain many large, metropolitan areas has resulted in a decline of its national significance. Furthermore, various parts of the area have tended to fall into the spheres of influence of the cities that have developed outside the Region. Consequently, it is less meaningful today to consider the Appalachians as a region in itself, since it is becoming increasingly segmented so far as its economic ties are concerned.[46]

Thus we return to an important point emphasized earlier in this chapter, namely, that Appalachia "is a collection of fringes of other systems which have some more or less common characteristics. More and more each of these fringes is being integrated into the particular system of which it is a part."[47] A regional policy that is primarily concerned with people would give high priority to integrating the growth of urban areas outside of Appalachia with their Appalachian hinterlands and to providing comprehensive relocation assistance. North Carolina provides a good example of what this implies.

The area of greatest economic growth in North Carolina is the polynucleated urban area known as the Piedmont Crescent. There are five major cities in this complex: Raleigh, Durham, Greensboro, Winston Salem, and Charlotte.[48] Under the present regional commission approach, the Appalachian counties of western North Carolina, which do not include the Piedmont, have been encouraged to try to solve their problems within the context of their own area. Similarly, the counties of eastern North Carolina have been grouped together to form a part of the region for which the Coastal Plains Regional Commission is responsible. The Coastal Plains Commission—which also includes counties in eastern South Carolina and eastern Georgia—is modeled after the Appalachian Commission and in principle its activities are to be carried out within the perspective of its own domain. However, Bishop points out that relocation assistance that attempts to guide migration to the Piedmont Crescent may well have a greater payoff than efforts to subsidize industry movements to lagging areas or to increase education at all levels. In North Carolina, he writes, "we are trying to alter the migration pattern. Instead of having our people concentrate in New York, Washington, or Philadelphia, we are attempting to encourage a shift into the Piedmont from the Coastal Plains."[49] He advocates more serious consideration of relocation assistance programs—"with job information and moving expenses—to be operated through the State Employment Security Commissions."[50]

Another lost opportunity is represented by the growth of parts of non-Appalachian Kentucky, particularly around Louisville, and in the Bluegrass area around Lexington. The cities in the Lexington-

Louisville-Cincinnati triangle are now linked to one another and to Appalachia by the interstate highway system and the Mountain Parkway in eastern Kentucky. Moreover, as shown earlier in this chapter, there is evidence that young people in eastern Kentucky have strong preferences to move to growing Kentucky cities outside of Appalachia, rather than to northern cities. The Appalachian Regional Commission has taken an interest in the commuting possibilities that have been and will be opened as a result of new and projected highways. However, Louisville is not within commuting distance of Appalachia, and there has not yet been any really systematic effort made to explore the possibilities of a comprehensive migration program involving growth centers in non-Appalachian Kentucky.

In general, it is to be expected that migrants will be less and less influenced in choosing their destinations by the previous choices of their families, and that they increasingly will become more sensitive to opportunities in the job market.[51] The Appalachian Regional Commission has taken account of the commuting possibilities that are and can be made available to residents of the region who live relatively close to growing urban areas on the fringe of the region. Many of its human resource investments within the region also imply that the beneficiaries may have to relocate to find gainful employment for their skills and training. But as yet there has been no systematic effort to guide migration, particularly if it involves movement outside the region.

For the near future at least, the principal response to Appalachia's lack of urban centers capable of providing the services, trained labor, and other external economies needed to support sustained growth apparently will be to encourage the development of such centers within the region. Each state has determined areas where it is believed economic growth is most likely to occur, taking account of commuting patterns, commercial activity, educational and cultural services, professional services, inter-industry linkages, government services, natural resources, physical geography considerations, and transportation networks. During the past three years the states have identified, throughout the sixty development and planning districts of the region, some 125 areas which have "significant potential for future growth." These areas taken together account for 80 percent of the people in the region, 88 percent of the bank deposits, 88 percent of the retail trade, 92 percent of the wholesale trade, and 92 percent of the major services. Between 1959 and 1965 these areas also accounted for 86 percent of the total increase in per capita income in Appalachia. An analysis of public investments during the first three years of the Appalachian program showed that only 4.9 percent of the outlays for non-highway investments were located outside of these areas, and that less than 5 percent of investments were in projects deemed to have low priority relative to regional problems. Thus, the Executive Director of the Appalachian Regional Commission states that with few exceptions, most of which occurred during the first months of the program, "the public facility investments during the first three years of the program appeared to have been properly located and their function directly related to development problems in local areas."[52] Yet some hard questions need to be raised in this regard.

The growth center policy of the Appalachian program is constrained by its district program. Instead of beginning by delimiting a select number of "areas of significant potential for future growth," it has been necessary to define growth centers so that each of the sixty-nine development districts has at least one center.[53] If each district really has a genuine growth center, then it would seem that there would be no need for outmigration from the region, nor for commuting to outside metropolitan areas. There would only need to be commuting—and perhaps some limited relocation—within each district, from the hinterland to the growth center.

Given the relatively low level of urbanization in Appalachia, given the great comparative advantages of larger urban centers in terms of external economies attractive to most firms, and given the enormous financial effort to bridge the gap between a "potentially promising" location and actually providing it with enough external economies to be competitive, it seems that greater selectivity could have been used in designating growth centers. When one considers that public capital investment in established metropolitan areas in the United States may range from a quarter to a third of the total capital outlay,[54] it becomes apparent that Appalachian program funds available for growth centers are not sufficient to make 125 centers attractive in comparison to those in more advanced regions, at least not by a process of balanced growth of public facilities within each center.

The Appalachian Regional Commission is aware of these problems and now distinguishes between 78 primary and regional "growth centers" on the one hand and smaller "district centers" on the other. Moreover, Commission growth center investments have been concentrated in thirty areas. Although large absolute expenditures have been made in some of the region's bigger cities, the highest proportion of Commission obligations has gone to growth areas in the 10,000 to 250,000 range. These areas account for 75.3 percent of all growth area obligations, compared to 15.6 percent for areas with populations over 250,000 and 9.0 percent to areas with fewer than 10,000 inhabitants. It is the policy of the Commission to invest more in per capita terms in communities of 250,000 or less than in larger cities because the impact of program funds is likely to be greater in these communities. Moreover, the most rapid growth in Appalachia is occurring in communities in the 10,000-50,000 population range, rather than in the larger cities or rural areas. Between 1960 and 1966, communities in the 10,000-50,000 range accounted for 40 percent of Appalachia's population growth even though they had only 24 percent of the region's population (see Table 14).

In practice, then, the distribution of growth center investments has been much more concentrated than might have been expected from an approach that gives each district at least one growth center and some districts more. However, some nominal growth areas are in fact hinterlands to more viable growth centers outside of their districts or even outside of Appalachia. The people in these nominal areas might benefit more from investments in health and education than from growth-type investments which might well be ineffective and which they are not receiving in any case. They might also be given more encouragement to commute or move to areas where employment growth is a viable prospect rather than a slogan of the local Chamber of Commerce. It is hoped that this question can be put in better perspective by the more general discussions in Chapters 9 and 10.

Summary and Conclusions

As in the case of the South, Appalachia's employment structure is heavily weighted in favor of declining and slow-growing sectors. The region's relative isolation, its failure to develop growing cities with attractive external economies, and its neglect of its human resources have combined to discourage more rapidly growing and better paying industries—particularly in the tertiary sector—from locating in Appalachia. For many of its residents, outmigration has been the only feasible response to high levels of unemployment and underemployment and low levels of income. The people of Appalachia have much the same values and aspirations as other Americans, and many are willing to move to areas where opportunities are better, or at least they feel that their children should move. Unfortunately, one of the main factors inhibiting Appalachian development—underinvestment in human resources—also makes it difficult for many Appalachian residents to find employment outside of the region. Residents of non-Appalachian regions who are helping to finance public works projects in Appalachia have reason to question whether these projects are really going to generate self-sustained growth in the mountains, much less help themselves. On the other hand, because the rest of the nation is an importer of Appalachia's people it has a stake in their quality. Considerably greater outside support is needed if the health and educational needs of Appalachia's people are to be met.

Many parts of Appalachia, particularly Central Appalachia, will not be able to provide decent jobs opportunities for many of their people. Increased skill and training will not be sufficient to attract rapidly growing, relatively high-wage industries in view of the many other disadvantages of these areas. Moreover, the magnitude of the public works projects that would be needed to put these areas on a par with their competitors in other parts of the country would be financially beyond the means of the Appalachian program. This is fortunate from an opportunity cost viewpoint in a national perspective.

The Appalachian Regional Development Act of 1965 was largely designed to attract economic activity to the region. Its primary emphasis was placed on highway construction, to open up the region to the "outside" world. However, because of the Vietnam situation appropriations for the Appalachian highway program have fallen far short of authorizations. Moreover, the Appalachian Regional Commission has been cognizant of the human resource deficiencies of the region and has moved to do more to correct this situation than might be supposed from a reading of the original Act. The Commission realizes that improving the quality of Appalachia's human resources may increase outmigration, but it has not developed a comprehensive labor mobility program geared to job opportunities outside the region. The Appalachian highway program provides links to growing metropolitan areas on the fringe of the region, but the Commission views these ties primarily in terms of commuting opportunities for Appalachian people living near the fringe or in terms of markets for Appalachian firms.

There are places in Appalachia with growth potential and the Appalachian Regional Commission can play a valuable role in stimulating, guiding, and coordinating their development. However, the future of many people of the region might be brighter if future legislation were to put more emphasis than is now given to linking the problems of Appalachia to opportunities outside of the region.

Chapter 5

The Regional Commissions

Introduction

The Public Works and Economic Development Act of 1965 authorized the Secretary of Commerce to designate, with the concurrence of the states involved, multistate regions that contain common problems of economic distress or lag that extend beyond the capability of any one state to solve. Among the factors used in considering whether a region has lagged behind the nation as a whole in economic development are: (1) a rate of unemployment substantially above the national rate; (2) a median level of family income significantly below the national median; (3) a level of housing, health, and educational facilities substantially below the national level; (4) an economy that has traditionally been dominated by only one or two industries, which are in a state of long term decline; (5) a substantial rate of outmigration of labor or capital or both; (6) adverse effects resulting from changing industrial technology; (7) adverse effects resulting from changes in national defense facilities or production; and (8) indices of regional production indicating a growth rate substantially below the national average.[1]

Once a region has been designated, the relevant states are invited to participate in a Regional Commission. The Commissions are patterned in structure after the Appalachian Regional Commis-

FIGURE 4: ECONOMIC DEVELOPMENT REGIONS

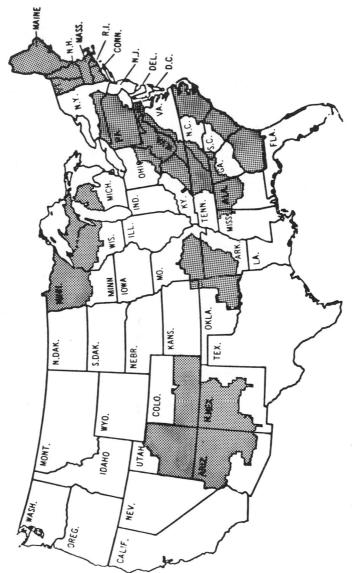

U. S. Department of Labor, based on data from U. S. Department of Commerce.

sion. They are joint federal-state organizations, composed of one member from each state (usually a Governor or his designee) and a federal member who is appointed by the President and confirmed by the Senate. The federal member serves as federal co-chairman and one of the state members, who is elected by his colleagues, serves as state co-chairman. Any action taken by the Commission requires the vote of the federal co-chairman and a majority of state members.

The Regional Commission approach assumes that the states know best the problems of their region. At the same time, it is assumed that the federal government is more likely to have an objective view of the overall plan in its relationship to national objectives. A joint plan combining these views is expected to be of greater value than a plan prepared alone at either level. Each Regional Commission is charged with analyzing the problems of its area's economy and developing an overall strategy for promoting the area's long-run growth. More specifically, each Commission is confronted with the following tasks: (1) identifying the reasons why the region's economy is lagging behind that of the nation; (2) identifying the human and physical resources available within the region; (3) determining overall developmental goals for the region in the light of its potential; (4) developing alternative programs for reaching these goals and identifying what should be done by the government and by private enterprise; (5) working with federal, state, and local governments for the implementation of the Commission's recommendations.[2]

In developing recommendations for programs and projects for future regional economic development, and in establishing within these recommendations a priority ranking for such programs and projects, the Commissions are supposed to take account of the relationship of individual projects or classes of projects to overall regional development. This includes locating projects in areas which have a significant potential for growth in the view of the states. Consideration must also be given to the population of the area to be served by the project or class of projects, including its per capita income and unemployment rate. In addition, the relative financial resources available to the state or political subdivisions which seek to undertake a project must be considered, as well as the importance of the project in relation to other projects which may be in competition for the same funds. Finally, there must be some prospect that the project will permanently improve the opportunities for employment, the average level of income, or the economic and social development of the area served by the project.[3] In this last instance, it will be noted that the focus is upon the development of the place in question, rather than upon its people, although in practice some of the Commissions are oriented toward human resource development.

On the basis of Public Law 90–103 amendments to the Public Works and Economic Development Act of 1965, the Commissions are authorized to give financial aid to economically lagging areas in financial difficulty by supplementing or substituting Commission funds for those ordinarily required from the state or local bodies in federal grant-in-aid programs involving the construction or equipping of public facilities or land acquisition. Thus, where a federal grant-in-aid program, such as public health services or vocational education, would normally be funded 50 percent by the relevant federal agency and 50 percent by state or local government, the supplemental grant program permits the Commission to assume a portion of the normal state and local matching share. The maximum allowable combined federal agency-Commission share is 80 percent. For example, under a maximum supplemental grant arrangement the funding for vocational education would be changed from 50 percent federal agency-50 percent state and local government, to 50 percent federal agency-30 percent regional Commission-20 percent state and local government. To carry out the supplemental grant-in-aid program, $5 million was authorized for each of the regional Commissions for the last part of fiscal year 1968, and $10 million was authorized for each Commission for fiscal year 1969.[4] However, actual allocations have fallen considerably short of these amounts.

Five Regional Commissions were established in 1966. The regions concerned are the Ozarks, New England, the Four Corners, the Coastal Plains, and the Upper Great Lakes. Because of funding lags many of the Commissions were not able to complete their staffs before 1968. The work of the Commissions is just getting off the ground at this writing, hence it is not possible to attempt any definitive evaluation of their programs. Nevertheless, it is instructive to examine their progress to date.

The Ozarks Region

As designated in 1966, the Ozarks Economic Development Region consisted of 125 counties in the states of Arkansas, Missouri, and Oklahoma. Nine Kansas counties were added to the region in 1968. These counties lie in the Ozark uplands, the Arkansas River Valley, the Ouachita Mountains and the border counties which merge into the bottom lands of the Mississippi River. The original settlers in the Ozarks were descendents of the early English colonists from the mountain regions of the eastern states. Although the Ozark Mountains, like the Appalachian Mountains, are geologically modest, they too have resulted in the isolation of many small settlements. Because of this isolation people of the region have been slow to assimilate urban values and ways of living, and economic progress has lagged behind that in surrounding regions.[5]

The Department of Agriculture has developed an index of farm-operator living standards based on average value of sales per farm, average value of land and buildings per farm, proportion of farms with telephones, proportion of farms with home freezers, and proportion of farms with automobiles. By these criteria the Appalachians and the Ozarks have especially poor living indexes. In relation to the rest of the country, the Ozarks region has poor soil, steep land, and small farms, conditions not suited to large-scale, mechanized commercial agriculture.[6] The region is still predominantly rural, despite the growth of urban population centers within it. In 1960, only about 40 percent of the population in the region was in urban areas, whereas the comparable national figure was 70 percent.

TABLE 22: SOCIOECONOMIC CHARACTERISTICS, OZARKS REGION COMPARED TO UNITED STATES

	United States	Ozarks Region	Arkansas Portion	Missouri Portion	Oklahoma Portion
Population, 1960	179,000,000	2,495,341	956,786	786,330	752,225
Population per square mile	50	28	31	27	26
Percent population change, 1950–1960	18	−4.8	−3.2	2.5	−13.1
Apparent net civilian migration, 1950–1960		430,754	164,490	70,553	195,711
Percent urban, 1960	70	40	46	32	41
Median age, 1960	29.5	32.5	32	33	33
Percent labor force change, 1950–1960	13	−5.5	−2.7	−2.4	−12.2
Employment pattern, 1960 (percent)					
Manufacturing	27	18	21	19	14
Agriculture	6	14	12	17	12
Wholesale and Retail	18	20	19	20	20
Finance, Insurance	4	3	3	3	3
Construction	6	7	7	7	8
Education and Public Administration	10	10	10	9	12
All Other	28	28	28	25	31
Median family income 1959	5,660	3,492	3,513	3,528	3,427
Percent change median family income, 1949–1959	82	101	105	105	93
Percentage housing units unsound, 1960	26	47	45	48	48
Median school years completed, 1960	10.6	9.3	9.7	9.3	8.9

TABLE 22—Continued

	United States	Ozarks Region	Arkansas Portion	Missouri Portion	Oklahoma Portion
Percent enrolled in school, 1960		78.1	79.4	74.4	80
Percent of families less than $3,000 income, 1960	21.4	44.4	44.4	43.1	46
Average size of farm, 1959, acres	303	203			
Percent of commercial farms with sales of less than $2,500, 1959	14	26			
Average dollar value of land and buildings per farm, 1959	35,000	13,000			
Per capita bank deposits, June 30, 1964 (dollars)	1,844	844			
Physicians per 1,000 population	1.4	0.9			

Source: Ozarks Regional Commission.

Only fourteen cities and towns have more than 10,000 population, and only four counties are parts of SMSA's. For several generations farming and natural resource extraction have been the major economic activities of the region. Because of technological changes and market shifts, the region's labor force has suffered increasingly from both underemployment and unemployment. A high proportion of the area's young people have migrated to places offering greater job opportunities; total population of the Ozarks declined by almost 5 percent during the 1950's, and by over 13 percent between 1940 and 1960.[7]

In 1959, per capita income in the Ozarks was $1,242, or 67 percent of the national average. Compared to the nation as a whole, the Ozarks Region has twice the proportion of families with an annual income of less than $3,000, but only one-third the proportion of families earning $10,000 or more. Furthermore, on the basis of projections of population and income to 1975, the Commission finds that the region's per capita income may fall short of the national mark by as much as $1,000. Low income is reflected in the standards of living of the region's people. For example, in 1960, 34 percent of the houses in the region lacked hot or cold running water, 32 percent lacked a flush toilet, 33 percent had no tub or shower, and 32 percent had no sewage system. Retail sales in the region in 1964 amounted to $1,138 per capita, compared to a national figure of $1,347. Of the 134 counties in the region, only one, Pulaski, Arkansas (Little Rock), is in the top 164 counties in the United States in total retail sales. In 1965 the federal government spent $236,-000,000 in public assistance grants to the Ozark states. The per capita cost was $25.43 in Arkansas, $21.71 in Missouri, and $36.51 in Oklahoma, compared to a national per capita cost of $15.75.[8]

The physical resources of the Ozarks do not provide a promising base for the region's future economic development. A large part of the land is unsuited to further agricultural development. Only isolated areas specializing in poultry, dairy, and intensive crops show some promise for the development of commercial agriculture and related industry. A great deal of the land that is adaptable to agriculture is forested. Much of the region is covered with slow-growing hardwoods, but there is sufficient pine to support an expanded forest products industry. The development of recreational centers for the populations of major urban centers of the mid-continent offers a promising potential use for the area's physical resources. Bauxite, iron, lead, zinc, coal, and natural gas are being exploited in the region, but mining employment has not contributed substantially to the economy and is not likely to expand. Manufacturing employment has increased in the urban areas of the region, but not fast enough to employ the large number of workers leaving the agricultural sector. Moreover, the region's manufacturing activities are concentrated in slow-growing sectors such as apparel. Public and private services sufficient to support sustained economic growth are available only in the larger urban centers of the region. Revenues from local sources alone are not adequate to support the public services needed for development. The need for additional education and training is especially acute, since the age composition, education level, and lack of marketable skills of the population tend to retard development in the region and also to keep workers from moving to where better job opportunities are available. Less than a third of the Ozark Region's residents twenty-five years of age or over had completed high school in 1960. The median number of school years completed was 8.9, compared with national median of 10.6.[9] In one of the most thorough economic surveys of the Ozarks region yet undertaken, Jordan and Bender find that "The major economic problem within the region affecting every type of adjustment is the amount and quality of education."[10]

In 1962, nearly 60 percent of local government expenditure other than capital outlay in the Ozarks went for education. The average was under 50 percent for all local governments in the United States. Nevertheless, the region's expenditure per pupil in daily attendance is too low to maintain an adequate educational system. The Ozark expenditure per pupil in average daily attendance in 1962 was $253, which was especially low in relation to school size (smaller schools need high expenditures per pupil if they are to provide the same quality of education as larger schools), and to density of population. Similarly, per capita local government expenditure (other than capital outlay) on education in the Ozarks in 1962 was about $65; the comparable national figure was over $83.[11]

The Ozarks Regional Commission's program for dealing with the region's problems has as its principal goal closing the gap in per capita income between the region and the rest of the nation. The strategy adopted in this regard includes (1) expansion and improvement of education, with emphasis on technical and occupational training; (2) identification and promotion of products and services to create the largest number of jobs, especially those that will appeal to educated, able young people; (3) development and upgrading of public facilities related to economic development in areas of significant growth potential; and (4) cultivation of attitudes favorable to economic growth and expansion.[12]

Road, water, and sewer systems are considered secondary to education in the Ozarks program. Dr. John Peterson, an economist who has worked with the program, points out that "A lot of people tend to think of resources as something tangible. I think the first resources are people—their training, education and ways of thinking. They have to want to improve their lot and then have the means to do so."[13] William McCandless, Federal Co-chairman of the Ozarks Regional Commission, testified before the Senate Committee on Public Works that "The Ozarks Region must place primary emphasis on the education and training of its people and an educational system that is responsive to a changing technology and society of the future."[14] School enrollment in the Ozarks as a proportion of the population aged five to seventeen years is not far below the national level, but the median educational level of the region's population will remain low so long as young people continue to leave the region once they complete high school. The Ozarks Commission has initiated a technical education program which, it is hoped, will create a reservoir of technically trained young people that will attract industry with the kind of jobs needed to lift the income level of the region. The first step in this program is planning for a system of occupational and technical skill training for each of the region's states. Substantial funds will be required to construct the new technical education centers that will be recommended. The Commission does not shy away from the outmigration issue, but believes that the job skills that these centers create will provide a foundation for the expansion of industry in the region. In the words of McCandless, "We are quite conscious that part of the investment made by the States will result in trained young people finding employment elsewhere. But, at the same time, we reiterate our conviction that the greatest asset that this Region can have is a preponderance of educated and trained manpower."[15] Considerable importance is also placed on developing research centers at the region's colleges and universities and in independent laboratories, and on developing cultural and recreational activities to help attract educated, skilled outsiders.[16]

The Commission is cognizant of the fact that the heavy priority given to education in manpower development means restricted funds for public facilities. "It would be most simple for us to generalize and state that all communities in the Ozarks need new and expanded public facilities and on a need basis, [and] we would be right. But I realize that the same plea can be made for virtually every community in the United States. The Federal Government already has numerous programs seeking to answer these community needs."[17] Thus, while the need for expanded public works in the Ozarks is recognized, the role of the Commission is to be one of coordination of existing federal grant programs and relating them wherever possible to realistic economic development goals. Where the Commission will engage in direct public investment, the location will be based not on community need but on economic development payoff. However, this does not imply a growth center strategy, since "In an open rural area such as the Ozarks, economic growth tends to be linear along transportation corridors. Certainly, there is a greater probability for growth at certain places in those corridors, but there are immediate opportunities in other places."[18]

The states of the Ozarks region have prepared their recommendations for a regional public investment plan, which is now being put together as one comprehensive recommendation. At the same time, a firm of economic and engineering consultants is making a developmental transportation analysis of the region. A navigation channel on the Arkansas River, scheduled to be completed in 1970, represents a potentially valuable new transportation resource for the region. Where industrial sites can be located, where loading facilities should be placed, and other questions related to the most effective utilization of the channel are all related to planning and constructing a highway system geared to economic development. The Ozarks region needs better access to the markets of the central part of the United States, and it needs improvements in its existing road system to link up growing areas within the region.[19]

Upper Great Lakes Region

The Upper Great Lakes Region consists of a 119-county area in the northern portions of Michigan, Minnesota, and Wisconsin. The population of this area is estimated at 2,700,000, or about 17 percent of the population of the three states comprising the region. Since the Great Depression, when many former outmigrants from the region returned because they had lost their jobs in the cities, population growth in the Upper Great Lakes has been relatively stagnant. From 1940 to 1950 the region's population grew by only 1.6 percent, compared to 18.1 percent in the nonregion segments of the three states and 14.5 percent in the nation. A similar trend prevailed during the 1950's. The region has long been characterized by heavy net outmigration. From 1950 to 1967, there was a net outmigration of nearly 300,000 people, more than 10 percent of the 1950 population. These outmigrants included more than half the people in the 20–24 year age-group, and over a quarter of those in the 15–34 year age-group. Continuing outmigration of the most productive and adaptable members of the labor force therefore represents a serious economic loss to the region. Accompanying the loss of people in the younger working age-groups has been an unfavorable shift in the age distribution of the region's population. The percentage of the population aged 65 and over has risen sharply relative to the nation as a whole. In 1960 persons over the age of 65 represented 11 percent of the region's population, compared with only 9 percent for the entire country.[20]

Employment trends in the Upper Great Lakes show a rate of growth substantially behind the national average. Between 1950 and 1960, regional employment growth was 1.7 percent, compared to a national growth rate of 14.8 percent. While the nation's labor force increased by over 6 percent between 1962 and 1967, the labor force in the Upper Great Lakes declined by several thousand workers. In March, 1966, unemployment in the region was 7.2 percent, almost double the national average of 3.9 percent. In the upper peninsula of Michigan the unemployment rate reached 10.4 percent.[21]

Per capita income in the Upper Great Lakes in 1960 was $1,420, or over $400 less than the per capita income of the three states as a group. In the same year, the region's median family income stood at $4,735, compared to the national median of $5,660. Over 40 percent of the housing units in the region were classified as unsound, compared with 26 percent for the nation as a whole.[22]

The relative stagnation of the Upper Great Lakes is related to a heavy representation of slow-growth industries in the total employment structure of the region. Although a high proportion of persons are employed in nonmanufacturing industries (63 percent), and manufacturing (18 percent), a sizeable proportion of employed workers is still engaged in agriculture, forestry, and fishing (14 percent). Chronic decline in agriculture is a major contributor to the region's slow growth. Farm employment fell by 40 percent between 1950 and 1960, while the comparable national figure was 38.5 percent. Total employment in farming, forestry, and fishing is continuing to decline; these activities accounted for 153,000 jobs in 1960, but only 120,000 jobs in 1966.[23]

Mining has also been in a state of long term decline. In recent years, however, large investments in the growing taconite industry have provided a new and solid base for the mining industry in the Minnesota portion of the region. Large steel and mining companies have invested or plan to invest over a billion dollars in plants and equipment to produce high iron-content, marble-sized pellets from the hard taconite, of which there is a three hundred year supply in the ground. Facilities at eight different locations will be in operation by the end of 1969, and facilities representing another half billion dollars of investment will probably be in operation by 1975. Despite the highly capital-intensive nature of this industry—an investment of over $100,000 is required for each new job—it is estimated that direct employment in taconite operations will be close to 10,000 by 1970 and close to 14,000 by 1975. Moreover, taconite production has also induced numerous other activities. In the process of grinding taconite rock, ten pounds of finished steel are consumed for every ton of taconite pellets produced. In the actual mining three tons of rock are needed for each ton of pellets, and spare parts are frequently required for the four hundred-ton shovels, and trucks, and the other equipment used in mining operations. Taconite producers spend $3.50 for replacement parts for every ton of processed taconite. In addition to expanding construction activities, the growth of the taconite sector has resulted in rapid service-industry growth. Because of the rising demand for manpower, workers have had to be recruited from other areas to augment the local supply of construction workers. Although business and union leaders felt that prosperity generated by the taconite sector would continue to grow for a considerable time, there has been a slackening of activity since 1966.[24]

During the 1950's manufacturing employment grew more slowly in the Upper Great Lakes than in the rest of the nation, but from 1959 to 1965 the region's sixth-year growth rate of 9 percent equalled that of the nation. However, most of the recent growth has been accounted for by the southern border of the region, which grew much faster than the country as a whole. Twenty-four southern counties had an increase of about 16,000 jobs from 1959 to 1965, which represented a growth rate of 21 percent. In contrast, the ninety-five remaining counties to the north had a net loss of 2,465 jobs, representing a decline of 3.8 percent. One reason for the rapid growth of the southern counties was the expansion of highways that provided quicker access to major markets farther south. In addition, pressures from expanding manufacturing industries in congested areas outside the Upper Great Lakes Region made its underutilized labor force attractive for branch plant locations. It is hoped that improved transportation and utilities will extend this industrial development farther north.[25]

In summary, with the exception of recent employment growth in the southern counties, major industries in the region have developed historically around the abundant forest and mineral resources of the region, and most industries still center around these resources. Areas that lack minerals or timber in productive quantities for the most part also lack any significant industrial activity. In consequence, opportunities for gainful employment are severely limited. This is probably the main reason why most graduates of vocational schools, colleges, and universities scattered throughout the region go elsewhere to find work; job opportunities simply do not exist for them.

In confronting the problems of the region, the Upper Great Lakes Regional Commission has established as its first-priority comprehensive goal narrowing the gap between regional and national averages with respect to unemployment rates and labor force participation rates.[26] It is assumed that once the job goal is reached other objectives, such as those relating to income and standard of living, will be closer to realization. In formulating the broad outlines of a strategy that will be the foundation for the Commission's plan for economic development of the region, the Commission points out that:

In regions such as the Upper Great Lakes, where a declining mining economy must be replaced or diversified through the introduction of an entirely new manufacturing industry or through the development of the tourist potential, the readjustment process must necessarily be long and agonizing, if it takes place at all. Meanwhile, people and resources remain unemployed and wasted and the Nation is deprived of the valuable productive contribution that the region is capable of making.[27]

Nevertheless, the Commission maintains that "Labor should be trained for jobs in the region rather than largely for export to other regions."[28] To encourage economic expansion in their region, the states which comprise the Commission have recommended a series of projects that fall into the general categories of industrial development, tourism development, agricultural development, and transportation development. In general, the public investment projects that are proposed are intended to induce increased private investment. In the industrial development category, the states have proposed geological mapping and forest inventory projects aimed at exploiting the natural resources of the area; expansion of vocational education facilities; and construction of water and sewage systems that would allow communities to take advantage of opportunities to expand industry and tourism. In the tourism development category, the states have suggested expansion of salmon sports fishing, rehabilitation of inland lakes, expanded training programs for tourist industry personnel, and creation of a new national park in the region. In the agricultural development category, the states have proposed soil surveys, creation of a plant research station, and a horticultural opportunities project. In the field of transportation development, new highways and airports are called for. In addition to these proposals, the Commission will consider suggestions received from various federal agencies and from members of Congress representing the region.[29]

Owing to its conservative attitude toward outmigration from the region, and owing to the fact that educational facilities are about on a par with those in the rest of the country, relatively little emphasis has been given to manpower and education in official statements by the Commission. Nevertheless, within the Commission serious attention has been given to these areas. A preliminary report[30] points out that a much larger percentage of the region's labor force is composed of workers over the age of 45 than is the case nationally, and calls for special emphasis on programs of adult and continuing education, and on facilities for retraining workers whose skills are now threatened by obsolescence. Special programs related to social, health, and other services may also be needed to link training programs for older workers to their place of work. The relative immobility of labor within the region is also a consequence of low population densities and low levels of per capita income. But the most serious obstacles to labor mobility are presented by an inadequate employment information system for matching men and jobs, and the lack of supporting services for those persons considering migration. An improved mechanism for transmitting job market and manpower information among centers within the region, and between these centers and such cities as Minneapolis and Detroit in nearby regions, is a prerequisite for increasing mobility. Existing information systems are deficient in geographical coverage, and they give little or no information concerning (1) identification and means of obtaining improved job opportunities; (2) minimum necessary entrance requirements for available jobs; (3) general socioeconomic conditions in the communities in which employment opportunities exist; and (4) availability, cost, and location of suitable housing in communities offering employment opportunities. Likewise, programs for relocation assistance and supporting services are either nonexistent or extremely inadequate. In order to provide the information and services necessary to increase mobility of labor in the Upper Great Lakes, it is recommended that the functions of the state employment security commissions be upgraded and expanded, and coordinated on a regional basis. The state employment security offices should develop region-wide mechanisms for transmitting information rapidly and clearly, and for insuring that it reaches the individuals who need it. In addition, the employment security commissions should establish working relations with the various social service agencies that can provide supporting services for relocated workers. On the other hand, for many members of the region's labor force, relocation will not be necessary; rather, workers can commute from smaller population clusters to available jobs in larger regional centers. Such commuting should be encouraged by providing reliable job market information and transportation assistance similar to that discussed for those being relocated.

In addition to greater labor force mobility, another priority need of the Upper Great Lakes Region is for expanded vocational-technical education. Many of the region's school districts cannot support either highly sophisticated academic courses or vocational-technical programs with any scope or depth because the districts have small student populations and only limited financial resources. This problem will become increasingly severe as the demand for highly educated and trained personnel expands. In order to insure provision of adequate programs to the region's population, programs should be developed on an area or multi-district basis to encourage merging of and cooperation among districts. Moreover, most programs financed by state and federal aid are too limited in duration and lack continuity and stability. To insure rational educational development, programs need to be approved for more than one year. Similarly, there is frequently a lack of lead time between project proposals and their approval. Finally, although funds are provided for the construction and expansion of physical facilities, there is often little provision made for the operational support necessary to make programs effective.

Because of the traditional philosophical orientation of many educators in the region, there tends to be a concentration on academic programs almost to the exclusion of vocational and technical education. Many schools have no vocational programs or only a limited number of courses, many of which are outmoded. Disproportionate emphasis is often given to providing staff and materials for "honors" programs, while inadequate attention is given to the needs and problems of the slow learners. Improved and expanded basic education and vocational-technical education will require more and better trained teachers and instructors at all levels. Where low population densities make area centers impractical, mobile classrooms and instructors may be used to supplement courses in the local school districts. Demonstration projects to study the feasibility and effectiveness of such innovations as televised instruction and programmed learning should also be undertaken.

The Coastal Plains

The Coastal Plains Region includes the coastal regions of North and South Carolina and Georgia.[31] Manufacturing industry and employment have grown rapidly in these states in recent years, but most of this growth has taken place in the Piedmont and other areas away from the coast. The Coastal Plains Region has traditionally been a low-wage area, and sharp and continuing decline in agricultural employment has resulted in a great deal of underemployment and poverty, particularly among the Negro population. In 1960, the five million people of the region had a per capita income figure that was $769 below that of the nation as a whole.

Since the states and counties which comprise the Coastal Plains have not been accustomed to viewing their problems and potentials in a common light, one of the first tasks of the Coastal Plains Regional Commission is to encourage and motivate state and local leaders to think in regional terms. At this writing, the Commission is still engaged in gathering data on the region's characteristics, needs, basic resources, and potentials.

The primary goal of the Coastal Plains Regional Commission is to narrow and eventually close the gap that exists between the region's per capita income and that of the nation. The initial strategies that will be employed toward this end will involve industrial development, marine resource development, education and manpower training, tourist promotion, and agricultural development. Programs which may later be considered include the region's transportation, capital resources, and housing and health needs.

A preliminary assessment by the Commission of factors affecting industrial potential in the region indicates that there are a number of favorable conditions to support new industry. The location of the Coastal Plains between the growing Gulf Coast-Florida region and the northeastern states is an asset from the viewpoint of consumer

and industrial markets. The region contains many towns of sufficient size to support a variety of industrial activities. In addition,
many smaller towns provide adequate personal and business services
for many types of manufacturing. Potential industrial sites and basic
utilities and transportation facilities are generally adequate for industrial development in many parts of the region. The Commission's staff has considered a number of possible ways to stimulate
industrial growth in the region, but at this stage more information is
needed regarding specific opportunities and barriers in particular
locations before a sound program for industrial development can be
formulated and implemented.

The Atlantic Ocean represents a major and largely untapped resource of the Coastal Plains. One of the main objectives of the
Commission is to assess the potential for increasing regional income
through the orderly development of marine resources, and to develop
and implement a program that will have the greatest impact on
the full exploitation of this potential. One of the main problems that
the region confronts in this regard is the conflict of interests among
various uses that can be made of the sea. For example, some persons
favor conserving and maintaining a natural type of marine environment. This position is in direct conflict with that favoring intensive
forms of recreational development. Such development often involves filling of estuaries and diverting water flows. This in turn up-
sets the delicate balance of nature and could have serious implications for future developments in the fishing industry and other forms
of recreation. The fishing industry in general consists of many
smaller fishermen with inadequate capital and management capability to remain competitive with other coastal regions and for-
eigners.

The Coastal Plains Commission regards the development of
tourism in the region as an integral part of economic development.
The region's temperate climate provides an extended season for
outdoor recreation, but its seashore and inland bodies of water and
its great variety of natural resources are relatively underdeveloped.
Its rich historical heritage has not been exploited to even a fraction

of its profit potential. On the demand side, untapped extra-regional markets will be easily accessible to all parts of the Coastal Plains by 1972, and people in these markets are enjoying increasing incomes and leisure time for recreation or retirement living. The Commission intends to produce the knowledge necessary to encourage profit-motivated private investment in those areas which offer natural, historic, transportation, and other opportunities. It will also seek to encourage enterprises offering the greatest potential in balanced-season activity, so as not to generate more short-season and sub-marginal employment.

The Coastal Plains is a region of traditional agriculture which has historically been oriented toward production of cotton, tobacco, and peanuts as the main sources of income. Large-scale mechanization in these areas has been undertaken only in recent years, but within a short time cotton and peanuts will be completely mechanized. Recent breakthroughs have been made in the mechanization of tobacco and more progress is expected in the near future. All three of the traditional commodities are under strict production control programs and a surplus of each exists at the national level at the present time. Thus, future developments within the region's agriculture are expected to involve some form of diversification of production patterns. The Commission feels that the region has a comparative advantage over many other regions of the country in the production of vegetables and horticultural specialty crops, but that this advantage has not been exploited sufficiently. Opportunities for expanded production in certain poultry and livestock products and soybeans are also considered promising. The agricultural economy of the Coastal Plains includes many large landholdings existing alongside an extremely large number of small farms. The small farmers, including tenants, have lacked management capacity and the capability to develop intensive, high culture crops. Small fruit and vegetable enterprises have not been really commercialized, and the production of poultry and hogs has largely been for consumption on the farm or for supplemental income. Until recently, large land-owners have had no strong incentive to mechanize or diversify outside of traditional crops. Although this situation is changing, many of them have found that in order to get into large scale production of nontraditional crops, they need high-quality labor on the one hand, and a large amount of low-skill labor during the harvesting season. Since many of the large landowners are independently wealthy, they have tended to regard change as being more trouble than it is worth.

Another problem in changing the structure of the agricultural economy is that the average age of farm operators in the region is over fifty. Most farmers in this age category have low levels of education and not much incentive to innovate. Many are merely struggling with traditional ways of doing things in the hope that they can continue to subsist in this manner and that their children can make it to the cities if they get a good education. Finally, in addition to production problems on individual farms, there has been a lack of organization to support adequate marketing facilities. The Commission hopes that it can promote agricultural development in the region by attacking some of these fundamental problems. Among the possible structural alterations that it envisages for the region's agricultural economy are: (1) changes in the mix of commodities produced and marketed in the region; (2) changes in the size and organization of farm units; (3) improved marketing facilities; and (4) improvements in technology as they relate to the agricultural industries of the region.

The future economic development of the Coastal Plains hinges to a great extent on the development of its human resources. Current projections indicate that approximately 50,000 agricultural workers will be released from the region's farms by 1975. At present most people in this category are not adequately prepared for industrial and business occupations where trained workers are in demand. For the region as a whole, 65 percent of those who begin school never reach college, and 85 percent never earn a college degree. In 1960 the region had approximately 478,000 adults with an educational achievement level of less than the fifth grade. Many thousands more had less than an eighth grade level of education. A few basic vocational training programs have been provided in recent years, chiefly through funding by the Manpower Development and Training Act, for those persons with at least a fifth grade level of education. Persons with less education have generally been rejected from most occupational training programs. Their only alternative remains basic adult education courses, but the response to educational opportunities of this type has not been very great. Consequently, many functional illiterates remain permanently in that classification. Moreover, the Coastal Plains lags behind other areas of the region's states in providing both technical and vocational training facilities.

The Commission believes that the greatest net return on regional investment would be obtained by upgrading the capabilities of those persons who are presently ill-equipped to contribute to the development of the region, but who represent a constant drain on its wealth through welfare programs. It regards an enlarged program of manpower development as a prime necessity for the region. In response, the Commission is sponsoring the development of multi-county Regional Manpower Training Centers. Such centers will serve as experimental training laboratories where, at one central site, a complete range of occupational and technical training below the college level can be provided. In addition, testing, counseling, evaluation, rehabilitation, and basic education for adult functional illiterates will be provided. The centers will serve as halfway houses through which illiterates will be transformed into literates, displaced farm workers will be introduced to the skills of industrial pursuits, and young people who do not go on to college will be provided with the basic tools needed for a trade or industrial career. The centers will maintain close association with technological advances in industry and the service trades and thereby avoid obsolescence of curriculum and faculty. In addition to the manpower training that the centers will provide on their respective sites, it is anticipated that they will be staffed to provide outreach into their surrounding areas to contact and motivate the population to upgrade its skills. Testing, counseling, and guidance for the new or potentially new enrollees will be provided, and persons who have completed any given level of training will be placed in suitable gainful employment and provided with follow-up services.

To implement this program, each state member of the Regional Commission will appoint to a special state manpower advisory council one or more citizens representing the fields of vocational education, technical education, adult education, vocational rehabilitation, and industry, respectively. The Employment Security Commission and professional social scientists will also be represented on the manpower advisory councils. The councils will work with the Commission and with professional consultants to provide the data required for the financing, location, program formulation and co-ordination, and program implementation for the proposed centers in the respective states.

In general, the Coastal Plains Regional Commission intends to place relatively greater emphasis on human resource and manpower development programs than on public works projects. The issue of outmigration of workers who seek to put newly acquired skills and training to work in areas outside of the Coastal Plains is not officially raised by the Commission. Nevertheless, the Commission is fully aware of this possibility and has no intention of resisting outmigration; neither does it intend to promote it.

New England

The six New England states form what is probably the most clearly defined geographic region in the United States.[32] It has been recognized as an economic region, sharing common attitudes, characteristics, and problems, for more than three hundred years. Five of the states share the Atlantic sea coast, which has served as a principal corridor for settlement and transportation. For the most part, watersheds lie totally within the region, the only significant exception being that of the St. Lawrence. The New England states share a generally common climate, including an abundant rainfall; they also have a common relative lack of natural resources.

New England was initially settled along the New Hampshire, Massachusetts, and Rhode Island coasts, almost exclusively by middle class English protestants. Although southern New England, in particular, has received large numbers of immigrants of diverse cultural and racial origins, a largely "Yankee" outlook and mentality have remained dominant in the region. With the exception of the French-Canadian subculture, the cultures of immigrant groups have generally been assimilated into the Yankee culture. Given its common geography and generally common culture, it is not surprising that the region also has a common history. The town and the town meeting institutions are shared by all of New England, and the entire region is characterized by weak or abolished county government.

The New England economy has gone through a series of historical phases and many of its past and present problems can be attributed to difficulties in adjusting to general economic changes. Two of the main factors affecting the present evolution of the region's economy are an infrastructure inherited from an older industrial economy, and a rapid evolution from older declining sectors, such as textiles, to advanced sectors such as services, electronics, research, and higher education. In the last century, mill-towns were scattered throughout the area wherever water power was available. A comprehensive railroad network was developed to service these communities. Later, about the turn of the century, electric generating stations and other public utilities were built to supply power to widely scattered, independent centers of urban industry. Much of the old infrastructure is inefficient by today's standards and the economic need for much of it has disappeared. The stage of American economic growth that was characterized by the steel and automobile industries bypassed New England because of its lack of raw materials and because, as population shifted westward, the region became increasingly removed from production and market centers. In addition, New England has lost many textile plants as a result of more attractive conditions in the southeastern United States.

The growth of employment in New England has lagged behind

that of the country as a whole for many years. Between 1961 and 1966 the average annual rate of growth in nonfarm employment was only 2.4 percent, compared to a national figure of 3.4 percent. In some places employment losses in declining industries such as textiles and leather have been more than replaced by job increases in technologically advanced industries. On the other hand, in Rhode Island, in parts of Massachusetts, and in eastern Connecticut there are reservoirs of skilled workers with the wrong skills who are located in the wrong places.

The brightest spot in New England's economy has been the rapid growth of economic activities based on advanced science and technology. Much of the growth in this sector has been concentrated around Boston, New Haven, Hartford, and other urban centers. Many of the new industries have clustered around universities and suburban areas, a development that has required a realignment of both private and public services. This shift in the industrial structure of New England has been brought about for the most part by the high educational qualifications of the region's labor force. Even the northern states of Vermont, New Hampshire, and Maine have higher levels of educational attainment than the national average. However, there are sharp contrasts between the rapidly growing research-oriented industries and professional and allied types of employment on the one hand, and the smaller industrial towns scattered throughout the area, with their economies still often based on textiles, leather, and other declining sectors, on the other.

The New England Regional Commission has commissioned a comprehensive review of the region's economy and its human resources. It has also commissioned an analysis of all types of transportation throughout the region. Unfortunately, neither of these studies is available at this writing. Meanwhile, each of the states is currently developing a state public investment plan for improving and strengthening its economic development programs. These plans, financed by grants from the Commission, include: (1) a statement of state economic and social development goals and objectives; (2) identification of potentials for growth and specific programs to achieve growth; (3) identification of important growth areas in the state; (4) determination of priorities among alternative investment; and (5) a statement of plans for improving the effectiveness of state economic and social development planning and programming. the respective plans will be coordinated on a region-wide basis by the Commission.

In terms of overall planning objectives, the New England Regional Commission has given top priority to human resource development. Despite the relatively high education and skill levels of the region's labor force, a great deal of retraining is necessary to adapt workers to jobs in expanding industrial sectors. In addition to industrial conversion in the southern states, an effort will be made to attract more industry to Maine, Vermont, and New Hampshire. The development of growth centers in the northern states will be promoted so that residents of these states can find good opportunities for employment closer to home; many workers from the northern states are now migrating to Boston and other metropolitan centers where, the Commission feels, the external diseconomies associated with increased congestion outweigh any concomitant external economies.

The Four Corners

The planning of the Four Corners Regional Commission is the least advanced of any of the commissions, so only the barest tentative outline can be given of its program.[33] The Four Corners area includes 92 counties in Arizona, Colorado, New Mexico and Utah. The region is remote and lacks industry. With the exception of Albuquerque, there are no large urban agglomerations or growth centers and its inhabitants are sparsely scattered throughout the area. In many respects, the area differs from the other designated regions in that it needs not so much redevelopment as initial development. Despite the region's dependence on declining agricultural and mining activities and its lack of urban centers, the Commission still has chosen for its principal goal raising the real per

TABLE 23: NEW ENGLAND ECONOMIC DEVELOPMENT REGION, ECONOMIC PROFILE

	Region	Connecticut	Massa-chusetts	New Hampshire	Rhode Island	Vermont	Maine
Population, 1965	11,132,000	2,833,000	5,349,000	669,000	891,000	397,000	993,000
Population per square mile, 1965	176.7	581.7	682.8	72.9	846.9	42.8	32.4
Population, percent change, 1950–60	12.8	26.3	9.8	13.8	8.5	3.2	6.1
Population, net gain or loss through civilian migration, 1950–60	31,212	239,895	−87,730	12,400	−25,742	−35,783	−71,828
Population, percent urban residence, 1960	76.4	78.3	83.6	58.3	86.4	38.5	51.3
Labor force, percent change, 1950–60	9.9	21.0	7.7	12.9	2.2	2.1	3.2
Total employment, percent change, 1950–60	11.7	22.1	9.5	15.7	4.2	3.1	5.8
Unemployment rate, February, 1966	3.6	3.1	4.3	2.3	4.1	4.5	4.2
Employment in manufacturing, percent of total, 1960	36.7	40.3	35.5	39.7	39.3	25.0	33.2
Employment in agriculture, percent of total, 1960	2.1	1.8	1.1	3.0	1.1	11.7	5.3
Median family income, 1959	$6,154	$6,887	$6,272	$5,636	$5,581	$4,890	$4,873

TABLE 23—Continued

	Region	Connecticut	Massa-chusetts	New Hampshire	Rhode Island	Vermont	Maine
Median family income, percent change, 1949–59	90.0	94.4	87.6	96.0	79.3	90.1	87.7
Percent of families with income under $3000, 1959	13.5	9.8	12.4	15.3	16.8	23.1	22.8
Percent of housing units unsound, 1960	21.3	15.2	18.9	27.2	21.3	31.6	38.8
Persons 25 years old and over, median school years completed, 1960	11.2	11.0	11.6	10.9	10.0	10.9	11.0

Source: Economic Development Administration, *Regional Economic Development in the United States,* Part 2 (Washington, D.C.: Government Printing Office, 1967). Section VII, p. 32.

capita income of the region to that of the nation as a whole by stimulating the existing economy and making it grow at a rapid and self-sustained pace.

The Commission has set eight priority targets; involving the development of transportation, tourism and recreation, education, agriculture, mining and natural resources, industrial development, health, and sociological improvements. However, it has not set any relative priorities among this all-inclusive list of variables, so it is difficult to say that it has any real priorities. Data on the region are very difficult to obtain; it might be best if the Commission were to give top priority to the collection and analysis of data on the region before assigning really meaningful priorities to the types of projects that compete for its limited funds.

As far as manpower programs are concerned, the Commission favors labor mobility assistance to facilitate worker movement *within* the region, as well as the creation of a regional employment data center to identify job opportunities and disseminate such information. In general, it intends to evaluate vocational training and manpower projects in terms of their contribution toward closing the income gap between the region and the nation. The Commission's planning efforts have not yet advanced to a point where consideration has been given to the role that migration might play in increasing the region's per capita income.

Summary and Conclusions

As is the case with the Appalachian Regional Commission and the Economic Development Administration, the legislation creating the new Regional Commissions is oriented toward place, rather than people. Moreover, whereas EDA at least maintains a genuine degree of concern for the lagging regions of the country wherever they may be, the Regional Commissions are more parochial in outlook. Although the new Commissions were created by the same legislation that created EDA, and although they and EDA have been linked by the latter's Office of Regional Economic Planning, the author encountered numerous instances where the Regional Commissions apparently wished to sever all connections with EDA and function as wholly independent entities. One reason for this preference seemed to be a natural desire to give one's own agency maximum visibility with respect to whatever accomplishments might be achieved. In addition, the Commissions seemed content with their mandate, whereas EDA officials tend to be more open in exploring the possibility that the legislation governing their activities might be too limiting or even erroneous. (These issues will be considered in the following chapter.)

A few of the Regional Commissions have given high priority to human resource development, but it is usually implicitly assumed that the people involved will, or should, remain within the regions they presently inhabit. Little or no effort is made to link human resource development and manpower programs to job opportunities in growth centers outside the respective regions, even if outmigration is not explicitly discouraged. Unless the Commissions can attract significant economic activity to their regions, rational resource allocation within the nation would be enhanced if greater attention were given by the Commissions to job opportunities outside of their regions. This same issue would seem to be a critical one with regard to all of the Commissions except that for New England, where intraregional opportunities are abundant. Given their limited budgets it is doubtful that the Commissions will have any great direct impact in any case. Nevertheless, the principles of rational resource allocation that are involved are important whether or not the levels of funding for the Commissions eventually permit them to have a greater impact on economic activity. Meanwhile, they can perform a valuable function by increasing efficiency through encouragement of multistate cooperation on problems and opportunities of mutual interest.

Chapter 6

The Economic Development Administration

Introduction

One of the more important aspects of the War on Poverty is the unprecedented effort that has been undertaken to help areas whose growth has lagged significantly behind that of the nation as a whole. The problems of many of these lagging areas have lasted too long to be considered temporary. They are chronic problems often caused by factors—technological change, resource depletion, changing demand, etc.—that are beyond the control of the local people. In response to this situation, Congress passed four major items of legislation between 1961 and 1965. The first, The Area Redevelopment Act, was a four-year program to alleviate conditions of substantial and persistent unemployment in areas characterized by chronic high-level unemployment and low levels of median family income. Among the tools employed in the ARA program were commercial and industrial loans, public facility loans and grants for infrastructure development, technical assistance to aid in local planning efforts, and training to upgrade labor force skills. By 1964, it was apparent that this essentially experimental program of federal assistance to depressed areas was producing only modest results. The program had a number of major deficiencies. First, its county-by-county approach resulted in excessive fragmentation. By focusing on a narrowing economic base, insufficient attention was given to the concentrated development of centers with significant growth potential. Second, the business loan component of the program provided inadequate incentives for the establishment of new job-creating industries. Third, funds were too limited to enable depressed communities to improve their infrastructures to a point where they would represent external economies sufficient to stimulate private investment. Finally, too much attention was given to specific projects to the neglect of long run development planning.[1]

The Public Works Acceleration Act, passed in 1962, was a two-year program to supplement the public works component of ARA activities. The intent of this act was to provide immediate temporary employment in eligible areas, while improving community facilities to encourage industrial development. The third major piece of regional legislation was the Appalachian Regional Development Act of 1965, which was discussed in Chapter Four. The fourth and most farreaching piece of regional development legislation was the Public Works and Economic Development Act of 1965.

The Mission of EDA

In the Public Works and Economic Development Act of 1965 Congress declared that the federal government, in cooperation with the states, should help areas characterized by substantial and persistent unemployment and underemployment and relatively low income levels to take effective steps in planning and financing their public works projects and economic development programs. The task of administering the Act was assigned to the Economic Development Administration, an agency within the Department of Commerce.

EDA, in keeping with the mandate of the Act, has attempted to be something more than the administrator of an attractive grant and loan program on a project by project basis; it has recognized the need for, though it has not generally acted on, an organized and logical strategy as a fundamental precondition to any successful attack on the problems of lagging areas. Within this perspective, EDA has developed five target goals for measuring the success of its program.

These goals include: (1) reducing the incidence of substantial and persistent unemployment and underemployment characteristics of certain designated and qualified regions, counties, and communities to a level commensurate with the levels prevailing in the national economy; (2) improving economic development planning, coordinating, and implementing capabilities at the federal, state, regional, and local levels; (3) providing a basis for improved coordination and continuity for federal, state, and local activities relating to regional economic development, and for more efficient utilization of all resources available for regional and local economic development; (4) providing a basis for rapid, effective, and efficient expansion of government investment at all levels to promote economic development if and when such expansion is determined to be desirable and necessary; and (5) developing alternatives to present patterns of migration of the unemployed and underemployed by expanding economic opportunities in more suitable locations.[2]

EDA has laid great stress upon local planning and initiative as evidenced by an overall economic development planning requirement, and the active partnership of government at all levels with private enterprise. Communities and areas are required to take the first steps in developing their own programs for economic recovery, for if they resist change the success of the development process is defeated at the outset. Public investment is viewed as an inducement to private investment, and the success of the development process is ultimately linked to increasing the amount of private investment activity in distressed areas. Furthermore, EDA regards overall planning as an essential element in the development process. Such planning requires analysis of the relevant areas' strengths, weaknesses, and opportunities. Selected goals should be feasible and realistic in terms of the resource capabilities of an area if given federal or state assistance. Comprehensive planning should reflect the views of all groups representative of the major interests of an area, and it should take into account such noneconomic factors as the quality of education and social patterns bearing on employment. Finally, although EDA is the federal agency primarily charged with the task of stimulating area and regional economic development, it recognizes that a great many other agencies and organizations also contribute to this process. Thus, it attempts to act as a catalyst, coordinating its efforts with those of other agencies.[3]

EDA Programs

To implement its goals, EDA has at its disposal a wide range of program tools, including grants and loans for public works and development facilities, industrial and commercial loans, and an extensive program of technical, planning, and research assistance to find solutions to economic development problems.

EDA is authorized to make grants up to 50 percent of the cost of qualified projects in designated areas for public works, public services, or development facilities, including related machinery and equipment. Qualified projects must meet a pressing need of the area and must tend to improve the opportunities for the successful establishment or expansion of industrial or commercial plants or facilities, or otherwise assist in the creation of new long run employment opportunities, or primarily benefit the long term unemployed and members of low income families. In addition, proposed projects must conform to the area's Overall Economic Development Plan (OEDP).

Frequently, communities that most need assistance experience difficulties in raising the funds required to take advantage of various grant-in-aid programs. EDA is authorized to make supplementary grants that may be used to reduce the local share required in financing federal aid programs. The amount of the supplementary grant depends both on the degree of economic distress of the area and on the nature of the proposed project, but in no case may the combined direct and supplementary grant exceed 80 percent of the project cost for any federal program. Most projects which qualified for federal aid but which would normally receive a federal contribution of less than 50 percent of the total project costs are eligible for EDA supplementary grants that will bring the total federal contribution up to that level. In cases where supplementary grants would increase the federal contribution to over 50 percent of the project cost, EDA has classified all eligible areas by the degree of their economic need. There are three groups of areas, which may be eligible for maximum grants of up to 60, 70, or 80 percent, respectively, of the project cost. Economic "need" is determined on the basis of median family income and the unemployment rate.[4]

EDA is authorized to make loans up to 100 percent of the costs of public works and development projects in redevelopment areas (defined in the following section). This loan assistance is used primarily to help communities that lack good, established credit ratings in the private capital market and is provided only when funds from alternative private or public sources are not available on terms that would permit the accomplishment of the project. These loans have a maximum term of forty years at an interest rate calculated in relation to current yields on comparable debt obligations.[5]

In addition to loans for public facilities, EDA also is authorized to encourage business and industry to build or expand their operations in redevelopment areas by providing such special incentives as low cost, long-term loans and working-capital loan guarantees. Loans may be made up to 65 percent of the total cost of the land, buildings, machinery, and equipment needed to establish or expand industrial and commercial facilities in redevelopment areas. These loans, which may run as long as twenty-five years, are made only when the project cannot be financed through other means on terms that would permit its accomplishment. In most cases, at least 20 percent of the project costs must be obtained from private lenders and a minimum of 15 percent must come from other private or public sources such as bank investment, company equity, or local development companies. Normally, 5 percent of the project cost must be provided either by the state or by a public or quasi-public community or area organization, though this requirement may be waived if funds are not available because of the economic distress of the area.[6]

EDA is not permitted to make loans for working capital, but it may guarantee such loans made by private lenders in connection with projects financed in part under the direct loan program. These guarantees are made only when it can be demonstrated that the borrower will be able to repay from project earnings the working capital loan as well as other related debt obligations.

A major part of the technical and planning assistance program consists of feasibility studies of specific economic and business problems affecting needy areas. In addition, technical assistance may include the identifying, planning, and programming of economic development projects; management and operational assistance; preliminary design planning and feasibility studies of development facilities; and demonstration programs of special methods to promote economic development. Priority consideration is given to projects that will have a specific effect upon employment or income in a relatively short time. In addition to technical assistance, grants-in-aid may be made to defray expenses connected with planning development programs.[7]

Finally, EDA conducts an extensive program of research on the causes and effects of chronic unemployment and underemployment. This program makes available the results of studies and technical assistance projects that may be of use in providing guidance for economic development efforts.

Total authorizations over the life of the Public Works and Economic Development Act of 1965 amounted to $3.25 billion. As of June 30, 1968, EDA had approved 1,242 public works projects amounting to $606.2 million. There were 211 approved business development projects, involving $138.9 million in loans and $14.3 million in working capital. A total of $29.3 million was provided for technical assistance and $9.7 million for planning grants. All programs together had received $818.7 million. California received the most money, $76.7 million, followed by Kentucky ($60.4 million) and West Virginia ($38.6 million). The pronounced tendency for EDA programs to favor small communities is illustrated by the fact that the number of public works projects (which accounted for three-fourths of all EDA outlays) going to communities with fewer than 10,000 persons was 963, or over three-fourths of the total, while the corresponding expenditures amounted to $364.2 million, or 60 percent of the public works total.[8]

Areas Eligible for EDA Assistance

The Public Works and Economic Development Act of 1965 defines four kinds of geographic entities that may be eligible for EDA assistance. These are redevelopment areas, Title I areas, economic development districts, and economic development regions.

A redevelopment area may be a county, a labor area, an Indian reservation, or a municipality having 250,000 residents or more. With the exception of Indian reservations, redevelopment areas must have a population of at least 1,500. Redevelopment areas are eligible for the full range of benefits described in the last section.

Redevelopment areas are designated on the basis of criteria that reflect chronic economic distress. These criteria include substantial and persistent unemployment, population loss, and low median family income. "Substantial and persistent unemployment" is defined by two criteria. First, 6 percent or more of the work force must have been unemployed during the latest calendar year. Second, the annual average rate of unemployment must have been at least 6 percent and (1) 50 percent above the national average during three of the last four years; or (2) 75 percent above the national average during two of the last three years; or (3) 100 percent above the national average during one of the last two years.

Areas that lost 25 percent or more of their population between 1950 and 1960 due to a lack of employment opportunities are eligible for designation as redevelopment areas, provided they did not have an annual median family income over $2,830 in 1960. An area where this figure was less than $2,264 in 1960 may be designated as a redevelopment area without regard to rate of outmigration.

When loss of a major source of employment causes the unemployment rate of an area to exceed the national average by 50 percent or more, or when such a loss is expected, redevelopment area designation is authorized. In addition, Indian reservations with a high degree of economic distress are eligible for designation as redevelopment areas. Finally, when a state does not have any area that qualifies on the basis of high unemployment, low family income, or population loss, the area in the state that most nearly meets these criteria may be designated as a redevelopment area.

Title I areas, which take their name from the title of the act that authorized their designation, are areas of "substantial" unemployment as defined by the Department of Labor. This designation includes labor areas with an annual average rate of unemployment of 6 percent or more during the preceeding calendar year. Title I areas are eligible only for public works and development facility grants assistance, and thus should be carefully distinguished from redevelopment areas.

The third kind of geographic entity eligible for EDA assistance is the multicounty economic development district. Individual redevelopment areas often lack sufficient resources to provide a solid base for their development. However, because of economic interdependencies among adjacent areas, successful development on a larger scale may be promoted by grouping together economically distressed areas and economically healthy areas. EDA has therefore encouraged groups of counties—usually five to fifteen in number—to pool their resources for effective economic planning and development. The district program offers incentives to promote the economic growth of the entire district, but it is aimed particularly at redevelopment areas. Thus, a district must contain at least two redevelopment areas. In addition to the benefits authorized for all redevelopment areas, those located within districts may receive up to 10 percent more of the total cost in grant assistance for projects that are consistent with the district program. With the exception of an EDA-designated economic development center, counties in the district that are not redevelopment areas are not eligible for project funding from EDA. However, all participating counties are expected to benefit from coordinated, district-wide development planning.

Each economic development district must contain an economic development center. The center must be an area or city with sufficient population, resources, public facilities, industry, and commercial services to insure that its development can become relatively self-sustaining.

The growth of the development center is then expected to carry over into the redevelopment areas within the district. Cities or contiguous groupings of incorporated places located outside the redevelopment area may be designated as economic development centers if they have a population of 250,000 persons or less. Once designated, development centers are eligible for EDA assistance on the same basis as redevelopment areas. It should be noted that EDA distinguishes between economic development centers and redevelopment centers; the latter lie within redevelopment areas while the former do not.

Counties that wish to form a district must submit a formal proposal for qualification to EDA through the governor of the state involved. In considering whether and to what extent a proposed district will effectively foster economic development, EDA considers a number of factors, including the percentage of district population living in redevelopment areas, district per capita income, the percentage of families with annual income of less than $3,000, trading area patterns, the character of the proposed development center and its ties to the redevelopment areas, and unemployment and labor force participation rates. Once a district becomes qualified, its major organizational task is to formulate a district Overall Economic Development Program, or OEDP, which must be approved by EDA before the district can be formally designated. EDA requires that the district organization be broadly representative of the major economic groups of the area, including business, labor, agriculture, minority groups, and representatives of the unemployed and underemployed.

When the district OEDP is completed, it is submitted to EDA's

Office of Development Districts in Washington for approval. Copies also are submitted to state agencies designated to handle EDA matters and to the appropriate regional EDA office. At this time the district organization requests a change in its status from "qualified" to "designated." When the district OEDP is approved, the district is designated and becomes fully operational. The district is required to maintain a currently approved district OEDP. A district's designated status will be terminated if EDA determines that it no longer meets the standards for designation, or if the district requests termination with the approval of the state affected.

The final kind of geographic entity eligible for EDA assistance is the economic development region. Economic development regions are multistate areas where long range planning can be carried out by joint federal-state commissions to solve economic problems too large or too difficult to be dealt with in narrower terms. An economic development region is eligible for supplementary grants, administrative expense grants, and technical assistance. The structure and objectives of the regional commissions were discussed in the previous chapter.

The "Worst First" Policy

Since the total need of areas designated for EDA assistance far exceeds the agency's available resources, it has developed as a part of its strategy an order of priorities known as the "worst first" policy. A number of EDA officials have told the author that the "worst first" policy has never really been implemented, while others maintain that it was never really taken seriously in the first place. Nevertheless, it is clear from a great deal of EDA's own literature that the agency has at least attempted to allocate funds on the basis of such a policy. And those who deny that a "worst first" policy was ever implemented generally are hard pressed to define the alternative strategy that might have been used in its place. In brief, it seems fair to say that insofar as EDA has had an overall strategy, that strategy has been based primarily on the "worst first" concept.

The "worst first" strategy seeks to reduce each area's problem in the order of its severity. Those areas with the worst problems in each of the categories of eligibility receive first priority in financial aid. To determine the order of priority within the categories, EDA first establishes to what extent each area lags behind the qualifying threshold. Then it devises a standard measurement called the "job gap" in each eligible area. The job gap is the number of jobs that must be created to lower the rate of unemployment or to raise median family income to a level that will remove an area from eligibility for EDA assistance. In areas where unemployment is the principal problem, the job gap represents the number of permanent new jobs that are necessary to lower the unemployment rate to less than 6 percent. In areas where low family income is the situation, the job gap is the number of jobs required to raise family incomes above a median level of $2,264. These job gaps are then used to set target budgets to indicate how much expenditure EDA can consider for an area during the planning period.[9] The "worst first" policy was devised by EDA on the basis of its experience that areas just meeting, or a little over, the qualifying level for assistance also are the most likely areas to benefit from vigorous national economic growth. In a number of such areas it was found that their economies improved to a point where they no longer qualified for EDA assistance, and they improved without the benefit of any operating EDA projects. The first evidence of this pattern appeared in the agency's first annual review of area eligibility in the spring of 1966. In its first ten months of operations, EDA had approved 650 separate projects, and 324 eligible areas received one or more projects. However, nearly a third of these 324 areas were terminated at the end of the first annual review because their unemployment rates had fallen below the 6 percent requirement for participation. This meant that they were terminated before any EDA projects had advanced sufficiently to be the cause of the economic improvement. Their economies had benefited from vigorous and sustained national growth. It was also found that areas in the 6 to 8 percent unemployment range had a much greater probability of being terminated than those areas with higher unemployment rates. The second annual review, made at the time when the "worst first" policy was being implemented, brought out a similar pattern. Of the 176 areas terminated in this review, 165 were in the 6 to 8 percent group. In the light of these findings, EDA decided that it could best use its resources to aid those areas that failed to benefit from growing national prosperity or did not receive the full impact of the expansion. These were the areas with the highest unemployment rates or the greatest proportion of low income families.[10]

In putting the "worst first" policy to work, fund allocations are made by EDA's seven area offices. EDA has divided its funds among the seven sets of problems that qualify an area for assistance —that is, so much for high unemployment, so much for low income, the Indian reservations, and other categories that were discussed above. Once these objectives have been set for each different problem, funds have been allocated to each EDA area office, generally in proportion to the part of the particular problem located within its jurisdiction. The area offices in turn have applied the strategy on the basis of problems within their areas. The amount of financial assistance actually extended in any part of the country has depended in principle on the merits of individual project proposals.[11]

The "worst first" policy is the guiding principle for EDA in the use of its resources. It has moved the agency away from the selection of projects simply on the basis of their individual quality and general contribution to economic growth. Instead, EDA is now oriented toward meeting particular geographic objectives.

That is, the goal is to improve the economies of specific places through a systematic application of specific solutions to specific problems, with stress on local planning, initiative, and support.[12]

These two brief paragraphs give considerable insight into some of the more questionable aspects of EDA policy. First, it is frankly admitted that a high quality program which promises to contribute a great deal to national economic growth might well have been rejected for EDA assistance. This is because EDA programs are not oriented toward people, but, as the statement clearly asserts, toward "particular geographic objectives," and "specific places." In other words, opportunity cost considerations from a national point of view are rejected in favor of efforts to shore up those pieces of the nation's geography that are the worst off. In addition, the "worst first" policy seems in conflict with the growth center feature of EDA's multicounty economic development district program.

EDA's Growth Centers

It has already been pointed out that each of EDA's economic development districts must include a development center of sufficient size and potential to promote the economic growth necessary to alleviate the distress of redevelopment areas within the district. EDA recognizes that economic growth tends to be concentrated in a relatively few areas. Because of this clustering there should be coordination of all government investment going into areas of potential growth. Indeed, the district growth centers are viewed as the key to solving the problem of rural-urban balance in the United States.

It has become increasingly apparent that problems of urban poverty and those of rural poverty are interrelated by the pattern of migration from rural areas to the large metropolitan areas. One approach to this phenomenon is to continue to concentrate on central city solutions. Measures such as public housing, more welfare, more training programs for the often illiterate and unskilled people streaming into the cities, and inducements to attract industry to the city core fall into this category. However, these programs are not likely to stem the tide of migration to the big cities nor will they in themselves eliminate the ghetto.

A second approach would be to create job opportunities for people in rural areas while continuing curative programs in the cities. But revolutionary developments in agricultural technology and growing urbanization have meant that the underemployed and unemployed in rural areas are increasingly unable to participate fully in the expanding market economy. Overemphasis on rural agricultural programs would probably only aggravate this problem.

The third alternative, that advocated by EDA, concentrates not on reversing the migration stream but rather on redirecting and channeling it. This policy accepts the fact that urbanization is a basic trend but strives to create a better urban-rural balance through the creation of urban alternatives. This does not necessarily imply the creation of new towns, since they are both expensive to create and of unproven value. Instead, EDA's alternative is represented by the economic growth center approach which attempts to link underdeveloped counties with healthy counties containing a regional growth center. By providing the economic districts with an urban alternative through the growth center, it is hoped that the growth center will help the economy of the depressed area. The growth center is expected to provide an economically efficient marketing and servicing center for surrounding counties by providing job opportunities for depressed area residents who could commute to jobs and by encouraging those rural area residents who do migrate to move to the growth center. It is hoped that the growth centers will provide definite and worthwhile migration alternatives within the urbanization trend and that they will contribute to a greatly improved rural-urban balance. Thus, EDA's program would relieve the pressure on the big cities while at the same time lift the rural areas by the bootstraps. This growth center approach implies that job opportunities can be induced easily because growth factors are already present even though the community may be located in a low-income area. It is hoped that migration flows can be channeled to the growth centers through a combination of forces including jobs, schools, transportation systems, social amenities, and improved equal opportunity programs. EDA's program can also be linked with parallel programs for resettlement assistance and manpower training and development to assist the rural migrant to adjust to the urban employment environment.[13]

How do the realities of EDA's development center policy compare with the strategy just outlined? First, while a development center strategy implies concentrating projects in a relatively few locations, EDA simply does not have the funds to create the many external economies that will be needed if rapid, self-sustained growth is to be induced or reinforced in development centers. As Duskin and Moomaw have pointed out, budget estimates for fiscal year 1968 allot $27 million to development center projects. "If we assume one development center per district, pro-rated, this would amount to an expenditure of approximately $225,000 to $270,000 per growth center. Hardly enough for a sewer line!"[14] Second, even if EDA had considerably more funds to devote to growth centers, the nature of the centers that are actually being chosen leaves great doubt as to their ability to provide a significant number of increased job opportunities for migrants from rural areas. The results of a study conducted by Brian Berry are instructive on this point.

Berry's analysis of the commuting behavior of the population of the United States in 1960 shows that all but 5 percent of the country's population resides within the daily commuting fields of metropolitan centers.[15] These fields spread over the entire land area of the United States except where population density is less than two persons per square mile or where there are national parks and forests, and Indian reservations. Berry finds that the degree of metropolitan labor market participation is the key variable in what he terms the "regional welfare syndrome," a pattern of urban influence on the surrounding hinterland's level of economic well-being as measured by such factors as income and unemployment. In general, degree of labor market participation declines with increasing distance from the city, as do the average value of farm land and buildings, median family income, median school years completed, rate of population increase, and population gain through migration. Proportion of families with annual incomes less than $3,000 and the unemployment rate are both directly related to distance from the city. The lowest levels of welfare are thus at the edges of metropolitan labor markets and especially in the nonurban interstices between them. When employment centers are closely spaced and their labor markets overlap, so that residents of one center can take advantage of employment opportunities in another, the decline in welfare levels that accompanies distance from centers is reduced or eliminated. Conversely, the wider the spacing of employment centers the lower the level to which the measures of regional welfare fall. Berry attributes these results to the lack of opportunities for economies of production in rural areas. His findings also support efforts to stimulate development in growth centers that can give inmigrants higher incomes and better job opportunities. He also concurs with the maximum size limit of 250,000 set by the Public Works and Economic Development Act of 1965 for development centers. "Above that size, the necessary conditions for self-sustaining growth seem satisfied. Perhaps the greatest payoff in terms of both employment and unemployment is in concentrating on cities close to 250,000 population rather than on those very much smaller. Generally labor markets appear to need a population of more than 250,000 to be viable parts of the urban system."[16] On the other hand, he finds that "The regional influence of smaller centers is too limited to justify putting public resources into them. Few cities of less than 50,000 population appear to influence the welfare of surrounding regions; those that do are located in the more peripheral areas."[17] In conclusion, he advocates policies designed to encourage migration from rural areas to viable growth centers, but not "to the cores of the largest cities, where isolation in ghettos produces a parallel and perhaps more debilitating isolation than in rural areas."[18]

The growth centers that have been designated by EDA are generally much smaller than the 50,000 population level that Berry finds to be a minimum for a city to have a positive influence on its surrounding hinterland. As of September, 1968, there were 52 designated Economic Development Districts and 80 Development Centers (64 Economic Development Centers and 14 Redevelopment Centers). The average population of Centers was only 38,192; the median was 24,145. Only four centers—Lafayette-New Iberia, La., Rome-Utica, N.Y., Knoxville, Tennessee, and Corpus Christi, Texas—had over 100,000 inhabitants. Only 13 Centers had more than 50,000 inhabitants.[19]

A Summary Critique

The present decade has been marked by an unprecedented effort on the part of the federal government to promote the development of economically lagging regions. Early experience under the Area Redevelopment Act indicated a number of major deficiencies in this experimental program. The ARA approach was highly fragmented in terms of both geographic and program considerations; its geographic reach was limited because of its tendency to deal with counties on an individual basis, and comprehensive long term planning was frequently precluded because of the tendency to emphasize the immediate effects of specific projects. The Public Works and Economic Development Act of 1965 attempted to overcome both of these difficulties. First, it called for the creation of multicounty economic development districts that would promote economic development on a larger scale by grouping together economically distressed areas and economically healthy areas. The counties, usually from five to fifteen in number, are to work cooperatively on problems and opportunities of mutual interest. In addition, to stimulate local initiative and to foster overall planning, each district is required to formulate an Overall Economic Development Program (OEDP), describing common economic problems and needs of the district and proposing solutions. The OEDP is supposed to give the area an opportunity to take a comprehensive look at itself, to see what is being done to stimulate economic growth, and to ascertain what still remains to be accomplished.

Unfortunately, the preparation of OEDP's by the districts has had little relevance to project proposals. Those who prepare the OEDP's tend to view them as onerous and time-consuming exercises which, once having passed review in Washington, can be permanently relegated to some remote bookshelf. The "economic analysis model" of the OEDP is in reality a lengthy series of tables that constitute an economic profile of the district. Since most of the data which go into these tables is available on computer tapes in Washington, it would be preferable for EDA to send the completed descriptive tables to the district staffs, and then require the staffs to prepare a written analysis of the implications of the descriptive data. For the most part, the persons who prepare the OEDP's have little training in economic analysis; nevertheless, they would probably acquire more insight into the problems and opportunities of their districts if they could give more time to exploring the meaning of the large amount of descriptive data with which they work, rather than merely filling out reams of tables.

In addition to furnishing the districts with data concerning their own areas, Washington should also furnish similar data concerning the border regions within which the districts lie. At present, the districts tend to be treated as if they were isolated from the rest of the world. At a minimum, they should be given data, comparable to that for their own districts, for two or three nearby SMSA's and for the Office of Business Economics region (defined on the basis of commuting patterns to metropolitan centers) of which they are a part.

Finally, the quality of the effort made in preparing OEDP's would be greatly enhanced if Washington would provide some real incentives in this regard. The fact that OEDP's are usually not related to project requests implies that Washington as well as the districts ignore their significance. Districts whose OEDP's represent well thought out analysis should be rewarded, and districts that do little more than feed back numbers and tables should feel the pinch in terms of projects. Of course, EDA freely admits that better off areas tend to submit better OEDP's and more attractive projects. Thus, EDA's "worst first" policy—a strategy of assigning top priority to the most stagnant areas—works against meaningful and effective planning. The worst off areas know that they will receive top priority no matter how minimal their planning efforts have been. EDA can and has financed the preparation of OEDP's by persons or groups outside the relevant districts' staffs. However, this often means that the OEDP is even less relevant than it would otherwise be because the staff officials directly responsible for implementing the OEDP have not been obliged to confront directly the problems of their areas.

The worst first policy also runs counter to the philosophy that calls for economic development centers within Economic Development Districts. The economic development centers are communities or localized areas with fewer than 250,000 persons where resources can be concentrated most rapidly and effectively to create more jobs and higher incomes for the population of the surrounding area. Since EDA admits that areas of top priority under the worst first policy are areas where growth responses are the least in evidence, it is inconsistent to favor them and to maintain that growth centers should be a proper focus for development policy. EDA maintains that the goal of the worst first policy "is to help place needy communities on a self-sustaining economic basis so that, when EDA activities are terminated in these areas, the communities will continue to grow on their own."[20] Nevertheless, it is conceded that not every rural area can make the transition from an agriculturally based economy to an industrial economy based on regional growth centers. Areas not suited to this type of growth pattern "can still achieve a high and rising level of per capita income in line with national economic growth, if they are willing to concede the need for outmigration of people."[21] EDA does not favor the movement of migrants from rural and small urban communities to the cores of large cities where, because of lack of job skills and education, they too often only add to unemployment, welfare rolls, and other problems. Indeed, EDA argues that it is necessary to stem and reverse the tide of migration that takes people to places where there are no jobs. The agency views the problem as one of seeking ways to encourage would-be migrants to the cities to seek opportunities in smaller communities, that is, in growth centers.[22]

Here there are two problems from a national perspective. First, because the United States still lacks a coherent and comprehensive regional planning framework, the approach taken by EDA leaves out of consideration areas that are neither congested urban agglomerations nor towns and small cities that are part of or in close proximity to lagging areas. This no man's land—in terms of policy considerations—has growth centers which probably can absorb more migrants more efficiently than the EDA growth centers, especially if they too were to benefit from federal aid aimed at helping migrants from lagging areas to find employment. Of course, it might be argued that rapidly growing centers obviously have no need for federal subsidies. This would be true if one were only concerned with the rapidly growing center and its own population. However, the relationship of concern here is that of centers of rapid growth to the people of lagging areas. If a federal subsidy can accelerate growth in a center which is already rapidly growing, and if this subsidy is made conditional on providing employment opportunities for residents of lagging areas, then it might well be more efficient for EDA to tie into the growing environment than to attempt to create growth in a relatively stagnant area by putting in water or sewer lines.

Second, it is not clear that the public works projects in which EDA is primarily involved, chiefly infrastructure in the narrow sense, will really lead to a rational migration policy. If the unemployment and welfare difficulties of rural migrants in large metropolitan areas are largely a function of lack of job skills and education, as EDA correctly maintains, why should the migration of these people to smaller growth centers not pose similar problems?

Here we come to the very heart of the problem of helping residents of our poorest areas. EDA, like the ARA and the Appalachian Regional Commission, was created on the assumption that what these people primarily need is improved public works facilities. Yet, as has been argued in previous chapters of this book, the greatest relative need of residents of depressed areas is for more investment in human resources and for expanded manpower programs. This point has been stressed in a great deal of recent research. Edward Denison, for example, has shown that increased education is "one of the largest sources of past and prospective economic growth," in addition to being "among the elements most subject to conscious social decision;"[23] and Theodore Schultz has pointed out that "investment in human capital accounts for most of the impressive rise in real earnings per worker" in Western countries.[24]

The dilemma proposed by EDA's espousal of both the growth center and "worst first" policies could be partially resolved if these respective types of areas were given priorities corresponding to their most pressing needs. Without greater investment in human resources and manpower programs in lagging regions there is little hope that industry will be attracted to such areas or that their residents can find jobs in other areas. The United States definitely needs a more integrated regional policy at the national level, as EDA implicitly recognizes by tying together the problem of outmigration from lagging rural areas and problems of large urban centers. Of course, it must be recognized that Congressmen who represent lagging regions will be reluctant to suggest, much less encourage, outmigration of their constituents. This has been made abundantly clear in congressional hearings concerning regional legislation. However, insofar as regional policy aims at increasing individual welfare rather than at maintaining a given level of population in a given area, outmigration should be viewed as a social gain rather than a cause for alarm.

Another problem that deserves more careful attention is that of criteria for EDA aid to redevelopment areas. It is often assumed that the unemployment of an area can be reduced by measures designed to increase employment. However, George Iden has shown that "except for extreme cases, the unemployment level is not closely related to the growth characteristics of the area."[25] He found that there were areas of persistent high unemployment that also had rates of population growth, employment growth, net inmigration, and male labor force participation similar to the corresponding averages among all areas. Gene Laber likewise has found that 36 percent of the nation's counties with an employment growth rate at or above the national average had an increase of one or more percentage points in their county unemployment rates.[26] Thus, it is evident that growth factors must be considered along with unemployment rates before it is determined that an area is "lagging" and therefore in need of aid.

It would be desirable and feasible to establish an independent agency at the national level to coordinate and watch over comprehensive regional policy formation and implementation. The public works projects that are the domain of EDA can play a vital part in the development of growth centers, though the centers that now qualify for EDA aid are unduly restricted. Responsibility for "worst first" areas, on the other hand, might better be placed with an agency or agencies more concerned with human resources and manpower problems. In any case, it is important that the coordinating agency be truly independent of any department. To place the coordinating function in any given department would create the obvious danger that it would give major attention to its own objectives and programs and then try to force—whether consciously or unconsciously—the accommodation of other agencies' programs to its own.

Chapter 7

The Indians

Conditions of Life

If the Economic Development Administration had ever consistently followed a "worst first" policy, it is virtually certain that the agency's budget would have been exhausted solely by projects for the Indians. Although there is no "typical" Indian or reservation, most reservations are located in sparsely settled areas that are poor in natural resources and job opportunities.

There is no general legislative or judicial definition that can be used to identify a person as an Indian. The Census has identified an Indian on a self-declaration basis, though in some instances they have been counted as Indians by enumerators if they appeared to be full-blooded American Indians or if they were regarded as Indians by the communities where they lived. To be designated as an Indian eligible for basic Bureau of Indian Affairs services an individual must live on or near a reservation or on or near trust or restricted land under the Bureau's jurisdiction, and be a member of a tribe, band, or group of Indians recognized by the federal government. For some purposes he must also be at least one-fourth of Indian descent.[1]

The 1960 Census reported 552,000 Indians, including 28,000 Aleuts and Eskimos. Of this total, slightly more than 300,000 lived on trust lands for which the Secretary of the Interior is the trustee.[2] A more recent estimate places the nation's Indian population at about 600,000 with approximately two-thirds living within the jurisdiction of the federal government and the rest living away from the reservations in varying states of assimilation.[3] In 1967 there were 290 Indian reservations under federal jurisdiction. This figure includes Indian areas such as the pueblos of New Mexico and the rancherias of California, which are not usually referred to as reservations even though they are for all practical purposes. Reservations range in size from a few acres to the 14 million acre Navajo Reservation in Arizona, New Mexico, and Utah. There are ten other reservations with more than a million acres; four are in Arizona, two each in Washington and South Dakota, and one each in Wyoming and Montana.[4]

The gross value of agricultural production—including crop and livestock production, as well as direct use of fish and wildlife by Indians—on reservations in 1966 was about $170 million. Indian operators received $58.6 million of this total, while another $16 million was received by Indians from rents and permits. Income from mineral rentals, bonuses, royalties, and other sources amounted to $31 million during fiscal year 1967. The principal minerals produced on Indian lands are oil, gas, uranium, sand, gravel, phosphate, limestone, coal, copper, lead, zinc, and gypsum. Approximately 800 million board feet of timber were cut from Indian land during fiscal year 1967, and timber sales yielded $15 million to Indians. In the same period, Indians received $4 million from private developers who leased Indian land for commercial, industrial, and recreational uses. Behind these aggregate figures is the fact that, while a few reservations have sufficient resources to support their Indian residents, most cannot provide them with an adequate standard of living.[5]

Even if the reservations were not for the most part lacking in natural resources, the economic advance of the Indian would be inhibited by traditional social and cultural values. For example, Indian values tend to downgrade the individual personality in favor of the group or community. In many tribes status and personal security are directly related to one's service in perpetuating ancestral usages and customs. In consequence, there is relatively little competitiveness or a pride in material possessions for their monetary worth. Indian values have not customarily included the amassing of valuables for private benefit because of the ingrained tradition of sharing. These attitudes perhaps account in part for the improvidence often attributed to Indians."[6] In addition, spiritual attachment to nature has made many Indians consider land to be something that its users have an innate right to enjoy, rather than as alienable property. "The Indian, for the most part, has a psychological and cultural relationship with the land which surpasses that usually understood by the non-Indian."[7]

Employers have noted that Indian work habits often reflect a lack of concern for time. This shows up particularly in a casual attitude toward reporting for work on time—or at all—if some "more important" alternative arises. A related problem is the inability of many Indians to reason in terms of cause and effect relationships.

Even in agriculture . . . modern methods are directly contrary to general Indian customs and beliefs. Modern agricultural development rests on research, improving seeds, use of fertilizer, on new ways of performing old tasks, and on an increased control of environment. But to the Indian cultures, which typically stress ancestral customs based upon a need to work in harmony with nature, such modern practices are often alien. The historic experience of the Indian has, in general, moved outside of traditions of science and technology; yet the individual must acquire an ability . . . to co-operate with a highly technical and competitive society.[8]

Despite the disadvantages they have faced, a few Indian families have gained relatively high incomes, educated their children, and found employment in good jobs in towns near the reservations. Others have made a good living in agriculture or ranching. But the great majority, who depend for the most part on seasonal work and welfare, are living in extreme poverty. About half of the Indian families have annual incomes of less than $2000 and about three-fourths have annual incomes of less than $3000. Approximately half of the Indians in the working-age population is chronically unemployed.[9] Some reservations have unemployment rates exceeding 70 percent of the tribal labor force. Among the Navajos, the largest of the tribes, the unemployment rate recently stood at 45 percent. Moreover, there is a great deal of underemployment on the reservations.[10] The housing conditions of the Indians are likewise worse than those of any other of the nation's minority groups. At least three-quarters of the 76,000 houses on Indian reservations and trust lands are below minimum standards of decency. Most houses are overcrowded and over half are too dilapidated to repair. Until 1961 little effort was made to alleviate the housing problems of the Indians, and even today the total of all federal programs directed toward improving Indian housing would not keep pace with continuing deterioration and dilapidation. The conditions under which they live, particularly the lack of safe, available water and adequate waste disposal facilities, are in large part responsible for the high incidence of preventable diseases found among Indian populations.[11] The most common infectious diseases among Indians are influenza, pneumonia and other respiratory infections, dysenteries, gastroenteritis, and streptococcal infections. Trachoma, which has virtually disappeared in the general population of the country, still affects many Indians. Tuberculosis is six times more prevalent among Indians than non-Indians, and ranks ninth as a cause of death among Indians. Whereas the average life expectancy at birth for the nation's population as a whole is 70.2 years, that for an Indian baby is only 63.8 years.[12]

It is universally agreed that substantial improvements are needed in Indian education. Despite significant improvements, the Indian illiteracy rate still stood at 12 percent in 1959. Indian children attend public, private, mission, and federal boarding or day schools. In 1967, 56 percent of all Indian children in school attended public schools, 34 percent attended federal schools, and 10 percent were in mission or other private schools. The Bureau of Indian Affairs encourages Indians to attend public schools, and operates federal schools primarily for those living in areas lacking adequate educational facilities or who require boarding home care in addition to educational services.[13] Although most Indian children are in school and are, or will become, literate, they compare very unfavorably to national averages in dropout rates and in achievement levels at all grades. Indian children attend schools where most of the teachers and administrators are non-Indians. The books and materials they use and the educational objectives of their classes are designed essentially to prepare them for life in the prevalent middle-class American society. The backgrounds of the Indian children, on the other hand, reflect the traditional values of their own cultures; most do not even speak English when they enter school. Instead of attempting to adapt the Indian children to changes within their own culture, the schools view their task as one of helping them to adjust to an alien culture. Toward this end, the children are helped to speak, read, and write English and are exposed to completely unfamiliar experiences. For example, most Navajo children have never seen a city, a boat, or an elevator before going to school. In addition, the children are helped to develop saleable skills and exposed to values quite different from their own; e.g., they are introduced to competitive roles that run counter to the traditional cooperative roles. As Striner points out, it is exceedingly difficult for the schools to bring the Indian children into line with those of the dominant non-Indian society. "There is evidence that the emotional pressure generated by this intercultural setting of Indian schools contributes to serious mental health problems, high dropout rates, and unsatisfactory achievement levels. Skill training and employability in adult years is seriously affected by these early educational deficiencies."[14]

The problems of educating Indian children are compounded by the lack of involvement of their parents, who generally are not encouraged to participate in the education experience of the children. They do not understand what is expected of their children in school and of themselves, other than to see that their children attend school. "Not surprisingly," Striner remarks, "most Indian parents have ambivalent attitudes toward the schools their children attend."[15]

In general, the children who attend Bureau of Indian Affairs schools are more disadvantaged at the outset than those attending public schools. Nevertheless, public schools are not more effective in educating Indian children and often they are less so. Racial prejudice in many areas where substantial numbers of Indians live is often a contributing factor in this regard. In view of these general considerations, Striner concludes that "the assumption that integrated education is invariably better than segregated education must be qualified by a careful assessment of local circumstances in Indian country before it can be accepted as valid,"[16] and that "the assumptions underlying the conventional approach to Indian education evidently have not been valid and a systematic search for more realistic approaches is clearly in order."[17]

Developing the Indians' Human Resources

Before the 1930's the Indian reservations were little more than concentration camps designed to keep the Indians away from the rest of the population. The Bureau of Indian Affairs was riddled with ineptitude and incompetence, and staffed by non-Indians with little know-how or means for dealing with Indian problems. Almost nothing was done to help the Indians achieve a standard of living more in line with that of the nation as a whole.[18] The Wheeler-Howard Act of 1934, frequently referred to as the Indian Reorganization Act, sought to improve conditions of Indian life by recognizing the importance of Indian society as a vehicle for preserving and encouraging values upon which the Indians could base their own innovations. It sought to transfer developmental initiative from the Bureau to the Indians themselves. The Act stopped the alienation and allotment of tribal land, authorized the purchase of new holdings, established a system of federal loans, confirmed Indian self-government, provided for the creation of tribal business organizations, and called for measures to conserve natural resources. Indians also became eligible for Bureau posts without regard to Civil Service Laws.[19] By 1953 a great deal of progress had been made in cases characterized by sympathetic superintendents, able tribal governments, and emphasis on local decision making. In that year, however, much of the progress that had been made was undone by House Concurrent Resolution 108, which declared it to be government policy to withdraw federal responsibility and services for Indians as soon as possible. Under this policy a major controversy developed over whether the federal government should press for prompt termination of tribes without their members' consent. During the middle 1950's mandatory termination appeared to be the government's goal; several tribes were terminated without tribal consent and thousands of Indians were relocated from reservations to urban areas where job opportunities were thought to be more plentiful.

The termination policy of the 1950's turned out to be a disaster for most of the Indians concerned and for efficient use of government funds. Many relocated Indians ended up in the slums without steady employment or else returned in bitterness to the reservations because they were totally unprepared through education or vocational training for urban job openings. As a result of the obvious failures of termination policy, Secretary of the Interior Seaton announced in September, 1958, that henceforth no tribe would be involuntarily terminated. During the present decade the termination question has been played down in favor of emphasis on the development of Indian resources. Yet programs for the employment of Indians have still not given adequate attention to education, training, and manpower programs in general. This is clearly seen in what was billed as the most important legislation concerning the Indians since the Wheeler-Howard Act, the Indian Resources Development Act that was submitted to Congress in 1967.

The main purpose of the Indian Resources Development Act was to enable the Indians to participate more fully in the life of the nation by providing them with managerial, credit, and corporate tools, and by encouraging them to exercise greater initiative and self-determination. Only one section of the Act, section 401, had anything to do with training and employment. This item provided an increase of $10 million for adult vocational training. As Striner correctly urges, this legislation "reflects a tragic misconception of the needs of the Indian population and the means which must be made available to Indians if they choose to move away from their traditional cultures and toward that of the non-Indian society."[20] Although the Act assumes a level of financial sophistication that is not found in many tribes, the "core of the problem is that this new legislation ignores completely the fact that a solution to the Indian problem calls for efforts in education, training, housing, welfare, and health at a level of funding never properly understood." The Act, he concludes, "is analogous to developing a repair manual for a 1967 Rolls Royce before we have successfully built a 1928 model A Ford."[21]

As one of the best recent studies of the Indian argues, the Bureau of Indian Affairs should take more initiative to help and encourage the Indians to develop their own potential. "Indian leaders must become versed in the scientific tradition of the age in order to possess tools for adjusting the shape and pattern of their own indigenous society and to allow them to participate in the life of the dominant society, while retaining the best of their own culture."[22] A simultaneous effort must be undertaken to improve the effectiveness of the education given to Indian children. This is an essential precondition to training for job opportunities comparable to those enjoyed by non-Indians. The basic requirements for an effective program have been set forth by Striner. First, the federally operated Indian schools should be made into models of excellence for the education of disadvantaged children. Second, per pupil costs will probably have to be doubled or tripled to achieve a really effective program, though such costs will be more than offset by consequent reductions in unemployment and increased personal income. Third, Indian parents must be involved to a much greater extent in the education of their children. Wherever tribes desire and have the evident capability to operate schools directly under contract they should be permitted to do so. A successful model for this approach already exists at Rough Rock Demonstration School at Chinle, Arizona. Fourth, the lack of solid data on Indian education must be remedied by a major research and development effort. And finally, educational materials and the curriculum for Indian and non-Indian children in Indian country should include more information on Indian culture and history and more factual material about current Indian life.[23]

Progress along these lines is already being made. The Bureau of Indian Affairs has been increasing its efforts to involve Indian leaders in decisions affecting their welfare and to create programs that will build on the strengths of the Indian heritage. For example, programs to teach "English as a Second Language" (ESL) are now being introduced. In 1967 ESL programs were established in each of the more than sixty Bureau schools in the nation's largest Indian land area, the Navajo community. One group of Navajo parents has even requested that an ESL program be established for adults. At the same time, Indian languages are being taught to teachers of Indian children. To further help Indian educational programs to correspond to the needs of Indian communities, a National Indian Advisory Committee, including tribal leaders from throughout the nation, was established in 1967 to assist in improving communications between the schools and the people they serve. A course of study is being developed to help Indian pupils understand the strengths and origins of their own culture. The Bureau has also increased its college scholarship aid by more than 50 percent in the past four years; about 2,400 students are now receiving such assistance. In fiscal year 1967 the Bureau's adult education program enrolled 12,400 persons in formal courses, 13,500 in informal courses, and held 13,700 individual counseling sessions.[24] Of the Bureau's 1967 budget of $214 million, over $111 million was allocated to education and welfare services, including relocation and adult vocational training.[25]

Federal agencies other than the Bureau spent more than $193 million on programs from which Indians received direct benefits in 1967. Approximately three-fourths of this amount was accounted for by two agencies directly concerned with human resource development: the Department of Health, Education, and Welfare

($112 million) and the Office of Economic Opportunity ($32 million). On the other hand, it is striking that the Department of Labor, under the Manpower Development and Training Act, spent only $1.4 million on Indian programs.[26]

Despite the profound change in attitudes toward the problems of the Indians, their needs are so great that an even more intensive effort must be made on their behalf. Moreover, more thorough consideration must be given to the problem of matching Indian manpower with job opportunities. Even so strong an advocate of incentives to attract industry to reservations as Striner admits that "Most Indian reservations are relatively unappealing locations for industry."[27] On the other hand, it is widely maintained that the Indians are particularly reluctant to leave their native habitat in search of opportunities elsewhere. What, then, are the relative merits of trying to attract jobs to the reservations versus programs to train Indians for jobs in urban areas and to relocate them to these centers?

Promoting Economic Development on Reservations

Since 1962 the Bureau of Indian Affairs has expanded its program to promote the location of manufacturing plants on the reservations. It works cooperatively with federal, state, and tribal agencies, civic organizations, and private firms in this regard, and it contracts for feasibility studies pertaining to potential development projects. Of course, competition from some 3,500 other community, state, and regional organizations—some with multimillion dollar budgets for industrial promotion campaigns—is formidable. One inducement to firms to locate on reservations is a program of financial aid to companies who provide on-the-job training for Indians. The employer may be reimbursed by the Bureau in an amount up to one-half of the federal minimum wage, and this subsidy can continue as long as it takes for the Indian employee-trainee to acquire the skill necessary for his job. In addition, the employer receives other assistance, including a recruiting and screening service paid for by the Bureau and cooperating agencies. Another inducement to industry is the offer to construct facilities according to the employer's needs and specifications. Such facilities are usually paid for by rental payments on a long-term loan, so that the tribe acquires ownership after a period of from ten to twenty years. The loan may be financed by a government agency or a private institution. Special tax inducements offered by non-Indian communities are offset by the fact that the reservation employer has no taxes to pay. Another point in favor of the Indians is their proven capabilities in many instances. Of all the factories employing Indians, the most successful have been those where Indians do precision work calling for exceptional skills and attitudes that they seem to possess in unique degree. Among the products and activities in this regard are jewel bearings and precision instruments used in space vehicles; electric components, principally transistors; precision gears; and diamond cutting.[28]

In 1960 there were only nine plants, with a total of 599 jobs, built on or near reservations. By September, 1967, the number of such plants had increased to 113, employing 5,510 Indians. The reservation unemployment rate, as defined by the Bureau, fell from 49 percent in 1962, to 41 percent in 1966, and then to 37 percent in 1967. When applied to the 1967 labor force of 132,000 this reduction means that 15,000 more Indians were at work in 1967 than would have been the case if the 1962 unemployment rate had persisted. Thus the Bureau's efforts to create employment opportunities on or near reservations, combined with sustained national prosperity, has resulted in significant gains. Nevertheless, the magnitude of the task remaining is formidable, especially when it is not known how many of the 82,500 Indians who were employed in 1967 were actually fully employed. Moreover, fragmentary information indicates that occupational upgrading is taking place, that fewer Indians are working at farm jobs, and that year-around employment is increasing, but that these gains are minimal in comparison with those of the nation's labor force as a whole.[29]

Another major effort designed to attract economic activity to the reservations is the joint Economic Development Administration-

Office of Economic Opportunity Selected Indian Reservation Program.

In May, 1967, a group of EDA officials visited a number of EDA-designated Indian reservations in an attempt to discover what assistance the agency could provide to Indians living in impoverished conditions and lacking job opportunities. As a result of the group's findings it was concluded that any workable program to aid the Indians would have to involve a deep commitment by the Indians themselves to planning for the growth of their communities. It was also apparent that no one federal agency could provide the resources necessary to induce economic growth on the reservations; the combined efforts of several agencies working jointly with a single action plan was needed. As a result, an agreement was reached between EDA and OEO to pool their resources in helping to select a number of reservations. The basic principle governing the selection of the reservations was to select the ones which exhibited a strong potential for substantial economic and social development. The criteria used in choosing the reservations included (1) evidence of an active, responsive tribal government with an interest in economic and social development; (2) availability of an adequate manpower pool and training facilities; (3) existence of community education and development programs; (4) minimum social, political, institutional, and cultural hinderances to growth; (5) current industrial activities; (6) availability of natural resources and raw materials conducive to the development of secondary and tertiary types of economic activity; (7) proximity of the reservations to regional growth centers with relevant inputs and markets; and (8) transportation linkages between the reservations and these centers.

On the basis of these criteria, an Action List of fifteen reservations was selected in May, 1967. In July, 1968, sixteen additional reservations—termed the Planning List—were designated to take part in the Selected Indian Reservation Program. Reservations on the Action List (see Table 24) will receive top priority in the implementation of projects addressed to the social and economic development goals of the tribes. Reservations on the Planning List (see

TABLE 24: OEO-EDA, SELECTED INDIAN RESERVATION PROGRAM,
ACTION LIST

Reservation	State	Population	Percent Unemployed
Navajo	Arizona	125,000	39.0
San Carlos	Arizona	4,473	74.0
Salt River	Arizona	2,212	43.0
Gila River	Arizona	7,113	55.0
Annette Island	Alaska	1,000	19.3
Zuni Pueblo	New Mexico	5,000	77.0
Mescalero	New Mexico	1,559	61.0
Blackfeet	Montana	6,381	39.0
Crow	Montana	4,097	44.0
Red Lake	Minnesota	2,538	38.0
Fort Berthold	North Dakota	2,657	79.0
Standing Rock	South Dakota	4,720	47.0
Pine Ridge	South Dakota	10,495	32.0
Rosebud	South Dakota	5,432	61.5
Lower Brule and Crow Creek	South Dakota	1,731	70.5

Source: Economic Development Administration

Table 25) will concentrate on developing the internal capacity necessary to formulate and execute the tribes' own development programs. Needed planning assistance is being provided to the tribes for obtaining professional staff to assist in formulating development programs. Before any projects are funded for any select reservation, the tribe must develop a plan outlining actions to be undertaken over several years and specifying priorities with respect to goals and projects to be implemented. The plan is to be updated as the economic conditions of the reservation evolve. Reservations also will move into and out of the Selected Indian Reservation Program. When a reservation on the Action List succeeds in developing a sound economy or sustained growth it will no longer need the special attention of the program and will be removed from the List. The vacancy may be filled by a reservation from the Planning List, and a new reservation may then be selected in turn for the Planning List. A

TABLE 25: OEO-EDA, SELECTED INDIAN RESERVATION PROGRAM,
         PLANNING LIST

Reservation	State	Population	Percent Unemployed
Cheyenne River	South Dakota	4,008	25
Turtle Mountain	North Dakota	7,187	52
Leech Lake	Minnesota	2,796	26
Papago	Arizona	5,358	23
Fort Apache	Arizona	5,407	43
Hopi	Arizona	5,556	48
Colorado River	Arizona	1,628	47
Eight Northern Pueblos	New Mexico	3,301	N. A.
Jicarilla	New Mexico	1,474	43
Nevada Reservations (22)	Nevada	4,418	N. A.
Fort Yuma (Quechan)	Arizona	1,634	35
Rocky Boys	Montana	1,149	50
Fort Peck	Montana	4,196	51
Flat Head	Montana	2,761	34
Fort Belknap	Montana	1,585	30
Northern Cheyenne	Montana	2,448	22

Source: Economic Development Administration

reservation on either list that does not participate effectively may be replaced by another reservation.

In the fall of 1967, EDA established an Indian Desk to coordinate its own and other agencies' Indian programs. Action plans have since been prepared for each of the Action List reservations. Five federal agencies—EDA, OEO, the Bureau of Indian Affairs, the Department of Housing and Urban Development, and the Small Business Administration—have cooperated in providing the data necessary to develop feasible programs. The tribal leadership on each of the fifteen reservations have been involved in the development of the plans.

The prospects for the success of the Selected Indian Reservation Program must be viewed against the actual conditions that promote or hinder economic development on the reservations. Some light can be thrown on this delicate subject by briefly summarizing some of the findings of an independent study of nine of the Action List tribes. Although these findings are often impressionistic and perhaps exaggerate some problems, they do illustrate some of the impediments confronting developmental efforts. Because the study is confidential the tribes will be designated by a letter rather than their actual name. Although the conditions perceived by the student who made the study may have changed since he visited the tribes in the summer of 1968, they are set forth here as he observed them.

Tribe A has received EDA funds for an industrial park, rebuilding a sawmill, a loan to a furniture company, and a planning grant. The industrial park has been completed but no firm has located there as yet. The furniture plant that is expected to be in operation on the site within two years may be too big to have a stable work force because of the high absentee rate on the reservation. The Indians work hard but it is difficult to get them to show up for work. A fence company on the reservation with a normal work force of about 25 persons has had over 300 different persons employed in less than four years. Only two workers from among the original employees were still with the company. The available work force figures for the reservation are misleading because so few of the Indians are psychologically or culturally prepared to hold down a steady job. Attempting to assess how many jobs will be created by EDA-financed activities is extremely difficult because the work force fluctuates so much that no one set number of jobs can be ascertained. In many respects, attempting to develop Tribe A is analogous to attempting to stimulate growth in an underdeveloped country with different cultural values, and government officials should not place too much reliance on the statements of tribal leaders who verbalize values more in harmony with those of the dominant society. EDA is viewed as one more agency from which the tribe can get money, but industry will have a difficult time making a profit on the reservation so long as there is no stable work force. Despite the fact that OEO jobs are used as part of the tribal council's patronage system, this agency's programs have proven valuable in encouraging local initiative in dealing with social problems. OEO's programs to overcome behavior patterns that are not conducive to holding a job are perhaps the key to Tribe A's future development; if OEO left the reservation tomorrow it would return to the way it was before OEO came. Moreover, there remains the problem that the most ambitious and acculturated people tend to leave the reservation.

Tribe B continues to maintain much of its traditional way of life. One of the greatest difficulties in communication is that although most of the people under fifty speak some English, they cannot articulate well in English and they are not as able to grasp the discourse of a white man as easily as most Indians. Nevertheless, the members of Tribe B have important assets, not the least of which is a recognition by the leadership of the tribe's weaknesses. Unlike poverty groups which have lost their sense of identity and self-confidence, these members have a strong sense of pride that can be directed toward developing the reservation. They are an energetic people and the one manufacturing firm on the reservation is pleased with the workers' efficiency. The expansion of this firm to a point where it would employ 200 persons, about five times the present number of employees, appears to be a reasonable project to which EDA could contribute. Such an undertaking would give the tribe a considerable psychological boost. The reservation also needs commercial facilities; 92 cents out of every dollar earned by members is spent off the reservation in the nearest city.

Tribe C is a good example of relying solely on economic development to eliminate poverty. The tribe has good plans for economic development, and over five companies have agreed to locate in the tribe's industrial parks. However, the tribe's plans are basically those of the Bureau of Indian Affairs and the tribal leadership; there is no evidence that the development program has been communicated to the general populace, which gives it negligible support. The population of the reservation is widely dispersed, there is a lack of transportation, and roads are poor. Many people, therefore, are unable to participate in social development or job training programs. In addition, the tribal leadership has done little to stimulate pride among its people. The local OEO program is small, and at present it lacks a program to overcome the psychological and social impediments to economic development. Thus, despite the fact that EDA has approved grants and loans for nine projects totalling $4.1 million, with one application for $1.4 million pending, there is little reason to be optimistic about the progress being made. So far only three jobs have resulted from EDA projects. Even though this is in large part a result of the incomplete state of most of the projects, it is not likely that EDA's potential new job estimate of 1,500 will be realized because of inadequate social development and the reluctance of members to travel to industrial sites.

Tribe D is rent by political factionalism among its own people and lack of cooperation between the tribe and federal agencies. The members' concept of an Indian is taken from the Anglo-Saxon stereotype, and they have little knowledge of their own history and traditions. The Bureau of Indian Affairs does not help with development plans and the superintendent feels that white society should dictate to the Indian how he should live. In view of these conditions it is not possible for the tribe to mount a community attack on its social problems. Despite EDA assistance it is most unlikely that this tribe will progress at even the average rate of the other selected reservations.

Tribe E is dominated by a conservative group which plans to obtain money from real estate developments in the outer areas of the reservation while maintaining an inner area that is to be unchanged from the way it is now. The tribe seems uninterested in training programs and industrial projects because of its goal of income without jobs. Without social education and jobs, however, the members will not be prepared for the responsibilities that money brings. Since they are not used to handling money, their lives may be disrupted by extravagance and then bill collectors. It is not in the spirit of the Selected Indian Reservation Program to try to change the plans of local leaders, so until a more forward-looking group gains influence over tribal policy the present approach of income without jobs will continue. The present leaders are not averse to taking EDA money, but they have no apparent intention of promoting genuine economic development.

Tribes F and G, located near one another, each have an industrial park with on-site improvements financed by EDA. Tribe F's park has one firm employing five persons and Tribe G's park has one firm employing seven persons, of whom only three are Indians. There seems to be little effort being made to expand either of these activities. Tribe F has submitted an application to EDA for aid in constructing a $2 million resort complex. An EDA-financed feasibility study indicated that the complex was not feasible. The tribe has submitted a proposal for a motel whose success seems dubious and whose job-creating potential would be small in any case. Because EDA has taken so long to render a decision on this matter—the tribe blames the agency for a four-year delay, longer than it has been in existence—tribal leaders are very dissatisfied. Tribes F and G have applied to EDA for planning grants that would be helpful if a competent staff were hired. Neither tribe has any definite plans for future EDA projects at this time. The leadership of both tribes tends to be lethargic, and neither tribe has well-designed economic development plans or well-coordinated social programs.

The Indians of Tribe H seem to have lost their sense of identity and pride and to have resigned themselves to being second-class citizens. The tribe has not been able to implement most of its economic plans because of internal institutional problems and a very conservative approach to investing tribal money, caused by the failure of a manufacturing firm it had financed. As on many reservations, alcoholism is a very serious problem. At the present rate of increase it has been estimated that over 90 percent of the members over age 15 will be problem drinkers by 1980. The reservation has a heterogeneous population, which, added to the Indians' own need for greater self-esteem, means that whites would probably enjoy the fruits of any economic development long before the Indian population. At present, Tribe H has two projects pending with EDA. One is for a plant that would be located off the reservation.

However, ARA undertook a similar project and it did not ease unemployment on the reservation. The second project involves an industrial park, but lack of a firm development plan and communications difficulties with EDA have stalled this effort. The OEO program on the reservation has failed to actively involve the general population in social and economic development projects, but it has made some progress in the area of social development. In general, the tribe has shown willingness to attack its social problems but its economic level has not been improved.

In contrast to many of the cases that have been cited, Tribe I's plans and general environment make it a promising prospect for future development. The tribe has problems common to many Indian communities, e.g., high incidence of alcoholism, limited attractiveness to industry and poor work habits, but it also is characterized by attitudes and methods that can serve as models to other reservations. For example, the tribal government is in close contact with the members; it provides effective leadership while at the same time taking account of the people's desires and ideas. After several bad experiences, the tribal council in all cases now hires those who are best equipped for job openings; it does not interfere with management's hiring practices or other activities. The various federal agencies on the reservation have an effective comprehensive and coordinated approach to the social problems of the community. The tribe knows that it wants to develop economically and socially, and its plans are geared to first-rate enterprises. It also knows how to get money from federal agencies. Each agency is presented with a project within its mandate while the tribe itself coordinates the various projects into an overall development program. The main objective of Tribe I is to have a year-around resort, building on the area's great natural beauty, skiing possibilities, proximity to a race track, and other attractions. Industrialization, cattle raising, and timber operations do not figure prominently in the tribe's goals. The resort concept seems feasible so long as it is implemented *in toto*. The estimated cost of this undertaking is $4,583,000 or about $3,000 per tribal member. The cost per worker would of course be a multiple of the latter figure. The chances for success on this reservation are good—if the government is willing to assume the necessary financing.

In reviewing these cases the difficulties of industrial development on Indian reservations are clearly evident, even if overdrawn. Nevertheless, progress is being made in attracting industry to some Selected Reservations. As of May, 1969, the Fairchild Semi-Conductor plant on the Navajo reservation employed 880 Indians (for the most part women), and upon completion of a new addition now under construction another 300 to 400 people will be employed. General Dynamics employs 148 Navajos, and three Navajo enterprises account for an additional 632 jobs. W. R. Grace employs 15 Navajos. On the Zuni reservation the Ami-Zuni Corporation employs 160 Indians and a new Dittemore-Freimuth plant will employ 35 persons. Forty-six Indians are employed on the Gila River reservation, but new activities will provide jobs for about 250 more Indians. A new plant on the Rosebud reservation will raise employment to somewhat over 200, while a similar number of jobs will exist on the Blackfeet reservation after a new plant has been finished. A division of the Mohawk Carpet Company plans to employ 200 Indians on the Crow reservation.[30]

Despite employment gains on reservations, it must still be remembered that most reservations are established in areas which have had little economic importance to white settlers. Moreover, as Striner has remarked:

The distances between reservations and major markets result in high transportation costs. Intrareservation transportation systems are minimal. There is an acute shortage of management skill on reservations. Much of the labor force is untrained and unaccustomed to the requirements of steady employment. Utilities and public facilities are only in the early stages of development. The Indian population is widely scattered; few Indian communities have a population of over 3,000.[31]

In view of this situation, Striner advocates strong incentives to attract industrial plants. These include tax credits, depreciation allowances, credit financing, and the creation of an Indian Development Corporation.[32]

In contrast to efforts to attract industry to reservations, little attention has been given to programs to relocate Indians to jobs off the reservations. This reluctance is probably a consequence of relocation experience associated with the termination policy of the 50's and the related problem of the Indians' lack of preparation for jobs and life off the reservations. Thus, what does seem apparent from any point of view is the need to give the Indian the sociological and psychological preconditions for participation in a disciplined labor force, and then the training corresponding to available job opportunities. Until these changes take place there will be no significant increase in economic opportunity either on or off the reservation. The better prepared Indians are likely to leave in search of job opportunities elsewhere and even if they stay and wait for jobs the many relative disadvantages of the reservations may still preclude significant industrialization. It is therefore necessary to consider the extent to which rising Indian expectations, which no one wishes to reverse, can be satisfied off the reservations.

Migration and Adaptation to Urban Places

The Bureau of Indian Affairs conducts a program of employment assistance to provide opportunities for Indians who wish to move to urban communities or to find work on or near a reservation, and to obtain adult vocational training in school or in on-the-job training programs.[33] Relocation for employment involves not only training and job placement for Indians who choose to resettle away from reservations where job opportunities are more abundant, but also financial help and counseling to ease the family's adjustment to the new environment. By the end of fiscal year 1967, over 61,500 Indian people had been given help toward direct employment by the Employment Assistance Program, and more than 24,300 had received adult vocational training.

The types of help available in the Employment Assistance Program share five common characteristics: they are (1) completely voluntary; (2) give extensive individual help to the participant; (3) are available only to Indians who are members of a tribe, band, or group recognized by the Bureau of Indian Affairs; (4) available only where there is demonstrated need; and (5) supplied only if the services cannot be obtained from other sources. Employment Assistance staffs are located at 65 Indian agencies and reservations. A staff makes information about the program available to the local Indian population, but no attempt is made to "push" an individual into the program, and only those persons with a sincere desire to take vocational training or find employment are encouraged to participate. Many applicants are given aptitude and interest tests to help in evaluating their attitudes and strengths.

The relocation program of the Bureau is intended for the person, either single or head of a family, who is prepared to leave the reservation for a job opportunity in an urban center. This program is divided into two services, the Direct Employment Program and the Adult Vocational Training Program.

The Direct Employment Program is intended primarily for the person who has a marketable skill for which there is no corresponding job available in the Indian community. Upon application for services, the individual is given help in selecting an appropriate relocation point; information on the environment and opportunities of the communities available is provided, and the client identifies the city to which he would prefer to move. Usually the city is one of the eleven where a Bureau field employment assistance staff is located. A wide variety of financial help is available to the participating Indian and his family. This can include the cost of transportation to the new job, a subsistence allowance, financial help for large families and for families that wish to buy their own homes, health examinations, and transportation of household goods. Several counseling services are available in cities with a Bureau field office. There is a vocational counselor who surveys current job opportunities and advises the client on securing employment. The client is informed of the nature, location, and salary of a particular job opening, and if he expresses an interest in it an employment interview is arranged. Before the actual interview the client is advised of what kind of questions to expect and how to fill out a job application form. There is also a community-living specialist who helps acquaint the Indian and his family with the community and its recreational and social opportunities. The Bureau provides temporary furnished living quarters, but a housing counselor accompanies the family within a few days after arrival in looking for adequate permanent housing. The counselor gives advice on such matters as proximity to transportation facilities, churches, shopping centers, and the job location. Once the family moves into its new home, the counselors begin a series of home visitations that last for two or three months. These meetings are primarily intended to help the family adjust to the new environment. If the employee is dissatisfied with his job or loses it, the cycle begins again and he is assisted in obtaining new work. If he remains employed his intensive contact with the Bureau is reduced as he assimilates into the community. He is entitled to use any of the Bureau's services for a period of three years after his arrival, but frequently he is independent after six months.

The second service offered under the relocation program is the Adult Vocational Training Program. The trainee is provided with the same forms of assistance as in the Direct Employment Program, but in addition he is given vocational training before finding a job. The Bureau contracts with established and accredited vocational training institutions to provide the necessary instruction. Training is offered in 115 fields at 437 institutions in 28 states. When the client has selected his program of training and is enrolled, his tuition and supplies are provided. Usually the training course lasts about ten months, but in some cases the trainee may remain in school for two years. During this time the Bureau defrays the living costs of the individual or family. Although this program has a higher initial cost, it increases the individual's capacity to hold down a job more than either direct employment or on-the-job training.

The On-The-Job Training Program of the Bureau is similar to OJT programs of other agencies. The Bureau usually pays 50 percent of the trainee's wage until he has completed training and is regarded as a qualified employee. This program usually does not result in a transferable skill, nor does it usually involve relocation.

During the last two years the Bureau has initiated more comprehensive and experimental programs to aid individuals who do not have the vocational skills, social and educational background, or motivation to compete effectively in the labor market. In late 1966 the Bureau entered into a contract with RCA to establish a residential training center for thirty families living near the Choctaw reservation in Mississippi. Day care centers take care of children while their mothers study community living, homemaking skills, child care, and other subjects to prepare them for urban life. If they choose, they may also learn a vocational skill to supplement the family's income. Meanwhile, the fathers are given a program designed to impart basic literacy, mathematical skills, an introduction to various kinds of jobs, and a social orientation. Counseling is given to the family as a whole, and a center political organization is encouraged to promote self-involvement by the participants. Before this program the participants lived in shacks and worked as sharecroppers. They lacked any opportunity for urban experiences, handled no money, and visited no banks. Their average level of schooling was 1.6 years. Of the initial group of families, eight have completed training and are now located in Cleveland, Chicago, and Memphis. There are now 55 families participating in the program and there would be more were it not for housing limitations.

The promising results of the Mississippi project led the Bureau to establish another residential training center for the hard-core disadvantaged at Madera, California. This center is operated under contract by the Philco-Ford Corporation and accommodates 31 families and 168 single persons. The programs at Madera are similar to those at the Choctaw Center, though the participants are drawn from all over the country. The educational levels attained by the Indians at Madera are higher than at Choctaw, but whereas the Choctaws are accustomed to long, hard work, this frequently is not the case for many of the Madera participants. Thus, prior to vocational training or job placement they need the experience of a "halfway house." The trainees are involved to the maximum with non-Indians in community activities. The typical participant stays at the center for nine months. Eighty-eight Indians have completed training and all but four, who are awaiting placement, have gone directly into jobs.

The newest residential training center is operated by Thiokol Chemical Corporation at Roswell, New Mexico, on the former Walker Air Force Base. The vocational skills that are taught are based on a survey of available jobs in the area. The program is similar to that at Madera, but more families will be involved. The training is designed to allow trainees to advance as far as they can and are able, or to drop off when they desire. At each level the individual is adequately prepared to enter appropriate employment. Aggregate costs, including contract, transportation, subsistence, furniture (which the family may keep), job placement, and follow-up assistance, are less than $5000 per adult trainee.

One of the main reasons for contracting the residential center programs to private firms is to promote a psychological transition from traditional dependence on the federal government to association with a large company. Even though the government provides the trainees' subsidies, the pay is provided on ordinary company checks. The experience of working for a company makes the participants more amenable to counseling and less dependent on government agencies.

The Bureau of Indian Affairs' relatively long experience with relocation programs has led it to the following generalizations concerning their success: (1) Prevocational and vocational programs should be flexibly tailored to the needs of individual persons and families. (2) The programs should be entirely voluntary and available in response to participants' interest and motivation, rather than on a scheduled basis. (3) Eventual employment near home is more desirable than long moves (half of all Bureau clients found work in their state of origin last year). (4) Pre-departure counseling is an important ingredient in the ultimate success of a move. (5) Counseling should be given to relocatees as long as they feel themselves to be in transition. (6) Counseling and aid to help the wife to adjust to the new environment may be equally or more important than the technical proficiency of her husband in assuring a successful move. (7) Group identification and the help of other Indian families are valuable assets during the transition to urban life. (In the early years of relocation experience individuals were encouraged to shun Indian organizations and involve themselves to the maximum with non-Indian organizations. That policy has now been drastically revised.) (8) Early involvement with private industry reduces dependence on paternal organizations and adds reality to the training experience. (9) Financial assistance before the first monthly paycheck arrives or to meet emergencies increases the probability of success. (10) Respect for the Indian's own culture should not be lost either by himself or those who work with him.

Because of the disastrous relocation efforts initially sponsored by the Bureau it is often still assumed that such programs are to be avoided. For example, one prominent study of retraining and migration states that:

the Bureau has not sufficiently evaluated their programs to yield benefit of experience to the newer retraining programs. However, from informal discussion one finds that the degree of success of the total program depends upon establishing job opportunities within the vicinity of the reservation for social reasons. Relocation, even when accompanied with acceptable training levels, has met limited success under the Indian Affairs program.

The experience is useful if it only serves to emphasize the obvious fact that retraining should be coupled with the provision of economic opportunity for the retrainees within their current environment, if at all possible.[34]

In fact, in the same year as these words were written, the Bureau did conduct a study[35] to determine whether and to what extent the families and individuals who participated in its Employment Assistance Program could be considered to be self-sufficient. The population sampled consisted of families and individuals who had received employment assistance in 1963. Data were collected and analyzed during the period January–June, 1966. This interval was selected because it represented a sufficient span to make the respondents' self-sufficiency status meaningful, but not so long as to make it difficult to locate and interview them. The sample included 327 individuals and family heads out of a population of 5,108. The sample, which was taken in consultation with the Bureau of the Census and the Bureau of Labor Statistics, was stratified according to whether the assistance recipients were placed directly in jobs, trained on the job, or provided institutional vocational training before beginning work. Samples of approximately 6 percent were randomly selected from each category.

The results of the study are summarized in Table 26. Of the total number interviewed, 52 percent had received institutional vocational training (IT), 37 percent direct employment (DE), and 11 percent on-the-job training (OJT). Fourteen percent of the interviewees were Navajos, 10 percent were Sioux, 9 percent were Pueblo, and 7 percent were Chippewa; other tribes accounted for 4 percent or less of the total. Thirty-five percent of the respondents lived in cities and towns surrounding Bureau area offices, while the remainder were in one of the seven urban centers where the Bureau maintains employment assistance offices (Los Angeles, Dallas, Oakland, Chicago, Cleveland, San Jose, and Denver).

The study showed that 70 percent of the study group who received services during fiscal year 1967 were employed during the January–June, 1966, period. In addition, 17 percent were attending school, in military service, caring for homes, or unable to work due to illness, disabilities, or family situations. Thus, 84 percent of those in the labor market were employed.

Eighty-five percent of the DE recipients chose an urban center for service, as did 64 percent of the IT group. On the other hand, most of the OJT group were trained and employed locally. The OJT group tended to be older than the participants in the other programs, which may account in part for this reluctance to move to urban centers.

Average annual earnings increased for all three groups, with the IT trainees showing a 358 percent increase and the OJT group 68 percent. The spectacular increase for the IT trainees reflects in large part the fact that before entering training they were often high school students. The relatively low increase for the OJT group may

TABLE 26: STATISTICAL SUMMARY IN PERCENTAGES FOR 327
INDIAN EMPLOYMENT SERVICE RECIPIENTS IN
FISCAL YEAR 1963

	Direct Employment	On-the-job Training	Institutional Vocational Training
Location:			
Within area	15	97	37
Urban centers	85	3	63
Marital status:			
Family	34	69	32
Single woman	18	14	35
Single man	48	17	33
Age:			
18–19	9	8	9
20–24	55	31	67
25–29	23	25	16
Over 30	13	36	8
Education:			
0–8	31	28	9
9–11	33	41	23
12 and over	36	31	68
Employment status:			
Working	69	80	68
Unemployed	20	6	10
Not in labor market	6	8	17
Unable to work	5	6	5
Attitudes:			
Question I. Are you living better now than the way you lived before you received services?			
Yes	61	61	72
No	5	8	5
Question II: Would you request the services again?			
Yes	71	61	78
No	9	14	7
Arrests:			
Percent decrease	59	33	38
Earnings:			
Prior	$1,039	$1,264	$ 681
After	$2,694	$2,119	$3,120
Increase	159%	68%	358%
Costs:			
Average recipient cost	$1,104	$ 648	$2,550

Source: "A Followup Study of 1963 Recipients of the Services of the
Employment Assistance Program, Bureau of Indian Affairs," Washington,
D.C.: Bureau of Indian Affairs, 1966, p. 49.

be related to its older average age, but also to the fact that these people did not leave for better paying jobs in urban areas. In any case, there is a direct relationship between the amount of money expended on a participant and his earnings.

Another indication of the success of the overall program is seen in responses to the attitudinal questions. Sixty-one percent of the DE and OJT group and 72 percent of the IT group felt themselves to be better off than before they received the program's services. The proportion who would request services again ranged from 61 percent for the OJT group, to 78 percent for the IT group. In other words, the most satisfied group moved to urban jobs and had had relatively more preparation before leaving.

In 1968, as part of the continuing evaluation of the Employment Assistance Program, the Bureau of Indian Affairs interviewed 85 percent of the trainees who were surveyed in 1966. The average actual annual earnings figure for the two years 1966–67 for the DE group was $4093, as compared to $2694 for the 1963–65 period. The comparable respective values for the OJT group were $2957 and $2119, while those for the IT group were $4027 and $3120. The proportion of the DE group that would request Employment Assistance services again rose from 71 percent in 1966 to 78 percent in 1968; the proportion of the OJT group responding affirmatively rose from 61 percent to 69 percent, and that of the IT group increased from 78 percent to 84 percent. Slightly fewer of the DE and IT recipients were off reservations in 1968 as compared to 1966, but the proportion of OJT recipients increased from 3 percent to 41 percent.[36]

In general, the Employment Assistance Program has been a success in terms of both return on the government's investment and the satisfaction of the Indian participants. Although the survey does not include the relatively new residential training center programs, it may be inferred that they will be even more successful than the previous relocation programs, especially in dealing with the problems of the hard-core disadvantaged. For example, a recent study indicates that the benefit-cost ratio for the Madera Employment Training Center is about 3:1 (see Table 27). Benefits were nar-

TABLE 27: COMPUTATION OF BENEFIT-COST RATIO FOR MADERA
         EMPLOYMENT TRAINING CENTER (per trainee)

Benefits:
  Present value of additional annual earnings, per trainee $11,078
    Prior to METC 45 trainees were employed at an average
    hourly wage rate of $1.84 or an annual income of $3800.
    After METC 57 trainees were employed at an average
    hourly wage of $2.19 or an annual income of $4550.
    Additional annual earnings per trainee =
    $$\frac{(4550 \times 57) - (3800 \times 45)}{120} = \$736.25.$$
    The present value of this amount for 40 years (assum-
    ing the average age of trainees is 25 and retirement is at
    age 65) at a 6% rate of interest is $11,078.
Costs:
  Training costs per trainee $2806.41
    Cost per month ($417) times average length of training,
    in months (6.73)
  Clothing allowance per trainee $94.50
    Allowance of $60 per trainee and child; an average of
    .575 children per trainee
  Foregone earnings per trainee $799.19
    Number of trainees working prior to METC times their
    monthly income times the average length of training
    divided by the total number of trainees
    $$\frac{45 \times 3800/12 \times 6.73}{120}$$
  Total costs $3700
  Benefit-cost ratio $\frac{\$11,078}{\$3700} =$ 2.994.1

Source: United States Department of the Interior, Indians, Job Training
and Placement Studies, Issue Support Paper No. 70–1, October 17, 1968,
p. 76.

rowly defined to include only the present value of future additional
earnings attributable to the program. Bruce Davie notes that "A
ratio of this magnitude is quite respectable, higher than those for
several other manpower programs whose analyses I am familiar
with."[37] He concludes that:

Substantial intangible benefits from this program, particularly for the
children, undoubtedly exist. Future follow-up studies might try to docu-
ment the educational progress of the children. In my judgment, impor-

tant as these intangible benefits may be, they need not be appealed to at
the moment to justify the continuance of the METC program. To date
the evidence shows that, purely on the grounds of economic efficiency,
the METC program is a worthwhile investment in human resources.[38]

Similarly, after a visit to the Madera Center in August, 1968,
Herbert Striner wrote to the Commissioner of the Bureau of Indian
Affairs that "My overall impression . . . was that this is a unique
project which should be duplicated many, many times over."[39]

Finally, it is instructive to take a closer look at the adaptation of
Indian migrants to urban life in Los Angeles, which has the largest
population of Indians in the country. In 1960, there were 12,400
Indians in greater Los Angeles but there are indications that their
number had doubled by 1966. A survey by John A. Price of 3,000
Indians in the Los Angeles area in 1966 showed that the great majority were migrants from other states—only six were descendents of
the aboriginal occupants of Los Angeles and only 77 were descendents of aboriginal Californians. The increasing mobility of Indians
was further indicated by the fact that only 19 percent of the respondents were born in the same state as their fathers.[40] According to
Price:

> A key to the great size of the post-1955 migration is the Employment
> Assistance ("Relocation") Program of the Bureau of Indian Affairs
> (BIA). . . . By 1962, the BIA had trained over 5,000 Indians and had
> relocated more than 40,000. Both programs have been intensified since
> 1962, and have been a massive stimulant to the growth of the Los
> Angeles Indian community. The BIA office in Los Angeles has, in recent
> years, been assisting about 1,300 Indians annually.[41]

Moreover, Price's survey showed that 42 percent of the Indians
coming to Los Angeles had received a brief BIA course on how to
live in the city. The main incentive for their leaving the reservations
was economic: they wanted jobs. As the years go by, they increasingly tend to idealize life on the reservations, but they increasingly
withdraw from previous reservation contacts. There is a tendency
for recent arrivals to the city to live in the central city, but longer
term residents move outward to the suburbs. Persons from tribes

located in the northeastern United States were found to be closest to a direct adaptation to urban life, whereas the Navajos showed the weakest degree of adaptation. However, the study showed that:

Indians fresh from strongly rural or reservation backgrounds tend, like the Navaho, to shift over time to patterns of life exemplified by the Five Civilized Tribes. Also, as the Indian community in Los Angeles matures, we may expect tribal groups such as the Navaho to shift toward tribal groups like the Five Civilized Tribes. The latter in turn is culturally close to the general population of Los Angeles, except for the particular ethnic identity.[42]

Thus, while the problems of the Indian's adaptation to urban life should not be minimized, conditions in the city lead him away from tribal patterns. As with other ethnic groups who have entered the "melting pot," the Indians tend to preserve certain values and customs that add to America's cultural diversity; but they, too, tend to be assimilated into the mainstream of American life as a consequence of the vastly greater range of choice available to them in the city.

Summary and Conclusions

Much has been made of the Indian's attachment to his people and his land, and there is a widespread assumption that Indians are unsuited for life off the reservations. This view was reinforced by the failure of the relocation policy of the 1950's, which moved a large number of Indians directly from reservations to cities without adequate preparation and training, and which explicitly or implicitly denigrated the Indians' own culture. More recently the rising tide of sentiment in favor of helping our Indian populations to attain a higher material standard of life while respecting their culture has tended to take the form of efforts to attract industry to the reservations. Despite some progress in this regard, Indian reservations generally have few if any attributes to make them attractive to industry. Moreover, Indians are not so reluctant to leave the reservations or as unable to adapt to city life as many believe. They do need, however, comprehensive programs to help them prepare for life and work off the reservation. There is a direct relationship between, on one hand, the amount of training and comprehensive assistance given to the Indian (and his family, which is equally important) and, on the other hand, his income after relocating and his success at adapting to the new environment. Moreover, the cost per job obtained by relocation programs is less than the government's cost per job in attempting to attract industry to the reservations.

While industry can hardly be said to be clamoring to get onto the reservations, even with government-financed incentives, there is at present a backlog of some 2,000 Indians on reservations waiting for training and probable relocation. There would no doubt be an even greater number if the 2,000 could be absorbed, since participants pass the word around that the programs are helpful and thereby generate interest among still other Indians.

All parties agree that what the reservations most need is expanded investment in human resources, including programs to change the sociological behavior of many Indians to bring it more into line with the kind of outlook needed to hold down a steady job. It is also agreed that the Indian culture must be respected and that any relocation program must be established on a voluntary basis. But sentiment about reservation life—which frequently is encountered more among older Indian leaders and well-meaning whites than among the younger, and especially better-educated, Indians—should not obscure the fact that the matching of workers and jobs demands a broader geographic perspective than is available by concentrating on the reservations themselves.

Chapter 8

The Mexican Americans

A Population Profile

The Mexican Americans constitute the second largest minority group in the United States, yet outside of the Southwest there has been little awareness of them and even less knowledge about them. Over one-tenth of the combined populations of Arizona, California, Colorado, New Mexico, and Texas is Mexican American, with the proportion ranging from 9 percent in Colorado to 28 percent in New Mexico (see Table 28). Of the nearly 3.5 million Spanish surname population in the Southwest in 1960, over 2.8 million lived in California and Texas. Outside the Southwest Mexican American communities are found in a number of cities, including Chicago, Detroit, Gary, and Kansas City.[1]

In the past Mexican Americans were for the most part agricultural workers, but they have now become urbanized to such a degree that the rural and migrant worker stereotype is outdated. The 1960 census showed that about the same proportion of Mexican Americans as Anglo Americans—80 percent—was found in urban areas. Moreover, Mexican Americans have a higher degree of differentiation in socioeconomic status than is commonly supposed. Leo Grebler has pointed out that "while the group includes large numbers of people with little formal education, few skills, low income, and other disadvantages, one finds in its ranks relatively well-to-do families and highly trained persons—a U. S. Senator and three Congressmen, others in responsible government posts, attorneys, physicians, teachers, social workers, and engineers."[2] The Mexican Americans "are also differentiated in regional terms. New Mexicans generally show patterns of behavior and attitudes that distinguish them sharply from their counterparts in south Texas or in Fresno, California, especially in the political arena. Mexican Americans are clustered in vast urban populations, but they are also scattered over hundreds of semi-rural and isolated *colonias* throughout the Southwest."[3]

TABLE 28: SPANISH-SURNAME AND NONWHITE POPULATION
AS A PERCENT OF TOTAL POPULATION, 1950 AND 1960,
FIVE SOUTHWEST STATES

Location	1950 White			1960 White		
	Anglo	Spanish Surname	Non-white	Anglo	Spanish Surname	Non-white
Southwest	80.4	10.9	8.7	78.9	11.8	9.3
Arizona	70.2	17.1	12.7	74.9	14.9	10.2
California	86.5	7.2	6.3	82.9	9.1	8.0
Colorado	89.0	8.9	2.1	88.0	9.0	3.0
New Mexico	56.0	36.5	7.5	63.8	28.3	7.9
Texas	73.8	13.4	12.8	72.6	14.8	12.6
United States	89.5		10.5	88.8		11.2

Source: Joan W. Moore, *Mexican-Americans: Problems and Prospects* (Madison, Wis.: Institute for Research on Poverty, University of Wisconsin, 1967), p. 4.

Nevertheless, the diversity of the Southwest's Mexican American population cannot mask the fact that in toto Spanish surname families are heavily overrepresented among the region's poor. The data in Table 29 show that over one-third of the Spanish surname group fall into the poor category as defined by the arbitrary but conventional criterion of family income of less than $3000. The rate of poor families is over twice as great within the Spanish surname

TABLE 29: NUMBER AND PERCENT OF POOR FAMILIES IN VARIOUS
POPULATION GROUPS IN THE SOUTHWEST, 1960

Population Group	All Families (1)	Poor Families[a] (2)	Percent of Poor in Each Group (3)	Poor in Each Group as Percent of All Poor (4)
Total	7,356,866	1,451,655	19.7	100.0
White	6,766,367	1,205,729	17.8	83.1
Anglo	6,068,340	962,826	15.9	66.4
Spanish surname	698,027	242,903	34.8	16.7
Nonwhite	590,299	245,926	41.7	17.0

[a] Families with annual Income under $3,000 in 1959.
Source: Frank G. Mittelbach and Grace Marshall, The Burden of Poverty
(Los Angeles: U.C.L.A. Graduate School of Business Administration, Mexi-
can-American Study Project, Advance Report No. 5, July, 1966), p. 3.

group as within the Anglo group, though it is still less than the
poverty rate within the nonwhite category.

In 1959 the median income of Mexican American males in the
Southwest was $2,768. This was 57 percent of the comparable
Anglo figure and only a little above that for the Negroes.[4] Interstate
differences in median income are considerable. For example, the
data in Table 30 show that urban male median income for the
Spanish surname population ranged from $2,339 in Texas to $4,137
in California. In Texas the Anglo median income is nearly twice that
of the Mexican American, whereas in California the Mexican
American value is three-fourths that for the Anglos. In general, the
relative incomes of Mexican Americans vary directly with the overall levels of income of the states. It is instructive to note that "Close
to 90 percent of the income gap between Mexican American and
Anglo men in California is associated with differences in level of
education, and the situation is much the same in other States. The
remaining relatively small income gap may be attributed to wage
and occupational discrimination, as well as to differences in quality
of education."[5]

TABLE 30: MEDIAN INCOMES[a] BY STATE, SPANISH-SURNAME,
ANGLO, AND NONWHITE URBAN MALES[b] IN THE
SOUTHWEST, 1959

	Arizona	California	Colorado	New Mexico	Texas
Spanish surname (1)	$3,322	$4,137	$3,340	$3,278	$2,339
Anglo (2)	4,757	5,421	4,719	5,276	4,593
Nonwhite (3)	2,581	3,580	3,190	2,563	2,282
Ratio					
(1)/(2)	.70	.76	.71	.62	.51
(1)/(3)	1.29	1.16	1.05	1.28	1.02

[a] All incomes are adjusted for *within-state* differences in age distributions.
[b] With income, age 14 and over.
Source: Walter Fogel, *Mexican Americans in Southwest Labor Markets* (Los Angeles: U.C.L.A. Graduate School of Business Administration, Mexican-American Study Project, Advance Report No. 10, October, 1967), p. 32.

Mexican American males are primarily employed in manual occupations. The white-collar jobs that they hold tend to be in small retail trade establishments, while those few with jobs classified in the professional and technical category hold mostly technical jobs. In 1960, about 30 percent of the males were farm and nonfarm laborers, and 40 percent worked in craft and operative jobs. In contrast, almost 40 percent of the Mexican American women living in cities were employed in white collar occupations. A survey made in 1966 by the Equal Opportunity Commission on the occupational distribution of Mexican American employees of firms with 100 or more workers in the Los Angeles-Long Beach and San Francisco-Oakland areas shows a continued concentration of Mexican American workers at the lower end of the occupational scale. Over half were employed as operatives or laborers and only one-fifth were in white collar jobs, mostly clerical and sales. In brief, Mexican Americans are concentrated in relatively low-wage sectors, though this phenomenon is less pronounced than it is for the Negro population.[6]

The most recent comprehensive data on unemployment in the

Mexican American population date from April, 1960. The urban unemployment rate at that time for Mexican Americans was 8.5 percent, compared with 4.5 percent for Anglos and 9.1 percent for nonwhites. However, some of the unemployed Mexican Americans in urban areas were probably only residing there temporarily, until they could obtain employment in agriculture. On the other hand, the *braceros*—Mexican agricultural workers who had contracts to stay in the United States on a temporary basis under a program terminated in 1964—were protected against extended jobless periods by their contracts. They thus experienced artificially low unemployment relative to the permanent rural population.[7]

Urban unemployment for Mexican Americans, as for other Americans, varies considerably with age. As the data in Table 31 indicate, unemployment tends to worsen with age, with the 65 and over Mexican American rate being particularly high relative to that for all comparable males. At the other end of the age groups, the 17.6 percent unemployment rate for Mexican American teenagers was considerably higher than that for all teenage males in the Southwest, but still not relatively so high as in the other age groups.

TABLE 31: UNEMPLOYMENT RATES, URBAN SOUTHWEST, 1960

Age Class	Spanish Surname (1)	All Males (2)	Ratio (Column 1/2)
14–19	17.6	12.5	1.41
20–24	11.3	7.8	1.45
25–34	6.6	4.1	1.61
35–44	5.9	3.7	1.60
45–64	8.3	5.1	1.63
65 and over	12.6	7.1	1.78

Source: Walter Fogel, *Mexican Americans in Southwest Labor Markets* (Los Angeles: U.C.L.A. Graduate School of Business Administration, Mexican-American Study Project, Advance Report 10, October, 1967), p. 20.

The lowest rates of Mexican American unemployment are found in Arizona and California, while the highest is in Texas. The situation in south Texas is particularly difficult because of the large supply of unskilled labor from immigration, natural increase, and commuting workers from across the border. Even the unlikely prospect of rapid economic growth in south Texas would not put an early end to depressed labor market conditions. In contrast, California's high wage levels mean a higher real return to wage earners, and there is more opportunity and less job discrimination.[8]

There is evidence of substantial gains in income and occupational status between the first and second generations of Mexican Americans, but similar gains between the second and third generations are not apparent. Occupational upgrading of third-generation males is slight and income gains do not show any improvement. In general, there is little ground for optimism that the economic gap between Mexican Americans and Anglos will be closed in the near future.[9]

Underinvestment in Human Resources

The employment problems of the Mexican Americans, like those of other minority groups, are in many respects tied to deficiencies in human resource development. As Robert Smith has argued, "The basic problem [in the Southwest's employment picture] is to raise the educational attainment and skill levels of the labor force, particularly among minority groups, to meet the needs of modern industry."[10] For the Mexican American, Miguel Montes has delineated five areas closely related to deficiencies in the education of Mexican American students. These are (1) a lack of experiences from which concepts grow, (2) an inadequate command of the English language, which is the language of the instructional program, (3) low self-confidence resulting from repeated frustration and failure, (4) an unrealistic curriculum which imposes reading and writing requirements in English before skills in listening and speaking fluency were attained, and (5) a lack of personnel sensitive to these problems.[11] Joan Moore points out that "while the overall ratio [in the southwestern states] is about one Mexican to seven Anglos, the child ratio was one Mexican child for every five

Anglos. The impact of this minority on the school system and other youth-serving agencies of these states therefore is far greater than ordinary population ratios imply. Historically, the schools have failed to cope with the educational problems of these minority children."[12] In addition, Mexican American homes have generally not stressed education or intellectual effort. Although more Mexican American parents are beginning to encourage their children to continue their schooling, such parents are still the exception.[13]

Illustrative of the educational deprivation of Mexican Americans is the fact that in 1960 their median years of schooling were even less than those of the Negro population. Mexican Americans 25 years of age and older had a median of 7.1 years of schooling, whereas the comparable figure for nonwhites was 9.0 and for Anglos 12.1. In Texas the median value was 4.8 years, only slightly above the cut-off level for functional illiteracy. Despite this discouraging picture, there has been notable progress among younger Mexican Americans. When only those persons in the fourteen to twenty-four year age group are considered, the median was 9.2 years. Moreover, current enrollment data for 1960 show Mexican Americans only slightly below Anglos in every state except Texas.[14] The relatively poor showing in Texas— a consequence of cultural factors, migrant work, and unenforced school attendance laws is illustrated by the fact that the median number of school years completed by persons 14 years of age and older in 1960 was 6.1 for Mexican Americans, as against 8.7 for Negroes and 10.4 for all categories.[15]

Rural areas show much less progress in educational attainment from generation to generation, in large part because of the disproportionate number of foreign-born Mexicans in the migrant labor force. Poor education of the rural parents prevents them from seeking better opportunities in the cities. "Thus, the children's schooling is poor, and without a massive effort to improve education in the farm areas, the children are trapped. Apparently, the local power structure in many of these areas is unwilling to invest in schooling that will almost surely reduce the supply of labor by an exodus to nearby cities. This problem can probably only be resolved by policy decisions at a higher level of government."[16]

There can be no doubt that education pays off for the Mexican American, especially since discrimination is much less a problem than in the case of the Negro population. As pointed out earlier, about 90 percent of the income gap between Mexican American and Anglo men in California is associated with educational differences. Moreover, the relative income of the Mexican Americans by state is positively correlated with schooling of Mexican Americans compared to that of the Anglo population.[17] Of course, it must be kept in mind that while Negroes have tended to encounter an occupational ceiling despite higher levels of education, few Mexican Americans may have had sufficient education to encounter it.[18] Nevertheless, Fogel has shown that given amounts of education provide larger incomes to the Spanish surname group than to other minority groups, i.e., Negroes, Indians, Chinese, Filipinos, Japanese, and Puerto Ricans. He attributes this phenomenon to lower levels of prejudice against Mexican Americans than against the other minority groups.[19] This does not deny the fact that, when incomes of Mexican Americans and Anglos who have completed the same number of school years are compared, the levels of the former are for the most part 60 to 80 percent of Anglo levels. Educational quality and discrimination undoubtedly account for the differences.[20] There is evidence that discrimination in employing Mexican Americans is directly related to size of firm, market concentration, and earnings. To a considerable extent Mexican Americans have low earnings because discrimination forces many of them to accept jobs in small, marginal firms.[21] Yet even in Texas, where discrimination is greatest, the Mexican Americans "are well aware of the fact that discrimination is becoming increasingly rare. All can remember the days of segregated schools, direct insult, and unequal rights before the law. The Mexican-American sees the current change as a result of his efforts rather than a product of increasing Anglo democracy."[22] Whatever the causes of declining discrimination, it is evident that future gains for Mexican Americans depend on how rapidly they can increase their educational attainment and job qualifications. The increasing level of education of the country's population as a whole and structural changes in the labor market make it imperative for the Mexican Americans to realize these gains.

The Problems of South Texas

An understanding of the economic position of the Mexican Americans requires an understanding of the nature and significance of immigration from Mexico. Approximately 1.3 million Mexicans are reported to have entered the United States between 1900 and 1964, but this is certainly an understatement, since early records are incomplete and many illegal migrants who remained permanently are unrecorded. In the second half of the 1920's and during the period from 1955 to 1964, Mexico accounted for about one-sixth of all immigrants to this country; in eight of the eleven years from 1954 to 1964, more people entered on a Mexican immigrant visa than from any other country.[23]

South Texas is particularly affected by Mexican immigration. Fogel remarks that:

Whenever residents of Mexico near the United States border perceive opportunities for a better life in Texas, they will emigrate to that state (unless immigration restrictions are tightened). Thus, though employment is likely to increase as rapidly in Texas as in the rest of the Southwest and the nation, and even though many Mexican Americans will share in these gains, the comparative position for the total Mexican American group in Texas will not change very rapidly because of the influx of immigrants from Mexico to the low wage jobs in the state.[24]

A particularly difficult situation is posed by the commuter or "green card" worker. This is a person who signs under oath at an American Consulate that he is coming to the United States to reside and work permanently, but who actually resides in contiguous Mexican territory and commutes to his job in the United States. Since the green card worker can live cheaper in Mexico he will work for less money than a domestic worker. Often a displaced domestic worker is driven to the north where he in turn displaces other local workers. Many Texas employers prefer to hire commuters because they are more easily exploited than American citizens. The wage that the commuter receives is very low by American standards, and he does not pay property taxes to support public facilities. No reliable estimate is available of the number of green card workers. Munoz, for example, gives a figure of 90,000[25] while Grebler cites a minimum number of 60,000 for the year 1960.[26] In addition to agricultural employment, the green carders serve in menial jobs in hotels, restaurants, and grocery stores, and as domestics. They also form a large part of the labor force in the garment industries of El Paso and Brownsville. The Department of Labor has estimated that they account for about 17 percent of the work force employed in El Paso, 23 percent in Brownsville, and 5 percent in San Diego. Their presence is related to high unemployment rates in all border areas. Complicating the issue is the spectacular growth of Mexican border cities, which have attracted large numbers of migrants from other Mexican areas as work opportunities across the border become increasingly publicized. For example, between 1940 and 1960, while the population of Mexico was increasing by 78 percent, the municipality of Piedras Negras grew by 159 percent; Matamoros, 164 percent; Nogales, 198 percent; Nuevo Laredo, 205 percent; Ciudad Juarez, 403 percent; Ensenada, 418 percent; Reynosa, 483 percent; Mexicali, 534 percent; and Tijuana, 654 percent.[27] Moreover, as Grebler maintains, it seems unlikely that economic conditions in Mexico will change rapidly enough over the next generation to reduce significantly the pressure to move to the United States.[28]

The other side of the green card issue is that restrictions on commuting could be harmful to American border towns. Those who have adopted this position argue that many of the manufacturing and service industries in these towns could not compete in their markets without low-wage workers from the Mexican side of the border. If they were forced to close by immigration curtailment then adverse multiplier effects would spread throughout the local economies and cause increased unemployment of domestic workers. Another argument in support of the present system is that Mexican nationals spend a great deal of their money on the American side of the border. If commuting were restricted the Mexican government could make it difficult for Mexican citizens to return home with purchases from American retail stores. Thus, according to these arguments, the American border towns may be better off on balance with the present "convenient fiction" of the green card workers, even if more tax money is required to support unemployed domestic workers and their families.[29]

Whatever the net impact of commuting on the local economies of American border towns, there has been mounting pressure to restrict the supply of commuters. Grebler summarizes the situation effectively and succinctly:

restrictionists can make a persuasive argument that there is no point in spending public funds for alleviating poverty among citizens or resident aliens if the effort is undercut by allowing commuters to take jobs at substandard wages. If the employment of Mexican commuters is considered an indirect form of foreign aid, the opposition can question the equity of such an arrangement. In this instance, the burden of foreign aid falls mainly on domestic labor competing in local job markets, instead of being distributed over the whole nation.[30]

The position of the Mexican Americans' leadership generally supports restrictions. As Robert Sanchez puts it, "we Mexican Americans feel that we have the right to reject the people involved in the commuter practice, even if they are of our own kind, and that we have the right to demand that our government do something about this very serious problem facing Mexican Americans today."[31]

If an effective manpower program is to be implemented in south Texas it seems clear that some restrictions will have to be placed on commuting and that illegal residence of Mexican citizens must be completely curtailed. Congress has already imposed a ceiling of 120,000 on Western Hemisphere immigration, though the effective maximum including relatives is probably closer to 145,000, or about the reported total number of New World immigrants in fiscal year 1964. The effects of this ceiling will depend in large measure on how it is administered. In any case, it should serve to check any sustained increase in Mexican immigration over the 40,000 annual average that has prevailed in the recent past.[32]

Another possible threat to efforts to upgrade wages and conditions of work on the American side of the border is the Mexican government's border development program. This is essentially a device to permit American companies to set up plants on the Mexican side of the border and use low-wage labor to assemble semifinished goods for the United States market. Under the program, factories that produce goods for export may import machinery, raw materials, and semifinished goods into Mexico with no payment of Mexican tariffs, and the items produced can be exported free of charge. The tariff applied by the United States is not based on the value of the product, but on the value added in the Mexican plant, which is primarily accounted for by low wages. The volume of these operations is not yet great, but it is expanding rapidly. As in the case of plants that benefit from commuters, it is not certain that firms would locate anywhere in the border area if they could not benefit from the services of low-wage Mexican workers. In any case, the program is unlikely to result in any positive gains with respect to the economic and social development of the American border area.

Despite the efforts of EDA and other government agencies to attract more firms to south Texas, it is difficult to imagine that enough economic growth can be generated in the area in the near future to increase significantly the wages and employment opportunities of the Mexican Americans residing there. The relatively underdeveloped human resources of the area and its remoteness from major centers of economic activity simply are not offset by attractive factors—other than low wages—that the region might offer to private firms. Still, numerous voices are raised demanding that south Texas be developed to a point where it approaches or equals the economic standards of the nation as a whole. Ernesto Galarza, for example, advocates "the creation by agreement between Mexico and the United States of a joint international border development authority to bring the border areas of both countries into balance by raising, at their point of contact, Mexican levels of income to American standards, not, as is happening now, by lowering American to present Mexican levels."[33] Such a proposal ignores not only the lack of attraction exercised by south Texas on American firms, but also the forces of internal migration within Mexico that would make it impossible for the border area of Mexico to achieve anything approximating the American standard of living. Similarly, the President's National Advisory Commission on Rural Poverty urges that "special attention should be focused on the welfare of migrant workers along the border in order to maintain health, housing, education, and labor standards prevailing throughout the country."[34] While it is justifiable in terms of both social justice and economic rationality to provide the Mexican Americans—whether migrants or not—with human resource development opportunities on a par with those in the country as a whole, it is not economically justifiable to demand that they be given equal job and wage opportunities *in the region* if it is not competitive with other regions. Human resource investment at least will give them the option of migrating.

Supporters of higher wages for farm workers in south Texas may be justified in calling for measures such as federal government withdrawal of all subsidies, contracts, and services from employers who employ illegal entrants or green carders to break strikes, but they also should recognize that higher wages will no doubt accelerate mechanization and increase unemployment. The stoop labor of the tomato fields has been displaced by machines and in some areas mechanical cotton pickers are harvesting 90 percent of the crop. "With shakers and air cushions two men can do in one minute what a crew used to do in one hour in the harvesting of nuts. Machines are picking grapes. Electric, not human, eyes are sorting lemons."[35] Unfortunately, the economic and social deprivation of the Mexican American migrant farm workers gives them little or nothing in the way of employment alternatives. The most recent Manpower Report of the President admits that despite efforts to strengthen services to the Mexican Americans, the MDTA program has not been very successful in reaching the most disadvantaged members of this group, particularly in rural areas. Projects are largely urban, applicants are often unable to meet training project entrance requirements, and many Mexican Americans appear to distrust the Employment Service in the belief that it cannot offer them jobs or will categorize them as farmworkers and return them to the migrant stream they are trying to leave. The Employment Service has been unable to change these attitudes due to a lack of adequate outreach facilities.[36] Poor job opportunities in south Texas have already resulted in a massive population shift to California.

Migration to California

In the 1960 Spanish surname population of the Southwest, 60 percent of the interstate movers lived in California, while only 17 percent were in Texas. Since two-thirds of the Mexican American population outside of California lived in Texas, it may be assumed that most of the movement to California originated in Texas. One three-county area in south Texas which had a population of 352,000 in 1960, slightly over two-thirds of whom were Mexican Americans, lost 10,500 persons to California between 1955 and 1960. The three counties received only 1,800 migrants from California. It has been estimated that net out-migration of Mexican Americans from Texas between 1950 and 1960 was 49,000, with most of these persons presumably going to California. The movement of Mexican Americans from Texas to California has been occurring for a considerable length of time. In 1900, Texas accounted for 69 percent of the Mexican-born population of the United States, but by 1960 this figure was down to 35 percent. Meanwhile, the California share rose from 8 to 43 percent.[37] In general, "most immigrants from Mexico now go directly to California, and there is a good deal of interstate migration from Texas (and to a lesser extent from other states) to California. Even many of the Mexican immigrants who settle initially in Texas move on to California."[38]

The flow of Mexican Americans from Texas to California has been in large measure a response to job opportunities. Between 1955 and 1959, for example, nonagricultural employment in California grew by 17 percent, while in Texas it grew by only 10 percent. In addition, Mexican Americans were attracted to California by higher wages, greater chances for social acceptance, and a familiar climate, though expanding job opportunities made it possible for these factors to operate.[39] Of course, the geographic mobility of the Mexican Americans drains young talent from less attractive areas, a problem already obvious in many parts of south Texas.[40] However, so long as this talent can be put to more productive use in California or other areas than in south Texas, migration will continue to benefit both the migrants and the nation as a whole. On the other hand, immigration of Mexican Americans without marketable skills contributed to the high unemployment rates in Los Angeles and San Francisco in the late 1950's and early 1960's, and it no doubt causes wage rates to be lower than would otherwise be the case in labor markets where Mexican Americans are a significant part of the labor supply. However, the depressing effect on wages of this immigration should not be exaggerated. Mexican Americans accounted for less than 10 percent of migration in the Southwest between 1955 and 1960. Thus Fogel concludes that "had there been no Mexican American migration to California in the past 20 years, wage rates and labor costs . . . would not be greatly higher than at present. It seems likely that other movers to California, many of them Negroes, would have filled the jobs now held by Mexican Americans."[41]

Cultural Barriers to Economic Advance

One of the main barriers to the progress of the Mexican American, as the Indian, is the widespread belief—often supported and promulgated by members of the traditional leadership—that ethnic cultural differences should be protected from all inroads by the dominant culture. This view not only discourages the introduction of modes of thought and action more conducive to rational economic behavior, but also migration which would tend to uproot an individual from his culture. Joan Moore correctly maintains that too often the isolation of the Mexican Americans "is sustained and perpetuated both by romantic anthropological nonsense about a poor and proud people who want to remain Mexican and by liberal notions of 'cultural pluralism.' "[42]

Among many Mexican Americans the notion of *la raza*—the race —functions as a kind of defense mechanism, emphasizing the uniqueness, solidarity, and loyalty of people of Mexican descent. Some equivalent concept is found in every underprivileged minority; the idea of "blackness" is another case in point. Unfortunately, many Mexican American leaders have tended to retreat behind this ideology.

The culture concept is easy to understand. It offers a comfortable sort of remoteness to the problems of Mexican Americans in a competitive world. It gives the leaders a vital role as a defender of an old and rich culture. It permits a comfortably "segregated" approach for many Anglos who prefer such an approach. And, to speculate for a moment: the self-segregating, strongly Spanish, anti-materialistic "little community"may offer a very pleasant sort of organizational Utopia both to Anglos and to Mexican-American leaders who must otherwise cope with a rapidly changing, often bewildering, modern industrial society.[43]

While it is difficult to measure the degree of adherence of an individual or group to traditional culture, it is generally accepted that the Mexican Americans residing in south Texas are more "Mexican" than those residing in Los Angeles. The rate of marriage outside the ethnic community is a good index of the disintegration of attachment and loyalty to the particular community. Data on marriages in Los Angeles in 1963 indicate that about 25 percent of the marriages involving Mexican Americans also involved an Anglo. The proportion of Mexican Americans marrying Anglos increased in the third generation, in higher occupational groups, and among younger people. Mixed marriages are becoming increasingly common, and the data imply that the social distance between generations of Mexican Americans is greater than that between some Mexican Americans and Anglos. While assimilation through intermarriage is still not imminent, the trends raise a serious question about the perpetuation of the Mexican American culture in Los Angeles. In general, "the findings indicate gradual assimilation of the Mexican-American population. Both the implied rejection of the traditional (especially by the young) and the implied acceptance of a social class culture rather than an ethnic culture among middle-class Mexican-Americans seem to spell out a growing dynamic of change."[44]

Similar movement toward acculturation and assimilation is also evident among the Spanish Americans of New Mexico. Nancie Gonzalez has found that:

> The period since World War II has brought about the greatest changes in the Hispano way of life, for the returning veterans, partly as a result of their experiences in the service, sought further technical and academic educational levels and went out to jobs requiring skills they had never had before. The continuing federal commitment to defense projects in New Mexico has helped to sustain an economy which is still not highly industrialized. Large numbers of Hispanos are entering the colleges and universities, as well as the technical schools, and many have left the state for better opportunities elsewhere. Intermarriage with Anglos has steadily increased, and many of the values and life goals usually associated with Anglo culture have been adopted by Hispanos.[45]

Even in south Texas, where many Mexican Americans are caught in a conflict between two cultures, an ever-increasing number are trying to find a respected place embracing the best elements of both worlds.[46] Still, there are far too many Mexican American leaders who promote the model of the Mexican American who "resists any and all attempts to erode his culture, his language or his life style just to satisfy the whim of a market-place morality."[47] In this vein, a great deal of emphasis is being given to resolving educational problems by raising the self-esteem of the potential Mexican American school dropout. However, it seems most unlikely that the problems involved in raising economic opportunities for Mexican Americans in our complex industrial society can be adequately dealt with by emphasizing the pride, language, and traditions of the ethnic minority. In any case, as Moore states, such an approach is simplistic, but it is politically acceptable. "And until more research is done, such thinking may well continue to dominate southwestern education."[48]

The same emphasis on Mexican American values also appears in discussions of manpower policy. For example, George Roybal urges that:

because of cultural difference and/or influence, regardless of degree, there exist significant differences in behavior, beliefs and preferences between the Mexican American and the Anglo.

The failure of government to understand the Mexican American is the cause of all failures in government programming that should affect Mexican Americans. The failure on the part of government to understand, appreciate and accept cultural differences—in terms of human values—is undoubtedly the major root of all our manpower problems.[49]

It is unquestionably important that the personnel of agencies dealing with the Mexican Americans understand and appreciate their culture, as Roybal insists. However, to "accept" all cultural differences may be to condemn the Mexican American to a continuing life on the margin of American society. Even the most sympathetic students of Mexican American problems acknowledge that traditional values tend to play down the importance of education and to foster a short time horizon that leaves long run welfare to forces beyond the individual's control. As we have seen, the more economically progressive Mexican Americans tend to adopt the values of the larger society and the trend seems to be accelerating in this direction. But this phenomenon is most apparent in Los Angeles and other areas where the advance of the Mexican American has been relatively rapid despite persistent—though declining— barriers to equal opportunity. The really hard core problem area is south Texas. In fact, much of the progress made by Mexican Americans can be explained by the shift in their regional composition from Texas to California.

Operationally feasible answers to the employment problems of south Texas, which includes the nation's largest concentration of migratory workers, are being sought by various federal, state, and local agencies. In fiscal year 1966, the Texas Education Agency, with OEO funds, developed an adult education program designed to give a group of 3,000 migrant farm workers a level of scholastic achievement as close to the eighth grade level as possible. However, only limited vocational training was included in the program, and most of the participants drifted back into the migrant stream because of their lack of marketable skills.[50] The 1967 Manpower Report of the President summarized the plight of the more than 125,000 migrant workers in south Texas in the following terms: (1) Mechanization is rapidly shrinking their opportunities for farm work, and, although their average earnings are less than $1,200 a year, they do not have the skills needed for alternative forms of employment. (2) Many of the workers have a language problem as well as low educational attainment. (3) There is insufficient demand for labor in general in the area to warrant training for local jobs. (4) Many of the workers are reluctant to move because of family and community ties. (5) Availability of low-cost housing (even though it is often substandard) in their present communities keeps them tied there. Finally, (6) training plus migration to industrial areas frequently represent their only real hope for employment and independence.[51]

What is particularly noteworthy in this evaluation is its frankness concerning the lack of job opportunities in south Texas and its advocacy of programs designed to train the migrants for employment in other areas. It would seem, however, that adopting this point of view as a policy approach would be blocked by the alleged reluctance of the workers to relocate, even assuming that their educational and skill levels were upgraded. Reluctance to migrate, as we have seen, is almost invariably raised as a reason to try to develop lagging regions rather than establish relocation programs. But we also have seen that this issue is not as important as it has generally been made out to be; the people involved are much more willing to move than their leaders or public policy makers seem willing to admit. Does this also apply to the Mexican Americans of south Texas? The great migration flow from Texas to California is itself evidence of the mobility of the Mexican American. Further evidence in this regard is available from a pilot mobility project that many federal and state officials hold to be the most successful to date in dealing with unemployed migrant workers in the Rio Grande Valley. Since this project could become a model for future policy programs, it merits detailed consideration.

Relocating Mexican American Migrants in Texas: The Ling-Temco-Vought Experience

The growth of the Dallas-Fort Worth area has been so rapid that trained and trainable manpower has become extremely scarce. Until recently, Vought Aeronautics, a Ling-Temco-Vought company, carried out its training programs within its Dallas plant, offering on-the-job training and a classroom curriculum. As its needs expanded, a new training facility was opened at nearby Grand Prairie, and its recruiting program was expanded to include areas that had been considered too distant. In 1964, L-T-V, under the spur of opportunities opened by the MDTA, increased its training program in cooperation with the Bureau of Apprenticeship and Training. In late 1965, L-T-V decided that a modular training unit—a school temporarily established in a locality of high unemployment—was the solution to its growing manpower needs. The Texas Employment Commission and the Federal Bureau of Employment Security suggested locating such a unit in the Rio Grande Valley. After initial reluctance because of the great distance separating the plant from the Valley, L-T-V decided to go ahead with a training program in the Valley. With the support of various federal agencies, L-T-V developed a pilot program to train 750 Mexican Americans from the areas surrounding McAllen, Rio Grande City, and Harlingen as aircraft assemblers who could work in the Dallas area upon completion of the program. L-T-V prepared training outlines, lists of tools and equipment, and the overall conceptualization of the program and forwarded this package of information to the Department of Labor, HEW, HUD, the Bureau of Employment Security, the Texas Education Agency, and the Texas Employment Commission. The public school system provided a training facility at McAllen, EDA financed the conversion and renovation of an old laundry building that is now the training facility in Rio Grande City, and a suitable building was found in Harlingen at an abandoned air base.[52]

As of August 26, 1968, 752 trainees had entered the training program in the Valley. Of this number, only 60 terminated their training while still in the Valley (28 in Harlingen, 16 in Rio Grande City, and 16 in McAllen). Inability to do the required work was only a relatively minor reason for termination. Data for the entire Texas Labor Mobility Project, for which L-T-V accounted for three-quarters of the relocatees, indicate that as of July 1, 1968, the average cost per relocatee was $550, of which $386 was for relocation assistance allowances. The average age of the relocatees was 26.2 years, and the average number of dependents was 2.6. The mean level of schooling was 9.4 years. Before entering the program, the average relocatee had earned $1.48 per hour in the last job held, but he had been unemployed for 9.3 weeks. The beginning hourly wage on the job for L-T-V workers was $2.50. Of the 477 workers who had moved to jobs with L-T-V in the Dallas area prior to July 1, 1968, 97 percent were still on the job.[53]

The L-T-V program was designed as a comprehensive training and assistance program. In addition to the company's own participation, the Bureau of Apprenticeship and Training acted as overall government coordinator and provided funds to assist in the on-the-job training program. HEW, in conjunction with the Texas Education Agency, provided funds to conduct classroom training through local school systems. HEW was also supposed to take care of the trainees' health needs in the Rio Grande Valley but failed to do so because of lack of funds. HUD was supposed to assist in finding housing for the workers in the Dallas area, but this agency also failed to live up to expectations because of lack of funds. In consequence, L-T-V took the responsibility for getting children into schools in the Dallas area and for the health needs of the workers and their families. The Texas Employment Commission lent assistance in finding housing agreeable to the workers. The Office of Economic Opportunity assisted in providing the basics of reading, writing, and arithmetic the trainees needed to assimilate their training. Counseling services were also made available to the workers and their families both in the Rio Grande Valley and in the Dallas area. The importance of comprehensive relocation assistance is illustrated by the fact that while L-T-V's retention rate was 97 percent, that for a Fort Worth firm which took 99 Mexican Americans from the Rio Grande Valley without adequate training or assistance was only 67 percent as of July 1, 1968. (Only three other firms took over four Mexican American relocatees, and the most that any one of these took was nine.)

The author visited the L-T-V training facilities in the Rio Grande Valley and talked with numerous company staff members and Mexican American trainees in September, 1968. The company officials and teachers were all enthusiastic about the possibilities for training migrant workers for permanent employment in urban areas where jobs are available for persons with the necessary skills. They found the trainees for the most part to be interested in advancing themselves and quite willing and able to learn. For their part, the trainees welcomed the opportunity to acquire a skill and find a ready opportunity to use it. When questioned about the alleged reluctance of Mexican Americans to leave the Valley, they generally replied that they would certainly be reluctant to leave if they had to go to an urban area with no training and no assistance in adapting to an urban environment. Both company staff and Mexican American trainees agreed without exception that the possibilities for training and relocating Mexican Americans out of the Valley have only barely been scratched. Several stated, with reference to unemployed and underemployed Mexican Americans, that "the whole Valley" could be moved out given "a program like this." L-T-V itself would have been willing to double the size of its program—and perhaps even go beyond that in the future—if the cooperating agencies had

had the funds to expand their participation accordingly. The company's experience is instructive for all who are quick to deplore policies designed to assist the relocation of persons from lagging areas to areas of economic opportunity:

We have always considered distance to be a major factor in prohibiting expansion into other labor markets. To the average individual, the very process of changing from one type of work to another can be a traumatic experience; however, this can be minimized if the man can daily return to the familiar, comforting environment of his own home. We have always felt it was out of the question to consider that he could survive the job transition and also go through a second traumatic shift of moving from his rural or small town habitat to the city.

However, with the assistance of the state and federal governments, we are now in the process of proving that theory to be out-moded.[54]

Another indication of worker mobility preferences is given by responses to a post-screening detailed interview schedule which is filled out for all persons who pass an initial screening for participation in MDTA labor mobility projects. Sample data for responses from participants in the L-T-V project as well as responses from persons who were rejected for one reason or another from participation (but who passed initial screening) were made available to the author.[55] In each case stratified samples were taken to assure that all classes of trainees (and time periods for those rejected) would be appropriately included. The sample of participants included 176 respondents, while that for rejected persons included 75 of the 156 individual files available on September 20, 1968.

In response to the question, "Since you last moved to your present community, have you ever thought seriously of moving from there?" 80 percent of the participants replied affirmatively (as did 91 percent of the applicants who were rejected after initial screening; the relevant proportions for this group will be given hereafter in parentheses). Eighty-nine percent (96 percent) of the participants who had thought seriously of moving gave no local employment or poor wages as their main reason. When asked why they decided to stay in their present community, 98 percent (97 percent) gave no satisfactory job elsewhere, lack of funds, or other economic considerations as the reason or reasons, though other factors—such as family considerations—may also have played a part in the decision not to move. In response to the question, "If you could do as you please, would you prefer to remain in your present community?" 41 percent (69 percent) replied in the affirmative. When the contingency of employment opportunities was included, the combined total of those preferring to remain in their present community was 52 percent (71 percent). The principal advantage that the participants found in their home communities was family considerations; 80 percent (79 percent) listed family considerations as a reason and most gave it as the sole reason. No local employment or poor local wages were given by 99 percent (100 percent) as the main disadvantages in staying in the present community.

All participants (99 percent) indicated a willingness to move to another area for a job if relocation assistance of the type provided by L-T-V were available. While many expressed a willingness to move anywhere in the country, 60 percent (61 percent) limited their response to a willingness to locate anywhere in Texas—which could still imply a move of considerable distance. Respondents were also questioned regarding the kind of place in which they would be willing to live. Four alternatives were given: a large city (250,000 and over), a smaller city (10,000–250,000), a small town (less than 10,000), or a farm. The smaller city was the clear favorite among these alternatives. Seventy-nine percent (81 percent) would be willing to live in a large city and 80 percent (77 percent) would be willing to live in a small town, but 95 percent (93 percent) would be willing to live in a smaller city. Only 35 percent (47 percent) would be willing to live on a farm. For those persons expressing a strong preference to live in one of the four alternative places, 50 percent (49 percent) chose a smaller city.

In general, these results indicate a high mobility potential for Mexican Americans in south Texas resulting from the push of poor economic opportunities at home and the pull of job opportunities elsewhere. This pattern was not limited to those who participated in the L-T-V project; if anything, those who were rejected after initial screening showed an even more pronounced willingness to move than those who were accepted. It was evident that the preferred place of residence would be a smaller city rather than a large city on the one hand, or a small town or farm on the other. While the trainees in fact moved to a large city, they nevertheless have been remarkably successful in adapting to their new environment, no doubt because of the comprehensive assistance that was provided.

In conclusion, it must be acknowledged that the L-T-V program does have some questionable aspects. As already indicated, the *de facto* cooperation of government agencies and the company fell somewhat short of the ideal envisioned on paper. One may also wonder if the jobs going to Mexican Americans from the Rio Grande Valley could not go as well to unemployed and underemployed Negroes from the Dallas-Fort Worth area or other areas closer than the Valley. In other words, the government may be subsidizing a project that serves to perpetuate Negro job market problems in the relevant markets. Some critics have also charged that L-T-V is obtaining government subsidies for a program that it would carry on to its own advantage even in the absence of subsidies. However, company officials indicated to the author that even though they would have desired more Mexican American trainees from the Valley, the 730 workers would be all they actually would take if the government did not continue to support the labor mobility program. Since these conversations Congress has agreed to extend the program, but no funding decisions have been made. Presumably, however, L-T-V will be able to continue to recruit, train, and relocate unemployed Mexican Americans, most of them from the migrant labor stream. In any case, it is fair to say that even if the L-T-V project would go on to the benefit of the company even without government subsidies, the Bureau of Employment Security still must be credited with initiating the project in the first place. With the advantages of employing Mexican Americans from the Valley thus demonstrated to L-T-V, it is quite possible that other companies might also wish to undertake similar projects. L-T-V officials have expressed willingness to consult with other firms who might wish to do so. There are still substantial labor shortages in the Dallas-Fort Worth area, and some companies apparently realize the need for and would like to emulate L-T-V's comprehensive approach to training and relocating Valley workers. But they simply do not know how to go about it. The Department of Labor and the Texas Employment Commission could perform a valuable service by acting as intermediaries for linking the information L-T-V is willing to share and firms desiring to know more about implementing a comprehensive relocation program.

It also has been argued that the project is skimming the cream off the top of the relevant population. In many respects this is true. The educational attainment and language problems of the relocatees—while very real—are still not so severe as among the more hard-core unemployed and underemployed in the Valley. Nevertheless, L-T-V cannot be blamed for desiring the potentially most productive workers available. Nor can training and relocation projects of this type be expected to solve the deep and long standing problems of the most deprived segments of the Mexican American population. Eventually relocation may benefit many members of the hard-core poor and unemployed, but in the interim a great deal more attention must be given to ameliorating their formidable social and educational problems. It must also be acknowledged that for some, particularly those in the older age groups, welfare is probably the only feasible type of assistance that the nation as a whole can offer.

Finally, it should be noted that there is one respect in which the L-T-V project may have an easier task than similar projects centered on other lagging regions. Since the trainees are drawn primarily from persons associated with the migrant labor force, the local leadership in the lagging area may be less likely in this case than in others involving full-time "permanent" residents to decry the loss of "their people." To be sure, some Valley merchants (and others) have complained that relocation involves a decline in demand for their goods and services, but such complaints do not appear to have exerted any real influence on the operation of the project. In other areas it is likely that political pressures against even voluntary relocation will be more formidable.

Summary and Conclusions

While considerable attention has been given to formulating programs to aid the social and economic advance of the Negro, relatively little attention has been paid to the often equally severe problems of our Mexican American population. The Mexican American is not handicapped by discrimination to the same degree as the Negro, but he still is at a disadvantage in the job market because of lack of education and training. The Mexican American also suffers from two difficulties that do not directly affect the Negro. First, although Mexican Americans constitute the largest minority in the Southwest, their geographic concentration in this area tends to make the rest of the nation unaware of their problems and therefore unresponsive to them. Second, pressures resulting from migrating and commuting from Mexico continually tend to depress wages and job opportunities of Mexican Americans on the United States side of the border.

There is a critical need for substantial upgrading of the quality and quantity of education received by the Mexican population. Although enrollment rates for Mexican American children are not much below those for Anglo children in much of the Southwest, greatly expanded adult educational and vocational training facilities are needed; and cultural factors, migrant work patterns, and poor enforcement of school attendance laws combine to make the education of Mexican American children in south Texas a national disgrace. There is clear and abundant evidence that increased education pays off in terms of concrete economic gains for the Mexican Americans, and their main hope for continuing progress lies in increasing their educational attainment and job qualifications.

If, as Fogel suggests, "in our society the flow of causation is frequently from income to education rather than in the reverse direction,"[56] then it is particularly urgent that the depressed economic conditions of the residents of south Texas be ameliorated. Migration to better economic opportunities in California and northern Texas is one means by which many Mexican Americans from south Texas have achieved some measure of progress, but so long as migrants and commuters from Mexico continue to flow into the area, wages will remain low and unemployment rates will remain high. Of course, with the exception of cheap labor, the advantages that south Texas offers to firms are so minimal that industrial employment opportunities would not be bright relative to the rest of the nation in any case. And any significant increase in agricultural wage rates will only accelerate the already rapid rate of mechanization. The implementation of any effective manpower program in south Texas requires that some restrictions be placed on commuting "green carders," and that immigration be reduced. Pressures within Mexico virtually assure that Mexican citizens will continue to move to the border in large numbers, and that many will seek work in the United States or in American plants attracted to Mexico under the Mexican government's border development program. Congress seems to be moving in the direction of greater restrictions to protect the Mexican American population, which heretofore has borne most of the brunt of our indirect efforts at foreign aid with respect to the commuter question. Perhaps the best approach to this question would be a gradual tightening of restrictions to permit the Mexicans to adjust to the new circumstances.

Of course, reducing pressures from the other side of the border will not make south Texas any more attractive to industry, nor will it do much to improve employment opportunities in the face of growing mechanization in agriculture. What is called for first of all is a good basic education program (including adult education) that respects and takes account of the minority ethnic culture and values, but does not use them as an excuse for evading the complexities of our urban-industrial society. Adequate job training is also a necessity, but this implies training for jobs that will most likely be found outside of south Texas. Finally, comprehensive relocation programs must be made available to those persons who choose to leave the region. There is considerable evidence that such programs are feasible and that they benefit the relocatees, the receiving firms, and even the government, since savings in welfare payments and increased revenue from payroll taxes more than offset the modest costs of comprehensive relocation assistance. These points also apply to many areas of the Southwest where poverty and unemployment among the Mexican American populations are at high levels, but south Texas nevertheless remains the principal problem area.

Chapter 9

The Industrialization of Rural America: Is It Feasible?

In the preceding chapters it has been emphasized that one of the common characteristics of the nation's lagging areas is their lack of rapidly growing urban centers, which increasingly have become the foci for expanding national economic activity. In this chapter, a more general view will be taken of attempts to stimulate economic growth in lagging, nonurbanized areas, and of both the economic and noneconomic arguments that often are used to justify programs of this nature. The nature and role of external economies and diseconomies will be given particular attention in considering investment efficiency from a spatial opportunity cost perspective.

Promoting Industrialization of Rural Areas

In recent years there has been a veritable outpouring of policy proposals to industrialize rural areas of the nation. For example, the 1968 Manpower Report of the President, while pointing out that some outmigration from rural and other lagging areas will continue to be necessary, proposes that the basic need of such areas is for programs designed to discover their economic potential and to promote their output and employment growth. It points out that:

222

Given financial and other help in their redevelopment efforts (and sometimes even without such help), labor areas with high unemployment have often demonstrated a capability for economic growth which reversed their previous decline. Within the large depressed regions, small cities have been identified as potential growth centers; it is hoped that these can be developed as employment and service centers for surrounding distressed rural areas.[1]

The Report goes on to argue that it is likely that within the next twenty or thirty years new growth centers will be established and existing small towns expanded into growth centers in rural areas. It points out that population sizes of from 50,000 to 500,000 have been mentioned in connection with such centers, but suggests that centers with a population of 10,000 to 50,000 may be adequate. (It will be recalled that Berry's findings indicate that an urban place with fewer than 50,000 inhabitants is unlikely to have any appreciable impact on its surrounding hinterland; see p. 153.) The Report calls for a "whole array of public and private measures" to transform the "potential demand" for the people and other resources of rural America into effective private demand. These measures would include improving transportation and other infrastructure and improving the educational and training opportunities available to rural residents. The alleged "vigorous growth potential" that "lies dormant in so many rural communities" may also need to be activated by investment grants, loans, tax advantages, and other special incentives.[2]

The Department of Agriculture has been giving particular attention to developing rural areas as an alternative to the growth of large metropolitan areas. In a recently issued report,[3] the Department argues that our big cities have more people and problems than they can handle, whereas many villages, small towns, and countryside areas are being drained of people and economic opportunity. Our urban centers, it urges, are congested, noisy, and full of tension, surrounded by polluted air and water, and burdened with too many people on relief, many of whom have come from rural areas without being properly equipped to cope with urban life. The report states (without referring to its source) that when a New Yorker moves to the suburbs, he costs (presumably in marginal terms though this is not indicated) the city $21,000 to provide facilities for his daily journey to and from work. In Washington, D.C., the marginal cost for each commuter is given at $23,000. In contrast, Fargo, North Dakota, with a population of 50,000, has an annual budget of $487,000 for all its transportation facilities. "Washington must spend that much to add only 21 commuter cars,"[4] the report concludes. Of course, Fargo probably does not need to provide extra facilities for a rapidly expanding population; its budget, which consists of a high proportion of operating expenses, should not be compared to the marginal capital costs of large cities. Nevertheless, it is clear that if these figures are at all reliable, the external diseconomies of large agglomerations are indeed formidable with respect to just this one type of public infrastructure. The argument is put in more general terms by Mayor Davis of Kansas City:

A city can get too big simply because the cost of providing services increases all out of proportion to total population growth. This becomes perfectly clear when put on a per capita basis, which is about $120 a year in Kansas City. In a city twice this size, per capita costs would rise to more than $200 a person.[5]

Similar results have been obtained by the present author from United States, French, and Belgian data.[6]

The Agriculture report finally maintains that, in addition to the financial costs, there are adverse physical and psychological effects that go with megalopolitan life. Here the eminent biologist René Dubos is quoted: "some of the most profound effects of the environment created by urban and technicalized civilization may not be on the physical health, but on man's behavioral patterns and mental development."[7] Dubos further fears that the impersonality of our large cities "is producing a gross impoverishment of individuals which could lead to the death of this civilization."[8]

What alternatives does the Department of Agriculture propose in the face of this "collision between man and his environment?" It envisages the revitalization of rural villages and small cities as well as the creation of new towns, so that each of these entities will have its own jobs and industries, its own college or university, its own medical center, its own cultural and entertainment center, "and with an agriculture fully sharing in the national prosperity."[9] These "Communities of Tomorrow," which may extend over several counties, will be capable of reversing the migration streams that presently are leading people to the big metropolitan areas.

The report correctly states that the major cause of the present "imbalance" of people and jobs between rural and urban areas is the relative availability of jobs in metropolitan areas and their lack in smaller cities, towns, and the countryside. Between 1945 and 1960 all the net gain in new jobs took place in large urban centers. New jobs in the smaller cities and in towns were offset by rural job losses in agriculture, extractive, and other resource-based industries. Although 400,000 jobs a year were created from 1962 to 1964 in counties with no city as large as 50,000 (compared to 800,000 jobs per year in large cities or SMSA's), this rate was still only about two-thirds of that necessary to halt the migration from the countryside to cities. In consequence, the report recommends that:

> Communities of tomorrow must expand job opportunities fast enough to absorb the countryside's natural population growth and to provide jobs for those who would prefer to move from impacted city centers to less densely populated areas.
> Jobs can be created by expanding industry, business, and agriculture; by developing health, education, and recreation facilities; by building new homes and community facilities; and by providing all the services demanded by a prosperous, progressive society.[10]

What is to draw private capital to rural areas and small towns beside government investment? The report maintains that the places that will be the "Communities of Tomorrow" already have numerous advantages, including plant sites that cost less to buy and build on, space for plant expansion and for packing, and the opportunity to live within easy commuting distance of both job and recreation areas.[11]

The desire to promote industrial growth and to limit outmigration from primarily rural areas also is apparent, explicitly or implicitly,

in some of the relevant scholarly literature. Gene Laber, for example, appears concerned that "counties experiencing employment
declines actually can be missed in the [EDA] designation process if
they adjust to their potential unemployment with out-migration or
reduction in labor force participation rates."[12] Why an area that is
adjusting to employment declines by means of outmigration should
be aided is not clear, unless it is assumed that federal subsidies
should be used to maintain the number of persons resident in any
given place, no matter how antieconomic such a policy would be.

William Nicholls, in his well-known study *Southern Tradition and
Regional Progress,* argues that the South's historical lag can only
be overcome by the industrial-urban development of the region.
This position is strongly endorsed by the present study (see Chapter 3). However, Nicholls goes far beyond urging promotion of
growth in the South's leading cities and SMSA's; he wants to emphasize the industrial-urban development of rural areas. Among the
reasons for his position is that it is easier to get rural people to
change occupations if they do not have to change their residences.
Moreover, local nonfarm jobs have a bigger impact on local incomes
than do distant jobs, and the drain on local human capital is reduced
if outmigration can be avoided. In general, Nicholls believes that
once industrial growth in rural areas is initiated it will become self-
sustaining.[13]

The most authoritative and most publicized study advocating
industrialization of rural areas is the recently published final report
of the President's National Advisory Commission on Rural Poverty.[14]
The Commission was composed of distinguished leaders representing various professional, occupational, educational, and political
organizations. The recommendations of the Commission were based
on information obtained from numerous public and private sources.
Members of the Commission's staff and leading students of rural
poverty from outside the staff assembled and analyzed an enormous
amount of data, including testimony of the rural poor. The Commission deliberated as a body to assess the facts of rural poverty and to
prepare its recommendations. With a few possible exceptions, the

Commission believed that its recommendations could be applied on a nationwide basis. In many respects these recommendations are well taken in view of the difficulties confronting the nation's 14 million rural poor. Nevertheless, as is the case with the studies discussed previously, the general perspective of the Commission's approach to rural poverty is distorted by its failure to come to grips adequately with the issue of population migration. The nature and consequences of the shortcomings in this regard deserve careful consideration.

The Commission's basic approach to the rural poor implies that solutions to their problems should not entail significant population migration. "There is plenty of work that needs to be done in rural areas. . . . The rural poor want jobs in their home community, or within reasonable commuting distance."[15] Although it is acknowledged at one point in the report that many of them do not mind moving to a small or moderate sized city for work,[16] the Commission avoids encouraging even such limited moves. Indeed, one of the "specific beliefs to which all members of the Commission subscribe" is that

> Every citizen of the United States must have equal access to opportunities for economic and social advancement without discrimination because of race, religion, national origin, or *place of residence* [17]

The Commission finds that in addition to widespread discrimination against minority groups

> Rural people in general, white as well as nonwhite, have been the victims of another more subtle kind of discrimination, based on location —the fact that they reside in rural areas.[18]

In response, the Commission recommends that rural people be given the same opportunity as urban people to participate in all social and economic programs designed to improve the quality of life.

The social costs of congestion in large urban areas constitute the principal justification for the Commission's position on migration. Thus, it finds that many migrants merely exchange "life in a rural slum for life in an urban slum, at exorbitant cost to themselves, to the cities, and to rural America as well."[19] The Commission is concerned that

industrial development within urban ghettos may trigger more senseless migration of the rural poor to equally depressed and socially isolated urban ghettos. Industrial development of, and job creation in, smaller cities and towns closer to where the rural poor now live and within commuting distance of their residences is the wiser alternative. But tax incentives are powerful tools to influence industrial location and should be used.[20]

In addition to arrangements to lower taxes, the Commission proposes that self-sustaining growth be promoted in rural areas by other types of subsidies, including grants, low interest loans, and the construction of industrial sites for new and expanding industries.[21] It believes that subsidies financed by the federal government should be much greater, because those which are locally financed often lower the ability of communities to finance and pay for public facilities and services, or threaten local tax revenues. Moreover, the effect of subsidies on industrial location increasingly tends to be cancelled out by the rapidly spreading practice of community utilization of industrial development bonds and concessions on local taxes. In addition, the more depressed communities are likely to be outbid by the more affluent.[22]

The Commission acknowledges that there are some rural areas that are not economically viable and therefore not capable of attracting industry. Nevertheless, it clearly believes that it is possible to attract sufficient industry throughout the country to a large number of smaller towns and cities in and near depressed areas. It also urges that "the Federal Government use a portion of its procurement expenses and investment expenditures for new installations to stimulate growth in particular lagging regions and areas."[23] No consideration is given to the opportunity cost that would be involved if this recommendation were followed, though it is certain that a large subsidy element would accompany politically determined preferential consideration for lagging regions and areas.

In view of the nature and magnitude of the forces influencing industrial location, how realistic is the Commission's faith in localized subsidies and strategies to induce industrial decentralization sufficient to absorb rural unemployment and underemployment?

Creating Jobs in Lagging Rural Areas: The Evidence

With the exception of a few programs, most notably the Tennessee Valley Authority, the United States is a relatively late starter in utilizing central government policy to guide the growth of large lagging regions. Thus the experience of other countries provides some valuable insights into the difficulties presented by such an approach. In France, for example, efforts have been made for well over a decade to promote economic activity in lagging regions, particularly those of the West, and to limit outmigration from these areas. French policy has included central government infrastructure investment, direct financial incentives to private enterpreneurs, measures to restrict the location of firms in the Paris region, and deliberate decentralization of government agencies and nationalized enterprises. These activities have been designed to promote the growth of economic activity in regions characterized by high outmigration levels, relatively low purchasing power, and relatively few household and public amenities.[24] Yet they still have not significantly improved the relative position of the regions of the West. The data in column 1 of Table 32 show that the ratio of inmigrant to outmigrant workers is lowest in the largely agricultural regions of the West, which accounts for the country's eight lowest ranking regions. Aquitaine benefits from the presence of Bordeaux, and the Center benefits from its proximity to the Paris region, yet even the values for these western regions rank relatively low in comparison with the other regions of France. The relatively low average household income values of the regions of the West are clearly seen in column 2. Moreover, as the index values in column 3 show, the growth in average annual wages between 1956 and 1964 was greater than the national average in only three of the regions of the West.

TABLE 32: MIGRATION, INCOME, AND INDUSTRIAL CONSTRUCTION
DATA BY FRENCH PLANNING REGION

	(1) Number of inmigrant workers for each out-migrant worker (1954–1962)	(2) Average household income (1962), in francs	(3) Average annual wage index in 1964 (1956 = 100)	(4) Industrial surface con-structed in 1964 (thousand square meters)[a]
Paris Region	2.56	16,369	200	572
North and East				
Champagne	0.73	10,040	194	236
Picardy	0.77	11,261	198	279
Upper Normandy	0.87	10,758	197	226
Nord	0.67	10,245	195	466
Lorraine	0.97	11,253	185	203
Alsace	1.10	10,798	205	209
Franche-Comté	0.95	10,709	202	148
Burgundy	0.72	8,284	194	231
Rhône-Alps	1.34	10,376	210	699
Provence-Côte d'Azur	1.23	10.970	202	229
West				
Center	0.87	8,515	206	372
Lower Normandy	0.51	9,283	199	183
Loire Country	0.58	7,503	189	350
Brittany	0.38	7,297	209	256
Limousin	0.52	7,429	191	43
Auvergne	0.66	8,255	192	135
Poitou-Charentes	0.60	7,134	196	187
Aquitaine	0.72	8,934	201	257
Midi-Pyrénées	0.62	8,523	200	175
Languedoc	0.58	9,512	205	97
France	—	10,823	202	5,553

[a] Includes only projects involving over 500 square meters.

Source: Régionalisation du budget d'équipment et coordination des investissements publics au regard des objectifs de l'aménagement du territoire (Paris: Imprimerie Nationale, 1966), pp. 328, 367, 455, 468.

The data in column 4 show that 37 percent of new French industrial surface construction in 1964 was located in the West; the West's population also represents 37 percent of the French total. Industrial surface created in the regions of the West in 1964 was 127 percent greater than that created in 1960, while the comparable value for all of France was 58 percent. However, in 1964 new industrial surface in the West grew by only 26 percent over the previous year's level, whereas for France as a whole it grew by 29 percent. The corresponding values in 1965 were 2.8 and 0.8 percent. In 1966 new industrial surface declined by 3.7 percent for France as a whole, and by 3.5 percent in the West.[25] Thus the growth of industrial surface in the West clearly is not sufficient to close the gap between its industry and that of the rest of France.

Italian efforts to promote the industrialization of the Mezzogiorno and thereby halt outmigration also have met with disappointing results. Schachter's thorough study of Italian regional development problems concludes that despite the government's efforts "over the last twelve years, the economic problems which for so long have plagued southern Italy remain unsolved. There are still nearly one million unemployed (and maybe more, were all underemployed accounted for), and the vast majority continues to live in abject poverty."[26]

Similarly, Benjamin Higgins notes the almost universal tendency for politicians to believe in the mutual consistency of policies to maximize national economic growth and to reduce regional disparities by investment in lagging regions. On the other hand, there is considerable reluctance to seriously explore the possibility that development of poor regions may best be promoted by investment in rich regions, or that the best way to help the people of lagging regions might be to encourage them to migrate to richer ones.[27]

The United States, with its Economic Development Administration established to help designated "distressed" areas (with express provision in the Act against encouraging out-migration), its Appalachia program and its antipoverty campaign, is no exception to the rule; area and regional development policy is designed primarily to help poor people where they are. Canada . . . is in general following the same format. . . .

Even the province of Quebec, despite its open espousal of French concepts and practices of regional planning, has come dangerously close to
making the same mistake. The Eastern part of Quebec, chosen as the
pilot region for the regional development of the province, is perhaps the
poorest and most stagnant area with similar population in the entire
province.[28]

However, Higgins notes that the Quebec planners have at least
attempted to establish growth centers in the more dynamic towns
within their pilot region, and they have recommended outmigration
from the more hopeless areas.[29]

It is difficult to find any case where hothouse efforts to promote
the development of large lagging regions have met with success.
Whatever advantages rural areas may have in terms of a stable labor
force that is relatively cheap and plentiful, of adequate and relatively
cheap land, and of easy access to work and recreation areas, they
still have a host of disadvantages to overcome. The cheap land and
low tax rates may be more than offset by low levels of services.
There are relatively few business contacts with other producers or
auxiliary business services. Labor may be plentiful, but it may prove
costly to adapt the relatively untrained labor force to the firm's
needs. The local market will probably not be significant, and frequently firms find it advantageous to locate near competitors rather
than at a distance, for reasons that will be discussed below (see
pages 234–5). Bad connections with long distance traffic may mean
higher transport costs and more time in transit, though these problems have become less important than in the past. Rural areas also
tend to be lacking in cultural and educational facilities. Finally,
there is often a great deal of mistrust of industrialization in rural
areas, including the mistrust felt by local "leaders" who do not wish
to alter the status quo.[30] Moreover, recent American and foreign
evidence concerning greater equality in the geographical distribution
of manufacturing does not indicate any corresponding lessening of
regional income differences or any relatively greater attractiveness
of small towns or lagging regions. Recent growth in total national
employment has been accounted for primarily by expanding tertiary

activities, which have been located for the most part in metropolitan areas. Those industries that have tended to leave metropolitan areas have been characterized by relative stagnation or decline; they frequently seek cheap labor in areas with surplus agricultural populations. Rapidly expanding sectors, on the other hand, have favored already concentrated regions because of their numerous external economies of agglomeration.[31]

It should be emphasized that the advantages of larger urban areas cannot be explained simply in terms of the traditional economic base approach, or in terms of classical location theory. The older export base approach never really came to grips with the process by which an area amasses overhead capital and by which it acquires new export bases. Similarly, classical location theory, including central place theory, relied on static analysis of the transport costs required to overcome distance under general equilibrium conditions, i.e., with "other things equal." More recently, greater attention has been given to the dynamics of urban-industrial growth. Thus, Wilbur Thompson effectively maintains that:

> The economic base of the larger metropolitan area is, then, the creativity of its universities and research parks, the sophistication of its engineering firms and financial institutions, the persuasiveness of its public relations and advertising agencies, the flexibility of its transportation networks and utility systems, and all the other dimensions of infrastructure that facilitate the quick and orderly transfer from old dying bases to new growing ones. A diversified set of current exports—"breadth"— softens the shock of exogenous change, while a rich infrastructure— "depth"—facilitates the adjustment to change by providing the socioeconomic institutions and physical facilities needed to initiate new enterprises, transfer capital from old to new forms, and retrain labor.[32]

The size and diversity of the large city also creates certain mutual advantages over rural areas for both employers and workers. While differing groups of workers in the city do not respond in the same manner and to the same degree to increases in employment opportunities or declines in unemployment,[33] they are more likely than workers in small towns or rural areas to find equivalent jobs in other firms if their employer leaves the area. This type of employment stability, which results from industrial diversity and which benefits both worker and employer, is to be differentiated from the stability that employers are alleged to find in the rural labor force. The latter is too often based on a lack of real employment alternatives for workers. Moreover, acquisition of skills and increased industriousness is encouraged by opportunities for mobility. This may explain, at least in part, Borts' finding that rising costs, particularly wages, that result from capital inflows are not a determining influence because they are offset by increases in productivity.[34]

The expanding role of the tertiary sector in urban growth deserves particular attention. Aydalot has argued that whereas industrial location in the past was primarily determined by factors such as energy sources, water, and transportation facilities, today entrepreneurs tend to be more attracted by agglomeration economies, and especially by tertiary services in the widest sense (including social amenities as well as business services).[35] As pointed out earlier, nearly all of the net growth in total employment in the United States since World War II has occurred in the service sector (trade, finance, insurance, real estate, general government, and personal, professional, business, and repair services), which now accounts for over half of both employment and gross national product. Moreover, in contrast to manufacturing, the firm in the service sector typically is small and owner-managed, and often non-corporate.[36] It is precisely these types of activity which, along with small manufacturing firms whose output is highly variable in both form and volume (for example, apparel, publishing and printing, sporting goods, toys), show the greatest tendency to cluster together in order to reap numerous external economies. The products or services involved are relatively unstandardized and cannot be stockpiled; frequent communication is necessary with both material suppliers and customers. In general, clustering creates a common pool for space, materials, and labor, meeting the inherent uncertainties of the small plants which accompany them. The supply of factors which are provided in the aggregate is more stable than the needs of the individual firms which make up the complex, resulting in a fuller average utilization of the productive factors available in the area as a whole.[37]

Among tertiary activities an increasingly important part is being played by amenities. "That the 'geography of amenities' plays an important part in the selection of location for people and a number of industries is increasingly recognized by students of statistics and by business managers."[38] Therefore, "the massive economic success of regions richly endowed with physical amenities seems a logical development at a time of rising standards of living, lengthening of leisure time for the mass, greater mobility of people, and better education for all."[39] If the growth of amenities may be regarded as indicative of progress, it is significant that this growth points in the direction of cities, that is, in the direction of a relatively few growth centers. The failure of stern legislation in many countries to stop a trend of concentration in small areas is clearly indicative of the power of the economic, social, and psychological forces shaping modern urbanization. It is also indicative of the increasingly footloose nature of economic activity. Joseph Spengler estimates that today only about 7 percent of the labor force needs to be located close to natural resources, whereas only thirty years ago nearly 30 percent were resource-bound. In other words, the great preponderance of the labor force now is potentially footloose or must locate in proximity to consumers who are themselves relatively footloose, and economic opportunity is associated less with land and natural resources and more with the presence of capital and human skill.[40] One of the principal factors underlying this phenomenon is the increasing nonlinearity of transportation costs with respect to distance. As Edgar Hoover has pointed out, the added time needed for an extra several hundred miles of personal travel, communication, or goods shipment is often less than the time required for the first ten miles. In general, Hoover finds a tendency toward less differentiation in economic and social structure, as well as locational advantage, among broad regions, but at the same time increasing differentiation among large and small centers within the urban hierarchy. In other words, the location of economic activity is more free with respect to major regions and less so with respect to size of community.[41] John Friedmann summarizes the situation in the following manner:

> This growing indifference among location points is counterbalanced by a weighing of extraeconomic elements which furnish a criterion for more refined distinctions among communities. I refer to the quality of life, especially the quality of the educational system, climate, and cultural and recreational opportunities. Except for climate, which is supremely place bound, these other elements are the result of community action and a will to attain high standards in the design of urban culture.[42]

Recent studies of the relative importance of various plant location factors from the viewpoint of industry have indicated the importance of markets, labor, and raw materials, with markets usually leading the list.[43] However, this does not contradict the importance of tertiary activities because market and tertiary factors are mutually reinforcing. As Perloff has pointed out, tertiary activities, dealing as they do with such functions as transportation and communications, construction, trade, finance, government, the professions, and recreation, are by and large closely tied to markets.[44]

Of course, many of these phenomena are recognized by advocates of rural industrialization. The President's National Advisory Commission on Rural Poverty, for example, points out that the industries that are generally attracted to rural communities are not rapid growth industries in terms of employment. Of the sectors that typically favor rural areas—textiles, food and related products, apparel, wood products, lumber, furniture, and miscellaneous manufacturing—only apparel manufacturing showed rapid employment increases between 1960 and 1965.[45] During the 1950's, 90 percent of the national increase in employment occurred in SMSA's. From 1959 to 1964 SMSA's accounted for about 72 percent of the national growth in private nonfarm employment covered by social security.[46] Given this situation it is difficult to justify the Commission's position that people should be guaranteed equal economic opportunity regardless of their place of residence. Rather, Perloff is correct in arguing "that activities inhibiting the needed adjustment of individuals, industries, or regions, can be serious drags on the required adaptation. Subsidizing industries for continuance in uneconomic locations would fall into this category, as would efforts to delay the migration of workers from areas with little employment opportunity."[47] A high capital-labor ratio is important in providing high wages, but relative use of capital is itself related to regional wage differentials. Low wages encourage labor-intensive activities rather than large inflows of capital. This is clearly illustrated by data on the rapid industrial expansion of the Tennessee Valley Region. From 1958 through 1966, the 170-county area served by TVA had announced new investment of $2.4 billion and a gross addition of 268,700 employees. Although the 133 rural counties in the region accounted for 42 percent of its total population, they received 52 percent of the newly created employment. However, over half of the new rural workers were employed in industries which nationally averaged less than $5000 per worker in 1966, whereas the corresponding value for all manufacturing was $6,631. Low-wage, labor-intensive industries tended to locate in the rural counties, while capital-intensive industries located near heavily populated areas. New investment per worker was $10,534 in SMSA counties, $12,020 in counties with a city in the 10,000–50,000 population group, and only $6,619 in the remaining, rural counties. Apparel, for example, accounted for only 7 percent of investment in rural counties, but it also accounted for 38 percent of the new jobs.[48]

Thus capital flows alone will not equalize interregional wage differences for similar levels of skill. Under such circumstances, only outmigration can be counted on to increase wage levels and per capita income. In general, where workers in rural areas and small towns are paid substantially less than they could earn elsewhere and where this situation is likely to persist, a policy of relocation assistance appears to be more rational than efforts to attract economic activity.

Of course, it is also necessary to consider the argument that outmigration from lagging regions includes the adverse effects and social costs of increased congestion and unemployment in industrial-urban areas. However, the assumption that the social costs of bringing industry to poorer regions would be less than the social costs involved in the migration of workers and the increase in congestion and unemployment in industrial areas might well be reasonable if there were only two basic types of region, lagging and congested. However, migration may be directed toward intermediate regions where growth is rapid but where congestion poses no immediate threat. The following chapter proposes a growth center strategy based on this approach.

Summary and Conclusions

The President's Advisory Commission on Rural Poverty is representative of rural industrialization advocates in that it "believes that industrial development of the smaller cities and towns of the country is essential, especially in our currently lagging regions,"[49] and it "would prefer to see the new rural industries subsidized by the nation as a whole, rather than the rural poor, who are now paid pitifully low wages."[50] Yet there is no convincing evidence that central government programs can attract enough industry to the countryside to provide people everywhere with jobs in proximity to their places of residence, even if this were desirable on grounds of value rather than efficiency. On the other hand, a good case can be made for federal subsidies for investment in education, health, and training in lagging regions, as well as for relocation subsidies and for information programs to facilitate rational migration. It is quite understandable that poor communities are reluctant to tax themselves for facilities and services that benefit regions to which their people migrate. On the other hand, if federal expenditures to attract industry to lagging regions are not only antieconomic but also largely ineffective, programs to influence the quality of human resources in lagging regions benefit the people of both these regions and the nation as a whole. The real problem in our current approach to rural poverty, as represented in the report of the President's Commission, is not so much that it neglects cost considerations or that it fails to specify overall priorities, but that it seems too concerned with the places, rather than the people, left behind.

Chapter 10

Urban Policy in a Mobile Society

Introduction

In the preceding chapter data were presented which indicated that the per capita costs of large urban areas are considerably greater than those of towns and small cities. It was argued that this should not be a justification for attempting large-scale industrialization of rural areas, since the rural resident is not limited to a choice between the countryside and a large metropolitan area; there are intermediate areas which offer rural outmigrants job opportunities without the disadvantages of large metropolitan areas. However, there are critics who argue that very few, if any, of our cities have become too big in terms of efficiency; essentially they argue that the greater costs of big cities may be balanced or even exceeded by the corresponding benefits.

This chapter considers the question of whether our large urban agglomerations are really too big in terms of economic efficiency and the personal and social wants and preferences that economic activity is presumably supposed to satisfy. Admittedly this is a very difficult topic because economists have almost completely neglected the issue of locational preferences (though they have given considerable attention to time preferences). Nevertheless, data are examined that relate to public residential preferences and to the always complicated question of efficient city sizes, and these issues are

239

related to public policy designed to improve resource allocation, including that of people over space. In particular, this chapter develops a growth center strategy based on rapidly growing intermediate-sized cities. The relevance of growth centers to workers in lagging areas as well as to problems of our large cities is also examined in some detail.

Is the Big City Too Big?

In defense of the big city. Jean Gottmann has estimated that over the next fifty years the population density of major urban agglomerations is certain to increase, and that on the average they will be closer to the present 30,000 people per square kilometer of Paris and Manhattan than to the 2,000 of Los Angeles. This assumption is based on distribution trends of various economic activities and also on the costs of dispersal. The city of the future will be densely populated, he believes, because this best suits its functions as a center of research, cultural, and managerial activities.[1]

Many students of urbanization are not particularly alarmed at this prospect. Hans Blumenfeld, for example, notes that at an average travel rate of 20 miles per hour, a radius of one hour's travel describes a circle with a total area of 1,250 square miles. No more than 312 square miles would be needed to house 10 million people in single-family houses on 30 by 100-foot lots. Streets, schools, and other facilities for residential use would add only about 200 square miles, and commercial and industrial facilities could be accommodated on 150 square miles. In all, this would leave almost half of the total area within an hour's distance from the center for parks, recreation areas, forest, lakes, and similar uses. If the travel speed were increased to 30 miles per hour, the area within an hour's distance from the center could accommodate 15 million people and leave 1,000 square miles of open land, under the conditions just described. Moreover, relatively few persons would live close to the periphery; the rest would be much closer to the center of the city than an hour's driving distance. The modern metropolis, Blumenfeld concludes, necessitates neither very high residential densities nor excessively long journeys to work.[2]

Werner Hirsch states that "To the best of my knowledge there is no study that shows that the social costs of huge urban complexes outweigh the benefits accruing to society. Nor do we know whether urban sprawl, or balance, is socially desirable or undesirable."[3] Similarly, a recent study of growth center concepts concludes that:

Certainly there is no evidence that there exists a city size beyond which marginal costs outrun marginal productivity, and in this respect we have nothing to tell us that an agglomeration is "too big," despite the attempts being made in Western European countries to decentralize their major capital cities. Indeed, there is accumulating a body of evidence to suggest that per capita income, productivity in manufacturing, wholesale sales per employee, and some other measures all continue to rise, without apparent limit, with increase in the size of agglomeration (measured, admittedly, in a cross-sectional sense).[4]

William Alonso likewise maintains that there are "good grounds for believing in increasing returns to urban size," and that "there is no basis for the belief that primacy or overurbanization *per se* is detrimental to the efficiency goal of economic development."[5] On the other hand, there are those who maintain that our large metropolitan areas can, and in some cases already may have, become too big.

The case against the big city. Edgar Hoover has pointed out that:

many of the most pressing problems of our larger urban areas today, ranging from traffic congestion to social discord, city/suburb conflict, and the fiscal crises of central cities, can be traced in some part to sheer size. .... It is clear that larger agglomerations, as such, raise increasingly challenging problems of divergence of private from social (and local from over-all) costs and benefits, in view of the intensified proximity impacts involving scarcity of space, pollution of water and air, environmental nuisances, and generally increased interdependence of interests.[6]

Elsewhere, but in a similar context, Hoover remarks that "quite clearly it is a mistake to count some people's gain, ignore others' losses, and use the result to rationalize *public* policies aimed at underwriting the growth of areas as such."[7]

There seems to be mounting evidence that crowding of people produces a variety of deleterious effects. René Dubos finds that crowded environments may promote an excessive secretion of various hormones, with a number of possibly harmful consequences ranging from sexual aberrations and cannibalism to complete social unresponsiveness. He believes that mob hysteria and juvenile delinquency may also be linked to crowding.[8] A study of the backgrounds of 1,660 residents of a middle-class neighborhood in New York City showed that stress and mental disorder were directly related; in a report on these findings to the American Psychological Association, Dr. Thomas Langner summarized the situation as "the more the unmerrier."[9] Likewise, Dr. John Christian of Philadelphia's Albert Einstein Medical Center has reported that overcrowding may lead to mass psychosis and psychological collapse; Dr. W. Horsley Gant of Johns Hopkins University gives some support to this view by his findings of indications of increased mental disturbance in persons who had lived under crowded conditions.[10] Kingsley Davis believes that the impact of giant agglomerations on people "is best indicated by their headlong effort to escape them. The bigger the city, the higher the cost of space; yet, the more the level of living rises, the more people are willing to pay for low-density living. Nevertheless, as urban areas expand and collide, it seems probable that life in low-density surroundings will become too dear for the great majority."[11] Of course, the fact that people desire or seek lower density sites within or near metropolitan areas still does not explain why people continue to migrate to metropolitan areas or why more people do not leave them altogether. The author has examined this issue at some length in a previous study, and a summary of that discussion will be presented here.[12]

One of the major conclusions derivable from the assumptions of classical economic theory is that factor mobility will equalize returns to various classes of homogeneous inputs, other things being equal. Space, however, is not homogeneous. Agglomeration of economic activities results in a wide variety of external economies, so that purely market forces tend to concentrate economic activities in a few focal areas. These external economies include relative abundance of public overhead capital, proximity to buyers and sellers, the presence of numerous auxiliary business services (banking, brokerage, insurance), educational facilities, and a well-trained labor force. The attraction of investment to already concentrated areas tends to raise the marginal product of capital in these areas, thereby inducing inmigration. Growth of a relatively skilled labor force, induced public overhead investment, and other induced activities further enhance the attractiveness of such areas for private investment. This cumulative process results in ever greater concentration of economic activity and population. However, it also entails numerous social costs, including traffic congestion, inadequate parks and recreation facilities, slum neighborhoods, natural beauty marred by buildings and billboards, and air pollution. Unfortunately, there is nothing in the nature of this process to halt these effects, because the external diseconomies of congestion are not usually internalized by private firms; or if they are internalized, they are not of such a magnitude as to offset the external economies of agglomeration. It is this disparity between social and private costs that causes jobs to be created in areas where the net social product is less than it would be in an alternative location (because external diseconomies outweigh external economies after a point), and that causes people to choose locations which they do not prefer (because the wage is higher in congested areas as a result of labor's increased productivity based on privately internalized economies; and because the wage may reflect a payment made to help overcome the external diseconomies borne by the individual. The latter phenomenon is most clearly seen in the supplements paid by oligopolistic firms to professional and managerial personnel to induce them to live in New York City).

It may be argued that individuals will increase their welfare by moving into concentrated areas so long as their marginal private gain in income outweighs their own internalized marginal diseconomies associated with congestion. However, this does not imply an increase in social welfare in a Paretian optimal sense, since such action, by increasing concentration, increases the diseconomies absorbed by previous residents. Some previously inframarginal residents might then prefer to leave the area. This would be the case where income loss from outmigration is less than the increase in marginal disutility resulting from increased congestion. On the other hand, social and economic rigidities, such as habituation to friends and surroundings and the costs of moving, will keep many of these people from moving; they will tend not to minimize their welfare loss unless increased disutility in the agglomeration is substantially greater than the private loss of relocating.

Public preferences and city size. Any consideration of whether big cities are too big should take account of public residential preference patterns. Such information as we have in this regard indicates a preference for medium-sized cities. Neutze's findings for Australia show that firms and families prefer centers with 2 million or more people to small towns, primarily because of the external economies available to firms and the cultural amenities and employment opportunities available to individuals. However, "for many, and quite possibly for most, the advantages of shorter journeys to work, less traffic congestion, and the like make the medium-sized centre more attractive."[13] By "medium-sized" Neutze means centers with populations of from 200,000 to one million.

French survey data also show that the social costs of urban congestion are considerable and that they are significantly felt by the populations involved. Most Frenchmen would prefer to remain where they presently reside or to live in a locality of more or less similar characteristics. In the Paris agglomeration, however, only a minority of the residents would really prefer to live in the Paris region. Seventy percent of the Paris residents favor a diminution of the population of the Paris region; similarly, in other areas of heavy urban concentration, such as Flanders, the Artois, and the Lyon region, there is also strong public support for a diminution of their populations.[14] From these and similar findings, Girard and Bastide conclude that "if the expressed aspirations could be satisfied, the movement away from the countryside, however vigorously condemned, would continue, but a regroupment would be made to the profit of medium and large provincial cities, and Paris would cease to grow. Thus . . . decentralization efforts conform to the wishes of the population."[15] It should be pointed out that even the largest provincial cities in France are not very large in comparison to the largest SMSA's of the United States. Even counting the populations in dormitory suburbs, industrial satellites, and municipalities situated along industrial or transportation axes closely tied to the respective metropolitan areas, the 1962 population of Lyon-St. Etienne was only 1,479,757; of Marseille-Aix, 934,700; of Lille-Roubaix-Tourcoing, 873,247; and of Nancy-Metz, 606,641. Thus, the French preference pattern, like that for Australia, clearly favors intermediate areas, in contrast to either rural areas or large urban agglomerations.

Such data as we have for locational preferences in the United States show a similar pattern. In Chapter 8, for example, it was shown that a sample of Mexican Americans in south Texas preferred smaller cities to either large cities, on the one hand, or small towns or rural areas on the other. Similar results were reported in the context of eastern Kentucky in Chapter 4. In Chapter 4 it also was pointed out that the Piedmont Crescent of North Carolina would be a feasible intermediate area to which Appalachian residents (as well as those of the Coastal Plains) who lack job opportunities could migrate. A sample of 385 people from two Crescent cities—Durham (1960 population, 78,302) and Greensboro (119,574)—were interviewed to gain an understanding of how they felt about their cities. Eighty-one percent of the Durham respondents and 82 percent of the Greensboro respondents indicated that they were either "satisfied" or "very much satisfied." Only 3 percent of the Durham sample and 4 percent of the Greensboro sample indicated any dissatisfaction with their cities. The respondents were also asked the question, "If you had complete freedom to choose the size of city in which you would live, which of these city sizes would be your first choice?" (A card was presented listing examples of Southern cities in various population categories.) For both cities

combined, 60 percent preferred a city in the 10,000–100,000 population range, and another 9 percent preferred a city in the 100,000–
500,000 range. Only 6 percent would prefer to live in a metropolitan city with over 500,000 people. The satisfaction of the respondents with their environment was also tested, using responses to
photographs of various types of residential areas. This study showed
that people do have preferences and are able to recognize gradations
of beauty, convenience, and other qualities that can be affected by
urban planning.[16] If the Crescent cities did not fulfill the full range
of livability preferences of the majority of respondents, it was
equally clear that "there is a greater challenge in meeting needs on
a much larger scale elsewhere where urban agglomerations have lost
many of the living qualities the Crescent cities still possess."[17] It is
noteworthy in the present context that a related study showed that
migrants to Durham and Greensboro had achieved a reasonably
contented existence. In this respect these cities were considered
representative of other cities in the Piedmont Crescent. Adjustment
of the newcomers was aided by the fact that most were natives of the
Southeast, and many were able to maintain frequent contacts with
friends and relatives in the areas from which they moved.[18]

In more general terms, a Gallup Poll survey released in May,
1968, showed that 56 percent of the American people would prefer
living in rural areas or in small towns—*if jobs were available.* In
comparison with a poll taken two years earlier, the proportion of
persons expressing a preference for city or suburban living dropped
by seven percentage points, whereas the proportion preferring a
rural location rose by the same amount.[19] No reasons were given
for this shift, but presumably increasing tensions of life in large
urban centers was a factor.

Finally, the *Wall Street Journal* reports that business executives
are increasingly reluctant to take jobs in the nation's biggest cities
because of their expensiveness and discomfort. Similarly, those
who are already based in cities such as New York, Chicago, and
Cleveland are the most inclined to leave for jobs in other places.
Many executives in big cities want to leave even at lower pay, and

many being transferred to big cities are given salaries, titles, and amenities far beyond what their job responsibilities would indicate in order to overcome their disinclination to move. While there have always been people who cannot endure large urban areas, "suddenly, to the growing dismay of corporations, executive talent hunters and management consultants, the metrophobes are legion."[20] There is evidence that as a consequence there has been an accelerated movement of companies from the city, but as yet "few companies are really adjusting to the problem. It isn't that they don't want to—they just don't know how," says one official of the American Management Association.[21]

In general, then, the limited evidence available suggests that, insofar as a public preference pattern with respect to alternative locations can be discerned, there is a definite tendency to prefer intermediate-sized cities. There also seems to be increasing aversion toward the big city.

A summary evaluation. While there is no hard "proof" that big cities have become too big from a social point of view, those who defend the "efficiency" of the big city generally base their arguments on the costs and benefits accruing to private firms. It is also argued that money incomes are frequently highest in big cities, though little systematic effort is made in such cases to determine real incomes. There are certainly many individuals who prefer to live in, say, New York or San Francisco, no matter what the inconveniences, to any alternative area. And their reasons are no doubt "good" ones, though the author does not wish to judge the reasons for people's location preferences. On balance, however, he agrees with Neutze that if market imperfections could be corrected to compensate for external effects there would probably be a less concentrated pattern of population and economic activity. "If we cannot correct the specific imperfections . . . , the indications are that there should be fewer people in large cities."[22]

Furthermore, although the density of some highly urbanized areas is falling because their areas are expanding by more than their populations, this does not mean that the congestion problem is solved. For example, New York's area expanded by 51 percent between 1950 and 1960 while its population grew by only 15 percent. However, Philadelphia, Trenton, Hartford, New Haven, and other metropolitan areas are also expanding. Thus, the population of the Eastern megalopolis cannot continue to expand without increasing population density, and without frustrating the search for large residential lots and suburban school grounds, sprawling shopping centers, single-story plants and broad expressways with space-consuming cloverleaf interchanges.[23]

Finally, it may be argued that it is capricious to use public policy to dampen urban growth, because even if it were possible to prove that there are external diseconomies of growth firms could be charged an amount equivalent to the difference between private and social costs. But this is not operationally feasible because it is generally not possible to measure the social costs of adding a plant to a given area. To make policy decisions dependent on our ability to make such measurements is in effect to preclude public action.

The failure of the free market to halt the growth of large metropolitan areas suggests that tax and credit policy and land-use controls might be used to limit private investment in congested metropolitan areas. However, the more feasible alternative from a political point of view might be to use tax and credit incentives to encourage private capital to locate in other areas; public overhead capital could also be used to induce the location of private investment outside of large metropolitan areas. Of course, some of these tools have been used by our federal agencies concerned with regional development. The problem is that they have been applied for the most part to promote economic growth in rural areas and small towns, and thus they have been not only economically inefficient, but largely ineffective too. To be sure, there may be some sites in rural areas with promising industrial potential, but the most efficient use of public funds might be to encourage the growth of medium-sized cities, especially those which have given some real evidence of growth characteristics.[24]

The Case for the Intermediate-Sized City

Brian Berry's work on spatial organization and levels of welfare (which was mentioned in Chapter 6) has demonstrated that degree of labor market participation, average value of farm land and buildings, median family income, median school years completed, rate of population growth, and percent gain in population through migration each decline with increasing distance from cities. In general, Berry finds that labor markets appear to need a minimum population of 250,000 to be viable parts of the urban system. Above this level cities appear to have the conditions necessary for self-sustained growth. On the other hand, few cities with fewer than 50,000 persons seem capable of influencing the welfare of their surrounding regions. On the basis of these findings, Berry draws a number of policy implications. First, the influence of small centers is too limited to justify public investment in them for regional development purposes. Second, an efficient development strategy might concentrate on cities just below the 250,000 population level. Public investment would provide the push required to get these cities over the threshold to self-generating growth. Third, those persons residing on or between the peripheries of metropolitan labor markets should be given adequate education and training, as well as relocation assistance, so that they can find employment in viable labor markets. However, care should be taken to discourage them from locating in big-city ghettos, where employment problems often are as difficult as those in rural areas.[25]

The 250,000 population threshold is also invoked by Wilbur Thompson, who points out that between 1950 and 1960, only seven out of 212 SMSA's lost population. If one of these, Jersey City, N.J., is regarded as part of the New York-Northeastern New Jersey SMSA rather than a separate entity, then there were no population declines in SMSA's with over 500,000 people, and only two declines in SMSA's with over 250,000 people (Johnstown and Wilkes-Barre-Hazleton, Pa.). He concludes that "if the growth of an urban area persists long enough to raise the area to some critical size (a quarter of a million population?), structural characteristics, such as industrial diversification, political power, huge fixed investments, a rich local market, and a steady supply of industrial leadership may almost ensure its continued growth and fully ensure against absolute decline—may, in fact, effect irreversible aggregate growth."[26]

Neutze's investigations employing Australian data indicate that most of the advantages of a city of 500,000 are probably also found in a city of 200,000, but that if a city gets much beyond the half-million level the external diseconomies probably begin to outweigh the concomitant economies. In any case, he suggests that many firms will maximize their profits in centers with populations between 200,000 and one million.[27] "Let us say," writes Neutze, "that 500,000 was the best size, or at least that most of the firms that could be diverted from locating in Sydney would prefer, as an alternative, a city of about 500,000. The objective should be to push the new centre as rapidly as possible through the early inefficient stages to get it close to 500,000 and to prevent it from growing past that size. More firms and families will suffer from further growth than will gain."[28] It should be pointed out that Neutze probably underestimates the attractive power of large agglomerations. More firms reap more gains from external economies in big cities than he admits —otherwise, so many of them would not continue to locate in metropolitan areas even after they pass, say, the one million mark. Government planners may be aware of the external diseconomies in such places, but this is different from saying that a firm will be at a disadvantage in locating there. It will not in many cases because it does not internalize many of the diseconomies. Thus, policy measures to induce firms to locate in intermediate areas have to go beyond simply trying to persuade them that it is to their advantage to shun the large agglomeration.

Finally, if we consider only government services, it is clear that intermediate areas are more efficient than either small towns or large agglomerations. Werner Hirsch estimates that the greatest economies of scale accrue to a government serving from 50,000 to

100,000 people. His findings are similar to those of the Royal Commission on Local Government in Greater London, which reached the conclusion that the optimum size of a city would be a minimum of about 100,000 people, and a maximum of about 250,000.[29] These results imply that cities that have passed the 250,000 mark may encounter diseconomies of scale in the public sector, but these will probably be outweighed by external economies in the private sector. On the other hand, small towns and rural areas once again are shown to be at a distinct disadvantage.

The foregoing analyses suggest that relatively rapidly growing intermediate-sized cities might receive much more attention in regional policy conceived from a national point of view. In these places public funds may be integrated with actual or potential external economies to produce rapid growth with a minimum of external diseconomies of congestion. As noted earlier, there are those who object to this policy on the ground that rapidly growing places do not *need* any form of government subsidy. This is quite true in the narrower sense, but if the growth of intermediate-sized centers can be accelerated with government aid by more than growth can be accelerated in lagging regions, and if the accelerated growth of intermediate centers can be made conditional on the granting of newly created employment opportunities to a significant number of workers from lagging regions (either by means of migration or commuting), then clearly it is economically efficient for the government to attempt to accelerate employment growth in intermediate centers. Finally, this policy would also be consistent with public locational preferences and with what little evidence we have concerning efficiency and city sizes.

A Growth Center Policy

One variant of the growth center approach would be to build entirely new towns. However, there are a number of reasons why this probably would not be satisfactory. Although new towns have received considerable publicity as well as a great deal of support from planners, they have been primarily a physical planning device. Too little attention has been given to developing an economic rationale for new towns. British experience has shown that location decisions for new towns have not been made so as to maximize their chances for industrial development, and insufficient attention has been given to developing their employment base. Moreover, most of the literature on new towns demonstrates that they are designed to appeal to people who already live in urban areas and are attached to them. They also seem to be repetitive and monotonous in terms of physical design, and to be generally dull relative to the more animated "downtowns."[30]

Reston, Virginia, one of the more highly touted experiments with a new town in this country, has proven to be a disappointment. It has had difficulty in attracting residents and it is, in any case, largely a dormitory community rather than an independent center with its own economy, as originally planned. Columbia, another new town near the nation's capital, may meet with greater success, but it is still far from being a center designed to divert migrants from large metropolitan areas. Columbia may prove to be a successful experiment in urban planning, but it is nevertheless part and parcel of the eastern megalopolis. Indeed, most new town proposals are geared to relocating people within metropolitan areas, and their costs are such that they have little relevance to people in the income groups in which most rural to urban migrants fall.

The material already presented in this chapter indicates that a more realistic approach to the problem of rechanneling migration streams might be to build on existing external economies in growing cities in, say, the 50,000–1,000,000 population range, and more particularly in the 250,000–750,000 range. These values are of course not magic numbers but rough indicators. As has been shown there is evidence for believing that self-sustained growth is more assured in a city with 250,000 people than in smaller places. On the other hand, external diseconomies may make expansion of alternative locations desirable from an opportunity cost viewpoint after a city passes the 750,000 mark. However, growing cities that are smaller than 250,000 or larger than 750,000 should not be automatically excluded from consideration; hence wider limits should be introduced for the sake of flexibility.

It has been specified that a growth center policy should build on cities that are already growing relatively rapidly. The simple reason for this is that such places are demonstrating their ability to create new jobs. There may be cities, and even rural areas, that have not been growing but which for one reason or another may have real job growth potential. Places at or near the intersections of interstate highways may fall into this category. Nevertheless, without preparing a detailed and costly case study of every county, village, town, and city that claims to have growth potential there is really no practical way to select a system of growth centers other than to rely on the record of the past, particularly the recent past. Sites that may benefit from interstate highway intersections, resource discoveries, or large-scale federal projects need not be automatically excluded if they have heretofore been relatively stagnant, but their case should be very strong if they are to be regarded as objects of growth center policy; otherwise, the Pandora's box of Chamber of Commerce salesmen will be opened.

It is not sufficient that a growth center policy be built upon rapidly growing cities of intermediate size. Their growth must be related to the employment of persons from lagging areas with high unemployment or low incomes. This implies that education and training programs in lagging areas be geared to employment opportunities in growth centers. In some cases workers in lagging areas may be able to commute to growth centers, but they often will have to move, in which case programs of comprehensive relocation assistance should be provided (more will be said in this regard in the following chapter). With these considerations in mind, it is necessary to point out that rapid growth is a necessary but not a sufficient condition for designation as a growth center. A rapidly growing, intermediate-sized city located, say, in the Midwestern corn belt may have little relevance to residents of any of our large, lagging rural areas. Workers from Appalachia, the Ozarks, or even the

Upper Great Lakes may be unlikely to be persuaded to move to this city, as would Mexican Americans, Indians, or Negroes. In this event, the City would not qualify as a "growth center." In brief, a growth center must be not only rapidly growing, but also a center which could be expected to benefit a significant number of people from lagging areas. Thus growth centers would have to be selected on the basis of commuting and migration data, as well as data on employment growth. The author is engaged in such a study for the Economic Development Administration, but the project is still in its initial stages. Of course, a growth center policy would not rely on reinforcing existing migration patterns; too often this implies movement from rural areas to big city ghettos. However, migration studies would give valuable insights into the migration streams linking lagging rural areas to rapidly growing, intermediate-sized cities, streams which could be reinforced by a growth center policy. For example, it was shown in Chapter 4 that many more young people in eastern Kentucky would prefer to live in Lexington—a city that meets our growth center criteria—than are actually going there, even though a fairly large number are moving to the Bluegrass city.

What measures could be undertaken to implement a growth center strategy? As indicated in Chapter 6, efforts to stimulate regional economic development, such as those that are now being made in lagging areas by EDA, should be applied to growth centers that conform to the conditions just discussed. However, the composition of the development aid tool kit should be changed, since the tools will be applied to areas which are already economically healthy and growing, rather than to areas which have relatively poor growth prospects. There would be more emphasis on measures that would appeal to growing industries and less emphasis on subsidies whose principal appeal is to small firms in slow-growing, low-wage, and labor intensive industries. There would be more money devoted to equipping relatively sophisticated industrial sites and less to building water and sewer lines (which may be sorely needed in rural areas, but which should not be such a central concern of an agency whose purpose is to initiate self-sustained growth). The kinds of tools would have to be more varied and flexible than those presently applied in small towns and rural areas. The latter often need so many improvements in order to make them relatively attractive to firms, especially the bigger and more rapidly-growing ones, that the limited resources of a development agency are not likely to change greatly the total "package" of factors that a firm considers when making a location decision. This is especially true to the extent that a "worst-first" policy is either explicitly or implicitly followed. On the other hand, the growth centers that are being proposed here would have a large variety of external economies. This means in the first place that a given type of aid extended by an economic development agency would not be so visible as it would be in a lagging area. However, if used wisely, a given type of aid can produce more employment opportunities in the growth center because it can be combined with these external economies. The development agency must seek out the bottlenecks that are hindering or preventing a firm from locating or expanding in the growth center and attempt to provide the assistance needed to overcome the resistance. The situation may call for a certain type of infrastructure, or for some form of investment or labor subsidy, or for some combination of aid devices. In any case, it is essential that the aid be made conditional on the extension of job opportunities to persons from lagging regions (and in part to the unemployed and underemployed residents of the center), and that comprehensive relocation assistance be made available to those who decide to move from lagging areas to growth centers.

The emphasis that is given here to the development of intermediate cities as the principal focus for a national regional policy is based not only on the job growth potential of these cities, but also on the fact that problems related to their growth are still amenable to solution. The massive renewal needs of our large metropolitan areas can still be avoided by careful planning in growth centers. "A city of 'optimal size,'" writes Benjamin Higgins, "must be big enough to be urbane in its range of activities and small enough to provide effective proximity to these activities for its residents, with the available techniques of city planning and transportation."[31] Unless the government knows what places are going to grow it can provide public facilities only after the demand has appeared. If there is planned growth of a few centers, then they can be provided with an integrated and coherent system of public facilities in advance of the demand. The conclusions to a comprehensive study of the Piedmont Crescent by F. Stuart Chapin, Jr., are highly relevant to all growth centers:

Apparently missing from numerous neighborhoods as now developed are qualities of appearance and beauty. But along with appearance and beauty, the qualities of the physical setting which seem to be highly prized also include privacy, spaciousness, and related considerations of density and crowdedness. From this study it would appear that from the standpoint of livability these are the qualities that people are seeking when they talk about the appearances of the downtown area, the city's main highway approaches, and their residential communities. It would seem therefore that action programs seeking to maximize economic growth will need to give much more attention to the living qualities a city has to offer industrial management, newcomers, and long-time residents.[32]

Finally, if a growth center strategy has much to commend it from the viewpoint of economic efficiency as well as that of public preferences, there still remains the problem of the consequences of migration from lagging areas to growth centers. The complexity of this issue requires that it be dealt with at some length.

The Migration Question

In earlier chapters it was shown in numerous instances that people are much more willing to migrate from lagging regions than has been generally acknowledged. However, this willingness is often made conditional upon adequate preparation to take advantage of job opportunities in areas where they exist. In a recent study of the geographic mobility of labor it was found that one out of five family heads would prefer to move if they could do as they please. However, the number who actually expected to move within one year was only half as large, or about one in ten. In fact, the actual mobility rate is about 5 percent per year for moves that cross labor market boundaries. In other words, actual mobility is only about half of expected mobility, which in turn is only about half of desired mobility.[33]

Unfortunately, the kinds of workers who are susceptible to unemployment have a relatively low propensity to move. Unemployment constitutes a "push" leading people to move if they are young, well-educated and trained, or live in a small town. But in the absence of such characteristics unemployment is not likely to overcome the reluctance to move. In general, John Lansing and Eva Mueller found that the depressed economic conditions of redevelopment areas inhibit inmigration more than they induce outmigration. The pull of better economic opportunities is the most influential economic stimulus to mobility, while the push of poor opportunities at home is less effective. The evidence indicates that young people who leave depressed areas have generally attained a substantially higher level of education than those who remain.[34] While some would use this as a justification for attempting to industrialize rural areas, the authors adopt a position in harmony with the position that has been urged in the present study. They state that:

Net out-migration of the kind that has taken place in redevelopment areas in the past and is likely to continue in the future leaves behind a population that is less and less able to cope with the already difficult economic conditions in these areas, *and* that is less and less likely to migrate. Educational and vocational training efforts as well as guidance programs are sorely needed to maintain or improve the quality and also the mobility potential of the labor force in redevelopment areas.[35]

Lansing and Mueller suggest two principal approaches for aiding lagging areas. First, in view of the fact that a great deal of the movement out of lagging areas is ill-directed to nearby areas with similar problems, there needs to be a program to expand information about job opportunities elsewhere in the country. If this information were more readily available it would help migrants to make more rational mobility choices. Second, since the workers who remain in lagging areas suffer debilitating effects both from local economic conditions and from selective outmigration, it is very important that their quality and mobility potential be improved and maintained. Guidance programs and special educational and training assistance are recommended, as well as general support for education.[36]

It is also pertinent to note an important distinction that Lansing and Mueller found between so-called section 5-A areas and section 5-B areas. The former, as designated by the Area Redevelopment Administration, were characterized by high and persistent unemployment, whereas the latter had a high proportion of low-income families. Although employment declined drastically in some industries in 5-A areas, it increased in others, especially in areas possessing rapidly growing sectors. On the other hand, the 5-B areas, which were generally rural and had long been depressed, gave little evidence of growth potential.[37]

Another recent study, concentrating on migration from agriculture, has come up with findings similar to those of Lansing and Mueller, but quite different conclusions are drawn from the data. Dale Hathaway and Brian Perkins found that, other things being equal, mobility rates from farm to nonfarm employment are lower for Negroes, older workers, farm operators, persons from low income rural areas, and persons in areas more remote from larger urban areas. They point out that many of the gross data which have shown other results have been limited to migration rather than occupational mobility, and they have not been adjusted for age distribution and other population characteristics. With these adjustments, it is seen that most farmworkers do not migrate far when they change to nonfarm work. Long distance moves are chiefly characteristic of Negroes and of the young, but there is no evidence that such moves really pay off economically. There is a very high rate of outmobility from farm employment, but many persons eventually return to farm employment at least for some time, principally because their expectations of higher nonfarm earnings have not been realized. Over 40 percent of the persons studied who changed from farm to nonfarm employment actually had lower earnings after the change. Thus, the return to farm employment that results from this experience reduces the net outmovement from farm employment to a fraction of those who are trying to leave. In the process, the income gap between commercial agriculture and the low income farmers seems to widen, as does the gap between the Negroes and whites who leave farm employment, and between income groups after they leave farm employment. Thus, Hathaway and Perkins conclude that the mobility process serves to encourage, rather than to eliminate, the transfer of low income problems from agriculture to rural nonfarm areas and urban ghettos.[38]

Because of the widespread interest in this study it is necessary to consider in some detail the policy implications that the authors draw from their findings. They conclude that there "is little in our results to suggest that the 'low income area' problem will be solved by the process of mobility; indeed the contrary appears more likely."[39] The principal reason for this position is that:

> The mobility process out of farm employment might be represented as "Many are called but few are chosen." The problem, then, would appear [to be] not to devise policies to increase the number of farm people who try nonfarm employment, but to develop policies whereby the proportion who succeed in their efforts at occupational mobility is substantially increased. . . . Of major importance is to find out why farm people with certain characteristics fare so badly in nonfarm employment and then develop policies to either change the characteristics of the individuals or the nature of the labor market they must enter.[40]

But there is little doubt concerning where the authors stand on this question. They state that:

> In order to improve the incomes of the lowest income groups more local development and employment opportunities are needed. Most farm people do not move far when they change jobs; but it still pays them best to move to large cities. Until this can be changed we can expect a continuing influx of rural people into large cities and a widening gap between the rural poor and our urban areas.[41]

Thus, while Hathaway and Perkins recognize that the nonfarm employment opportunities available to farm people can be improved by policies designed to "change the characteristics" of the individuals involved, they say nothing more about human resource development and nothing at all about improving job information systems or relocation assistance. Instead, they conclude on the theme that "more local development and employment opportunities are needed." They fail even to raise the question of why firms should want to move to the countryside to employ people who have already shown themselves to be relatively unproductive in their employment efforts in the cities. In the case of the Negroes, lack of urban opportunities is often a matter of discrimination rather than productivity, but again it is difficult to imagine that this situation would be improved simply by having firms move to the rural South. In brief, the central farm manpower problem, as Theodore Schultz has urged, is not that the amount of mobility between the farm and nonfarm sectors is too small, or that farm workers are the victims of monopoly power exercised by employers of farm labor, or even that of structural maladjustments resulting from rapidly increasing agricultural productivity. Rather, the most acute problem is "the low level of marketable skills of the farm labor force generally."[42] Garth Mangum is correct in maintaining that too few of these persons being trained for farm occupations will remain on the farm, and that the funds for such training can be better spent on training for other occupations. "Considering the growing demands, the efforts to develop training in such critically labor-short areas as health and technical occupations and some of the skilled trades have been surprisingly limited."[43] And, as Marion Clawson has pointed out, "One is hard put to think of any federal program that has been directed specifically toward the farm-to-city migrants."[44] In brief then, there is a crying need for educational, training, and manpower programs to develop our rural human resources and to link them to expanding job opportunities in growth centers. Appeals to industrialization of the countryside are not only economically undesirable but serve to divert public policy from programs which should have top priority if farm workers are to share in growing national prosperity.

While outmigration, under the proper circumstances, may help the persons who are migrating, the economic conditions of those who remain behind may improve or worsen, depending on whether a new equilibrium can be attained that adjusts to the new labor market situation or whether there is a cumulative disequilibrium. Peter Blau and Otis D. Duncan are among those who take the positive side of the case. They find that outmigration benefits not only the migrants, but also those who remain behind in rural areas, because outmigration lessens the competitive struggle for jobs.[45] Harvey Perloff maintains that efforts to delay the migration of workers from areas with little employment opportunity can be a serious drag on needed adaptation. He notes that low wages do not attract a large inflow of capital into poorer areas, so that capital movements need not bring about an equalization of wages for similar skill levels.[46]

This suggests why additions to, and even existing members of, the labor force within a given region may not be fully employed and wage levels may be depressed. Under such circumstances, it is only through outmigration that upward pressure on wage levels can be exerted and per capita income raised.

As a general principle, it can be said that in a town or rural area where workers are paid substantially less than they could make elsewhere and where basic change in five years or so is unlikely, the shift of some of the population out of the area might be just as important to the region's economic future as efforts to promote economic activities.[47]

On the other hand, the selective nature of outmigration from lagging areas means that such areas lose their most vital people— the best workers, the young, the better educated. Moreover, in addition to the initial reduction in employment (or, if the migrants were unemployed, the reduction in transfer payments of a welfare nature) there may be adverse multiplier effects. If outmigration leads to absolute declines in population, the tax base will be decreased, leading in turn to higher average tax levels or to a deterioration in public service standards. In either case the area's attractiveness to industry is likely to be reduced. Marginal firms may even leave the area and create further adverse multiplier effects. The value of real estate may decline with depopulation, causing banks and other financial institutions to be more strict in granting credit. Depopulation and declining purchasing power may also cause some market-oriented producers to curtail production and cause still more unemployment. Outmigration may also fail to produce a permanent solution to unemployment problems because of reverse migration. There is evidence that when employment opportunities appear in a lagging area there is a return movement of workers. Since these returnees are frequently more highly skilled than the members of the local work force, the hard core unemployed of the area may find little relief for their problems.[48] Thus, outmigration may cause cumulative difficulties in a lagging region, and the benefits from an increase in local employment opportunities may help return migrants more than it helps the local residents. Of course, the positive multiplier effects of any new activity will indirectly benefit the community as a whole, especially if leakages to other areas are minimal.

Finally, the results obtained by direct movement of unemployed workers from one sector to another can also be obtained by a decline in the number of people who try to enter the less desirable sectors. Lowell Gallaway has found evidence that a similar phenomenon may be occurring on a regional basis. Inmigration into areas experiencing chronic unemployment

is markedly less than that into other areas which are similar except for their level of unemployment. At the same time these chronically depressed areas do not have levels of out-migration which are greater than those of other areas. Thus, the net effect is one of out-migration from these areas despite the fact that there is no apparent unemployment-induced increase in out-migration. Regardless of how the transfer is effected, the impact on the labor market is the same, a redistribution of unemployment.[49]

Whatever may be the consequences of outmigration from lagging areas, it is still clear that policies that merely try to check migration —even by attempting to subsidize the industrialization of rural areas —do little service to either the nation or the individuals concerned, at least from an opportunity cost viewpoint. The remigration problem in particular shows that the real problem of lagging regions is underinvestment in their human resources, rather than migration as such, which is a symptom rather than a cause. Hopefully, a national regional policy would aid areas with problems occasioned by out-migration to attain new equilibria with a minimum of friction. The nation may also deem it desirable to aid persons in these areas whose prospects for either local employment or for retraining and migration are not bright; older workers in particular would fall into this category. However, it must be recognized that we are talking here about welfare and not about economic development policy.

The main thrust of public policy in lagging regions should still be in the direction of active manpower and human resource programs, including comprehensive job information and relocation assistance. Even among those who are fairly pessimistic about the economic viability of small towns and rural areas, and who favor manpower policies for such areas, there is a tendency to play down the relocation issue. For example, Wilbur Thompson writes that it is especially critical to design local manpower policies that will make net out-migration neutral with respect to population quality. "Some of the brightest young men," he suggests, "might be kept at home with premium pay and with travel and education allowances that permit these ambitious people to maintain intellectual contact with the rapidly advancing technology of their chosen professions (e.g. attendance at professional meetings and post-graduate seminars at leading universities)."[50] It is difficult to imagine a typical community in a typical region where outmigration is a major problem subsidizing its local intellectual(s) in his (their) quest for excellence. One can well imagine the town council members' reactions as the professor proposing such a plan confirms their worst suspicions about such types. Jocular skepticism would not, of course, necessarily imply the unworthiness of the professor's scheme. On reflection the council itself might even decide that the policy is a good one—if the federal government would finance it. A good teacher (or local leader), for example, may well be worth a subsidy from the community if his contribution to upgrading the economic value of the community's human resources exceeds that of the best alternative teacher by an amount at least equivalent to the subsidy. But given that outmigration is a principal characteristic of the community, it is understandable that the community might prefer to invest in a road or a subsidy for a textile mill rather than in highly mobile human resources. On the other hand, it is equally understandable that the citizens of Chicago or Peoria would be reluctant to subsidize the local intellectuals—or leaders of whatever stripe—in Searcy, Arkansas, especially if the subsidizers are supposed to accept tacitly the condition that they are not to let their urban external economies entice the subsidized. But, then, the whole tortuous business could have been avoided in the first place if the location of skilled and able people had been left to the interplay of their own preferences and the market system within the context of a growth center policy.

Northern Ghettos and Southern Growth Centers

If the departure of workers and their families poses problems for lagging regions, it is widely agreed that "receiving areas may benefit greatly from geographic mobility, in increased production and in the demand for goods, services, and facilities. Although some costs are also transferred from depressed areas along with the migrants, there are indications that an area's benefits from inmigration greatly outweigh its costs."[51] There is also the argument that migration from rural to urban areas promotes the occupational mobility of the migrants themselves, as well as that of the already resident urban population. This position is usually based on the experience of inmigrants at the turn of the century. Rural migrants to the cities, it is maintained, achieve higher occupational status than persons remaining in rural areas, but not so high as the urban natives. Because of their poorer education and training, the rural migrants are employed in the lower ranges of the urban employment hierarchy. However, this permits more of the better qualified city-reared workers to move into relatively higher occupational positions than would otherwise have been possible. Thus, the role that immigrants from Europe once occupied in the cities has been assumed today by migrants from rural areas, to the advantage of both the city natives and the migrants.[52]

Appealing though this argument may be, it does not hold for Negro migrants, at least not without severe qualifications. The large influx of Negroes to central city ghettos, particularly during the 1940's and 1950's, paralleled on the surface the experience of earlier white immigrants. However, the experience of the Negroes has been different in a number of fundamental respects.

From the outset the Negroes have been more highly segregated than their European predecessors. Between 1940 and 1960, 33.0 million whites and 6.4 million Negroes were added to all metropolitan areas. However, 84 percent of the Negro increase occurred in central cities, whereas 80 percent of the white increase was accounted for by the suburbs. In the 24 largest SMSA's, which contained over half the nation's urban population in 1960, whites increased by 16.0 million persons and Negroes by 4.2 million. But only 0.2 percent of the net white increase was accounted for by central cities; the corresponding value for Negroes was 83 percent. In some metropolitan areas there is an even sharper contrast. For example, between 1950 and 1960 Cleveland's central city gained 103,000 Negroes and lost 142,000 whites, while the suburbs gained 367,000 whites but only 2,000 Negroes. In all of Cleveland's suburbs, there were only 6,000 Negroes, as compared to 900,000 whites, in 1960.[53]

The high and persistent concentration of Negroes in central cities has been accompanied by lack of job availability. The situation of the urban Negro today is different from that of earlier immigrants in that jobs are not as available now. Today, the occupational structure of the male Negro work force bears more resemblance to that of all male workers in 1900 than it does to that of all male workers in 1960, even accounting for shifts in occupational structure. Despite the low esteem in which foreign-born immigrants were held, they made considerable progress from the start. In 1900, a larger proportion of second generation Irish, Polish, and Italian male household heads were in trade, professional, and clerical occupations—and a smaller proportion in service and laboring jobs—than was the case in the first generation. Similarly, in terms of occupational structure the Chinese and Japanese probably had lower status in 1930 than did the Negroes in 1960. However, by 1950 Chinese and Japanese had made much greater strides in obtaining jobs in prestige occupations, and by 1960 these oriental groups had outpaced even the white population in terms of concentration in professional and technical employment and in white-collar employment in general. About 18 percent of the Chinese and Japanese were in professional or technical work in 1960, compared to 11 percent of the white population and only 3 percent of the Negroes.[54]

Historically, the tendency for lower income groups to locate in the central cities has been related to a highly centralized employment structure. However, as was shown in Chapter 2, job opportunities today are accelerating in the suburbs, out of reach of the central city poor. There is considerable evidence that high Negro unemployment rates are at least as much an effect of housing discrimination as of employment discrimination.[55] The data presented in Table 33 show that the proportion of low income whites living in the suburban rings of the ten largest metropolitan areas is much greater than the proportion for low income Negroes. In other words, it is simply not true that Negroes are concentrated in central cities because they are poor. Kain and Persky remark that

this finding is consistent with the work of numerous researchers who have concluded that little of the existing pattern of Negro residential segregation can be explained by income or other socioeconomic characteristics. One of the authors has estimated that on the basis of Negro employment locations and low income white residential choice patterns as many as 40,000 Detroit Negro workers and 112,000 Chicago Negro workers would move out of central ghettos in the absence of racial segregation.[56]

It follows, therefore, that any long run solution to problems of central city poverty must involve a major dispersal of its low income population. This runs counter to the proposals of segregationists,

TABLE 33: PERCENT OF WHITE AND NEGRO FAMILIES (TOTAL AND
          POOR) LIVING IN THE SUBURBAN RINGS OF THE TEN
          LARGEST URBANIZED AREAS, 1960

	White	White Families with Incomes Below $3,000	Negro	Negro Families with Incomes Below $3,000
	All Families		All Families	
(1) New York[a]	27.8%	16.3%	9.4%	8.2%
(2) Los Angeles	65.2	61.6	27.3	23.3
(3) Chicago[a]	47.6	37.2	7.7	5.9
(4) Philadelphia	50.8	37.4	15.7	14.2
(5) Detroit	58.9	44.9	12.1	11.3
(6) San Francisco-Oakland	57.8	48.8	29.2	25.8
(7) Boston	74.3	64.0	19.2	13.9
(8) Washington	75.7	59.6	9.8	10.4
(9) Pittsburgh	70.5	63.3	29.4	27.1
(10) Cleveland	59.2	39.3	3.1	2.4

[a] For New York and Chicago the suburban ring is the difference between
the SMSA and central city. For all other cities it is the difference between
the urbanized area and the central city. Both San Francisco and Oakland
are counted as central cities.

Source: John F. Kain and Joseph J. Persky, "The Ghetto, the Metropolis
and the Nation," Harvard University Program on Regional and Urban Economics Discussion Paper No. 30, March, 1968, p. 4.

black militants, and many well-meaning whites who concentrate on
refurbishing the ghetto. The present writer agrees with Kain and
Persky that

nothing less than a complete change in the structure of the metropolis . . .
will solve the problems of the ghetto. Indeed, it is ironic, almost cynical,
the extent to which current programs that ostensibly are concerned with
the welfare of urban Negroes are willing to accept and are even based
upon the permanence of central ghettos. Thus, under every heading of
social welfare legislation, education, income transfer, employment, and
housing we find programs that can only serve to strengthen the ghetto
and the serious problems that it generates. In particular, these programs

concentrate on beautifying the fundamentally ugly structure of the current metropolis and not on providing individuals with the tools necessary to break out of the structure. The shame of the situation is that viable alternatives do exist.[57]

What are these alternatives? The first steps advocated by Kain and Persky include improved information made available to Negro job seekers, strong job training programs linked to employment opportunities in industry, and improved transportation between the ghetto and suburban employment sites. Instead of urban renewal and public housing projects that reinforce racial and economic separation in metropolitan areas, the supply of low income housing outside the ghetto should be greatly expanded. Rent subsidies and vigorous enforcement of open housing laws would give developers, lenders, and realtors an excuse to act in their own economic self-interest. Even if residential segregation is maintained, or if Negroes prefer to live among other Negroes, there can be suburbanization of the Negro without housing integration. The creation of a number of dispersed Negro communities would place Negroes closer to suburban job opportunities and, by reducing pressures on central city housing markets, improve the chances for private renewal of middle income neighborhoods. Along with these measures, it is imperative that Negro educational levels be upgraded so that they will be prepared to take advantage of favorable job opportunities.[58]

Antipoverty and ghetto dispersal efforts will have a better chance of success if the flow of poorly educated and trained migrants to metropolitan areas can be greatly reduced. This is not to say that Negroes have not benefited by moving to the North. Many have developed their potential much more in the North than they ever could have in the South. Ginzberg points out that even an industrious worker on a poor southern farm is hard put to use his time productively at some times of the year. A northern worker who is employed usually has regular full-time work, and the values and habits that he develops in this regard are passed on to his children. The urban Negro family in the North has three times the income of the average Negro farm family, and though living conditions may not be three times better, exposure to a wider range of available goods and services is likely to stimulate greater efforts to raise living standards. Urban Negro families are generally smaller than farm families, so there also is more income per family member. The North has also given the Negro a wider range of job opportunities, more contact with the white population, better educational facilities for his children, and greater status in the community. The Negro in the North is still the victim of serious inequalities of opportunity, but Ginzberg believes that on balance "the rapid movement of Negroes to Northern cities represents a substantial contribution to solving the problem of developing Negro potential."[59]

Ginzberg's argument again reflects the either-or approach that is commonly taken toward interrelated problems of rural and urban areas. Ginzberg would have the Southerner move to the northern metropolis to escape the debilitating conditions of his rural life, while those who want to "save" the family farm and the small town would have people stay at home in order to escape the debilitating conditions of metropolitan areas. The growth center policy that has been advocated in this chapter would have workers, black and white, leave areas where job opportunities are dim for rapidly-growing intermediate areas where labor is in relatively short supply. In the case of the Negro, a national policy to develop human resources and to create job opportunities in southern cities would (1) relieve pressures on northern metropolitan areas while they upgrade the education and skills of their ghetto residents and redistribute them so as to make jobs more readily available, and (2) give the rural southern Negro a viable alternative to the northern ghetto.[60] As was shown in Chapter 3, urban-industrial growth in the South is moving at a much faster pace than in the rest of the country. Public policy should build on this growth to give Negroes an opportunity to contribute to the building of the "New South." As northern firms expand their operations in the South, and as northern managers and technicians move into the South, there is likely to be less discrimination, or at least less desire to discriminate, in employment. As to worker attitudes in the South, Emory Via reports that the stereotype of white workers resisting job desegregation is inaccurate. There are numerous situations where Negroes and whites work amicably together, and there are repeated instances of on-the-job mutual help. Negro and white workers can have confidence in each other as craftsmen and fellow workers and personal respect for one another. It is senseless to deny the presence of resistance to job claims by Negroes, but it is a mistake to focus exclusively on such responses.[61]

Recent Southern experience shows that job integration can be made to work if management stands firm in implementing nondiscriminatory policies. Significant desegregation has taken place in the apparel, textiles, auto and farm-implement manufacturing, aerospace, and tobacco sectors. A strong government posture on job rights and a firm management policy of employment equality have been shown to be decisive with employees in the great majority of cases.[62] Of course, employment discrimination is often a reflection of discrimination against Negroes in education, housing, and the very nature of some social and political practices. The nation as a whole has a vital stake in upgrading the quality of our Negro human resources, and in removing artificial barriers to the Negro's ability to take advantage of the investment made in his resources. One advantage that the southern Negro has is his youth. In 1964, Negroes in the farm population had a median age of 17.6 years, whereas that for whites was 31.9 years.[63] Hopefully the South and the nation will not neglect the opportunity that this represents. That the South is making progress in providing opportunities for Negroes is indicated by the fact that during the period from March 1, 1966, to March 1, 1967, two Negroes moved into the South for every three who left. The South lost 149,000 Negroes through migration, but it gained back 93,000.[64]

Chapter 11

Promoting Labor Mobility

The Need for Relocation Assistance

Many students of manpower problems have urged the adoption in this country of programs for relocation assistance. R. A. Gordon, for example, in summarizing the findings of a number of papers on manpower policy, writes that "Supply needs to be related to demand regionally as well as by occupation and other characteristics. It is clear that American manpower efforts thus far have not put sufficient emphasis on the geographical relocation of workers."[1] Among the conclusions that Arthur Ross draws from a similar set of papers is that although persons who are young and well educated can and do move about the country in response to better job opportunities, this is not the case for many middle-aged workers. They are not used to travel and have long attachments to familiar surroundings and friends. It is expensive for them to move their families and belongings, and, unlike younger people, they cannot afford to shop around the country for better opportunities. Thus, to Ross, "The case for relocation allowances is that displaced middle-aged workers need special assistance or they are likely to vegetate and decay in areas where employment opportunity has permanently dried-up."[2] C. E. Bishop, drawing on papers prepared for the President's National Advisory Commission on Rural Poverty and on his own research, points out the need to make the migration process operate so that a higher proportion of those who migrate actually benefit from migration. In advocating a nationwide comprehensive manpower program that would provide improved job information to potential employees, he states that

> The meager evidence that is available suggests that the return received from investments in mobility assistance programs far exceeds the return from investments in education and training. Public assistance in defraying certain mobility costs may contribute greatly to the success of mobility efforts. In particular, a system of relocation payments provided through, and based upon the advice and counsel of the Employment Security Commission, could yield very high returns for society.[3]

Even *The People Left Behind* recommends that the public employment offices integrate mobility and relocation assistance into an area manpower planning and development program. Relocation payments are advocated in the form of (1) travel and living allowances for persons seeking job interviews for jobs recommended by the public employment service; (2) relocation allowances for moving workers, their families, and their households to permanent jobs, with both moving expenses and minimal settling-in expenses being included in the allowances; (3) travel and subsistence allowances for employment service-recommended training outside of the worker's area of residence; and (4) supportive services, including help in straightening out the worker's affairs in the place he is leaving, information and counseling on living conditions in the new community, referrals to social agencies, and other newcomer services. However, in keeping with the spirit of its report, the President's Commission recommends a relocation program for disadvantaged workers only as a last resort.[4] Even so, the report contains a "memorandum of reservation" by two Commission members stating that "Providing jobs and opportunities for rural people where they are is a thread that winds through the entire report. It appears self-defeating to suggest this cannot be done and therefore provision should be made to subsidize, even as a last resort, movement of the rural poor to other places."[5] The relocation recommendations are indeed incongruous with the rest of the report, but it is gratifying that most of the Commission members were willing to let them stand in spite of it.

Wilbur Thompson maintains that even though characteristically small-town depressed areas are probably not viable economically, we have programs designed to attract industry to these areas with no programs to help redundant workers move from them to tighter labor markets.[6] "When more spending leads to overtime for Cleveland machinists while barely touching the plight of unemployed West Virginia coal miners," he writes, "counseling, retraining and relocation become the mainstays of a new employment policy."[7] However, he argues that while the federal government should have a supporting role, programs involving relocation should be primarily the responsibility of local governments. "A sophisticated response to structural unemployment requires . . . a bit of meddling in the lives of people, in contrast to the relatively impersonal federal deficits prescribed for cyclical unemployment. And 'meddling' is best done at the local level."[8] Furthermore, he asserts that "the sheer size and scope of a comprehensive retraining and relocation effort would almost surely prevent the creation of anything more than a nominal direct *local* role for federal personnel."[9]

While there is a great deal of substance to Thompson's position, there are a number of reasons for believing that he underestimates the role that the federal government will have to assume in any comprehensive national program of retraining, job information, and relocation. In many local communities in economically lagging regions, those who need help must have little reason to expect any positive initiatives from local leaders or officials. The Negro in rural Mississippi and the Appalachian living in a county controlled by a clique that seeks only to preserve the status quo would be surprised to learn that "meddling" on their behalf is "best done at the local level." Thompson clearly recognizes that it is unrealistic to ask any one community to pay the costs of services that benefit another community, yet since this issue is at the heart of any retraining and relocating program, it would seem that the direct and active involvement of governments above the local level would be a necessary condition for the successful implementation of such a program. But even state governments have shown little or no interest in programs involving relocation. Since Thompson singles out West Virginia as a state that particularly needs a relocation program, it is instructive to note that this state's antipoverty programs have refused to recognize the necessity for population migration, and nothing has been done to help migrants.[10] Whether or not federal personnel would assume a direct local role in a comprehensive relocation and retraining effort, it is necessary that local functions be performed in harmony with national policy as determined at the federal level.

European Relocation Programs

One of the most important differences between manpower policy in western Europe and that in the United States has been the greater emphasis given to worker relocation programs in western Europe. This phenomenon was dismissed in some quarters on the ground that European workers are relatively immobile and need more encouragement and support from public programs. However, a study by the International Labor Office[11] has shown that European workers are in reality quite mobile. Frequency of moves in West Germany between local districts and *Länder* are about the same as those between counties and states in the United States. West Germans were found to be more mobile than French and Italian workers, but even in these two countries 1.5 million people change communes annually, and about half a million change regions. Moreover, as Jack Steiber has remarked, a case can be made that it is even more important to give assistance to promote geographic mobility in the United States than in other countries because of the greater distances and higher costs of moving.[12]

A survey of relocation programs in ten western European countries indicates that one of the principal reasons why more European workers have not made use of relocation assistance is that employment opportunities are usually found in areas with the greatest housing problems. As might be expected, reluctance to leave the home area is a deterrent to mobility, but this primarily affects older workers. Cultural and religious differences among the regions of a country may also inhibit mobility. The number of workers who take advantage of relocation assistance is limited by lack of knowledge. Only in Sweden is information on relocation assistance publicized by all employment offices; in other countries no particular publicity on its availability is given. In some cases allowances have not been sufficient to induce workers to leave their home areas. However, experience in Sweden and Great Britain has shown that applications for relocation assistance have increased in response to increased allowances. For those countries examined in detail, the rate of return after relocation assistance seemed to average about 20 percent. In addition, there were indications of considerable job switching in new areas; in Sweden less than 40 percent of the workers who had received relocation assistance were still in their original jobs a year after moving.[13]

Sweden's policies for encouraging labor mobility are particularly noteworthy. Despite relatively full employment, employment declines in forestry and agriculture have resulted in high unemployment in some areas of the country, while there have been labor shortages in others. In response the government has established a comprehensive program to assist unemployed workers in lagging areas in moving to labor-short areas and to give them skills that are marketable in the latter areas. Financial assistance includes travel and moving expense allowances, family allowances, starting allowances, and special settlement payments to induce people to move from lagging regions. Workers who are unemployed, or who are likely to become unemployed, are informed of job opportunities in other areas by the Employment Service. Frequently Employment Service officials from labor-short areas visit labor surplus areas to describe the opportunities available.[14]

A worker and his wife may obtain financial aid to go and look over a job opportunity in another area and to find housing, and then return home. If the family moves, the Labor Market Board pays the cost of personal transportation, as well as for packing and moving the family's belongings. If a worker is not able to take his family to a new area immediately, he receives an allowance from the Board to compensate for the cost of maintaining two households. This allowance can amount to a maximum of $40 a month for the wife and $9 a month for each child for a period lasting up to nine months, though it cannot be more than the actual rent or housing costs. It is paid directly to the family in the home area. "Starting allowances" are paid to tide transferred workers over until they receive their first paychecks. The amount varies according to whether a job is temporary or permanent, but the maximum amount is $100. Finally, "settlement grants" of about $400 are available to persons in the five northernmost counties, where unemployment is particularly high, if they agree to move to other parts of the country acceptable to the Labor Market Board. Workers who do not remain in their new locations are required to repay money received as relocation assistance. In the case of starting allowances, a worker must pay $1 per day for each day less than a hundred that he does not work on his new job. However, if he moves to another job with the approval of the Board, he does not have to make any repayment. Likewise, travel or family expenses for temporary moves do not have to be repaid.[15]

As indicated earlier, one of the major obstacles to mobility is housing problems. The Labor Market Board and communities have used emergency funds to provide housing for new workers and their families. In some areas communities are given extra building loan credits on condition that they provide dwellings to relocated workers. Transferred workers are sometimes given preference on housing waiting lists, especially if they are construction workers engaged in building other housing. Relocated workers also are given assistance in selling their homes; the Labor Market Board has even purchased homes from workers in labor surplus areas.[16]

Labor Market Board reports indicate that in the course of a year about 0.3 to 0.4 percent of the civilian labor force makes use of some form of financial assistance to aid relocation.[17] The funds spent to encourage geographic mobility amount to between 1 and 2 percent of the total cost of employment programs, which include emergency public works programs as a major item. The success of relocation programs in Sweden is due in large measure to the fact that the Employment Service is an integral part of the organization of most communities, and that it provides many services beside matching workers and jobs.[18] In the last analysis, however, the appeal of relocation programs resides in the fact that, in the words of a Swedish Minister of Finance, "It is cheaper to move manpower to jobs than to move industries into labor surplus areas."[19]

Labor Mobility Demonstration Projects in the United States

In 1963, the Department of Labor requested and received authority to conduct a limited, experimental labor mobility program that provided financial aid on a need basis. The program was made possible by an amendment to the Manpower Development and Training Act of 1962 and a Congressional appropriation of $5 million each year since 1965 for administrative and allowance funds. During the fiscal year that ended in June, 1968, the U.S. Employment Service (USES) and eighteen affiliated state employment service agencies jointly participated in labor mobility research projects that incorporated knowledge acquired from earlier projects. In the twelve of these states that are east of the Mississippi River, projects were linked by a compact that provided for common payments procedures, eligibility criteria, and other standards. This set of twelve projects has been designated the Interregional Labor Mobility Project. The Project was established to provide information on how the USES could best operate a national program involving interstate coordination.[20]

For the most part, recruitment of relocatees depended on the regular flow of applicants to local employment service offices. The local office interviewer first explored with the applicants the prospects for local employment, including possibilities for occupational change or relocation. Only after all local alternatives were explored were applicants asked to consider relocation. If it appeared that relocation might be feasible, applicants were referred to a labor mobility representative, who interviewed them to determine if they were eligible and willing to move and if they could be given appropriate jobs outside of their areas. Any involuntarily unemployed worker who was unable to secure suitable employment within normal commuting distance was considered eligible for relocation assistance.

In addition to the normal applicant flow, a number of other recruiting techniques were used by various projects. These included call-in cards and letters sent to potential recruits after a review of applications on file, the use of posters and pamphlet hand-outs, and referrals by other agencies. The most successful method of recruiting proved to be hiring interviews conducted locally by representatives from firms in other areas. In some projects it was found that up to half of the respondents to this type of recruitment were not even registered in the local employment office. Many of these persons who were not selected for relocation were able to fill local job needs.

"Positive recruitment" does at times create problems. Employers sometimes want workers on the job in distant places within a few days. This makes it difficult to process mobility assistance, and in some cases provides too little time for proper counseling and evaluation of applicants' reasons for wanting to relocate.

Once it is determined that applicants are eligible and willing to move, a project must find suitable job opportunities. One means is to use the employment service interarea recruitment system. The project reviews the inventory of job openings for its state and then for other states to determine whether appropriate opportunities exist. Other local and state offices may also be requested to investigate job openings for potential relocatees. If these methods do not work, a project may rely on direct contacts with employers. Some projects send resumés of applicants to prospective employers, and in some instances want-ads from out-of-town newspapers have been used with success. When employers required interviews on their premises, most projects provided pre-employment expenses, in-cluding round-trip transportation and subsistence. In some cases where employers had had good results with previously hired workers, hiring authority was delegated to project directors or inter-viewers. A small number of persons were hired on the basis of telephone interviews. In Missouri a "hire day" was used with good results. A group of relocation applicants in a given occupation were brought together in a central place in an area where their skills were in relatively short supply. Employers were invited to interview and hire the potential relocatees on the date fixed for the meeting. The positive recruitment approach mentioned earlier was found in a number of projects to be particularly useful for disadvantaged workers, since most employers of unskilled labor do not want to hire workers without some face-to-face contact. Many of the em-ployers who engage in this type of hiring provide thorough training, relatively high wages, and opportunities for occupational upgrading and better pay.

Table 34 lists some of the relevant characteristics of relocatees who participated in five projects which together accounted for about half of all mobility project relocatees. The author has been told by an independent Department of Labor official that these data, which are taken from the USES publication *Moving To Work*, probably overstate the degree to which project relocatees as a whole are dis-advantaged. However, they represent the most complete tabulation available at this writing.

The success of any relocation program rests in large measure on the proportion of stable relocations that it generates. The experi-ence of the USES mobility projects over the past three years indi-cates that because of the complex problems surrounding moves, a minimum return rate of between 5 and 10 percent can be anticipated within the first few months. The number of relocatees that have participated in projects under Title I of MDTA by fiscal year are shown in Table 35. *Moving To Work* states that the proportion of successful relocations has increased steadily from 70 percent in fiscal year 1965 to 88 percent in fiscal year 1968. However, these

TABLE 34: CHARACTERISTICS OF WORKERS RECEIVING
RELOCATION ASSISTANCE FROM LABOR
MOBILITY DEMONSTRATION PROJECTS[a]

	1968	1966–67
Average age	26.4	30.0
Percent married	50.1	33.6
Average number of dependents, excluding relocatee	2.1	2.6
Average number of weeks unemployed	21.3	16.9
Average years of schooling	10.4	11.7
Percent receiving welfare assistance at time of relocation	17.3	11.0
Percent receiving unemployment insurance at time of relocation	19.4	—[b]
Percent MDTA trained	18.3[c]	15.9
Percent handicapped	9.0	—[b]
Percent males	90.3	93.1

[a] The data are based on a sampling of projects. They concern five projects which together moved half of all relocatees.
[b] Not available.
[c] Of those relocatees who received MDTA training, 68 percent were placed in training-related jobs.
Source: Moving To Work (Washington, D.C.: Labor Mobility Services Unit, United States Employment Service, 1968), Appendix 1, p. 1.

figures are suspect in view of the fact that the total number of re-locations given in this report are inflated. In the most thorough study of the labor mobility projects, which unfortunately examines only fiscal year 1967, Audrey Freedman found that for relocatees who responded to a questionnaire two months after relocation, 13 per-cent were unemployed and about half of these persons had returned and were unemployed in their home areas. The remaining 87 per-cent were still employed in the new areas, although one-quarter of them had changed jobs. Eighty-two percent of the respondents stated that they were satisfied with their relocation. While these results indicate a high rate of success in placing workers in perma-nent employment and in settling them satisfactorily in new com-munities, they are somewhat clouded by the fact that no response was obtained from a quarter of the relocatees. Whether lack of response was related to some failure of relocation was not known.[21]

TABLE 35: NUMBER OF RELOCATEES IN LABOR MOBILITY
DEMONSTRATION PROJECTS, BY FISCAL YEAR

	1965	1966	1967	1968[a]
United States Employment				
Service projects	228	1064	2175	6201
Private contract projects	347	574	1361	1296
Total	575	1638	3536	7497

[a] Includes the period to September 1, 1968.
Source: Department of Labor.

Workers who return home may do so for many reasons. A worker may not like his shift assignment or may not have properly understood the nature of his job when he was hired. In a few cases employers changed the work assignment or the wage rate so as to reduce the worker's expected take-home pay. If, upon investigation, the employer was found to be at fault, the worker was assisted in finding a better paying job. Community related reasons for unsuccessful transfers included inability to find suitable housing, high costs of living, shopping and transportation complexities of urban centers, and feelings of alienation. Personal problems related to health, returning to school, entering the armed services, and simple homesickness were also instrumental in some return moves.

To improve the rate of stable relocations, mobility project staffs have increasingly endeavored to investigate working conditions, pay rates, and living arrangements before approving relocation allowances. Moreover, all projects are now required to interview the wives of potential relocatees to ascertain the families' attitudes toward moving. Travelers Aid Association services—visits to the home, visits with friends and neighbors, and inquiries into family reliability and stability—have helped many projects to eliminate high risk relocatees. In the West Virginia project, for example, Travelers Aid assistance has been an important factor in increasing the relocation success rate from 50 percent to 91 percent.

Relocation costs have varied from project to project, depending on the nature of the services provided. In general, however, costs have been reduced as the project staffs gain more experience.

Average individual allowance costs for all projects amounted to $442 in 1966–67, but in 1968 this figure was reduced to $325.[22] Some of the factors that have contributed to this reduction are better screening of applicants, more intensive pre-employment interviews, and better spreading of payments. No precise cost-benefit analysis has been applied to the projects. However, the average relocatee in the projects covered in Table 34 had been unemployed for 21.3 weeks and had probably been collecting welfare payments or unemployment insurance benefits. According to *Moving To Work,* the average weekly wage that he earned on his last regular job was $72.00, whereas the corresponding amount after relocation was $90.00. Freedman's analysis of fiscal year 1967 data indicates that in general, relocation appears to have shifted workers from low-paying jobs held prior to unemployment preceding relocation to moderate-wage employment.[23]

The findings of the labor mobility projects indicate that a wide range of specialized supportive services will be needed in any nation-wide mobility program, especially where the rural poor or ghetto residents are involved. These services include pre-relocation counseling, assistance in obtaining housing, orientation in the demand area, health aid, financial counseling, help in obtaining transportation, clothing, furniture, and, in some cases, help in preparing applications for employment, school enrollment, public assistance, and other public and private services. Nearly all relocatees need some form of assistance, even if it only be information about the housing, educational, recreational, and other facilities in the new area. Many of the more disadvantaged relocatees have little ability to cope with situations that differ from those to which they are accustomed in their own community; these persons need considerable assistance if they are to overcome the complicated problems they experience both before and after moving. Workers involved in the mobility projects have expressed their desire for more services in the demand area. Housing is a universal problem, and some projects have prevailed upon employers to create home-finding services within their personnel departments.

There has not been a great deal of public or political reaction to the mobility projects because they have not been given much publicity. Some employers in supply areas have expressed concern that moving workers would dry up their source of cheap labor. However, the workers were unemployed in their home communities, and the employment service staffs have usually been able to convince the employers that relocation was really best for the community and the relocatee. Some businessmen and other citizens in demand areas have expressed concern about disadvantaged workers moving into their communities. This concern has also been reflected by their Congressmen, but objections were usually withdrawn when it was pointed out that the inmigrants were needed to fill long-standing job vacancies that apparently would not be filled by local persons.

In view of the experience obtained thus far from the mobility projects, the USES has suggested a number of features that should be incorporated into future mobility programs. The organizational structure recommended by most states is a strong central mobility office with area representatives covering a number of local offices, and, in some cases, a full-time staff assigned to larger supply area offices. This is preferable to the system that utilizes central project officers with fractional or full-time staff assigned to specific offices. The latter system is often characterized by lack of control by the project director and by the need for staff members who are not assigned full-time to mobility activities to perform too many other functions. In procedural requirements the projects have shown a need for a stronger clearance system into which current supply and demand data can be fed. Tie-ins between MDTA and mobility programs have proven desirable and feasible. The project reports indicate that applicants should be trained in supply areas for eventual relocation to demand areas if there are no foreseeable local job opportunities. All projects have emphasized the need for comprehensive supportive services. The success of mobility programs is also dependent on maintaining good relations with community organizations, and on enlisting the cooperation of employers in helping disadvantaged relocatees to adapt to their new environment. All projects pointed up the need for an adequate and flexible budget; inflexibility in allowance schedules have resulted in "overpayments" to some relocatees and insufficient funds for others. Finally, several states have recommended that the mobility program be moved from a pilot to a permanent basis, and that it be made national in scope, with adequate publicity.

The Labor Mobility Services Unit of the USES believes that the USES is ready and able to take on a permanent nationwide mobility program to include a high degree of specialized, supportive services. The cost of these services will be high, but the Unit finds that such a program is self-supporting in the sense that the benefits that accrue to the relocatees, as well as to society as a whole, are far greater than the effort and expense involved.

The United States Employment Service and Labor Mobility

In its platform proposals sent to the Republican and Democratic Conventions in 1968, the AFL-CIO correctly pointed out that:

Despite the fact that the solutions to our manpower problems require an integrated, national approach, the public employment service—our single most important instrument for manpower programs—is, for all practical purposes, 50 different state systems. Under its present structure the public employment service inhibits efforts to establish an effective national approach, or even a regional approach, to manpower problems. And because its activities are geared to the boundary lines of local communities and states, instead of being patterned according to job markets which often cut across state lines, even local job markets are sometimes fractured by the existing administrative arrangements of the public employment service.[24]

The AFL-CIO went on to recommend the establishment of a permanent program of adequate relocation allowances for unemployed workers and their families to enable workers who so desire to move to areas where job opportunities exist.[25] The great differences that exist in unemployment rates among labor areas make such a program a necessity. In January, 1966, for example, Lexington and Louisville, Kentucky, had unemployment rates of 1.9 and 3.5, re-

spectively, whereas some eastern Kentucky counties had unemployment rates near 30 percent.[26] Yet no systematic effort has been
made to establish permanent comprehensive relocation programs
even within this one state.

The relatively heavy use of state employment services by Negroes
and their high rates of outmigration from the South mean that the
USES could perform a vital role in making more adequate job information available than is now given concerning different labor
markets. The southern Negro often moves to other areas without
any information other than what he gets from family and friends,
who themselves may be recent migrants. As a result, he frequently
goes into an area with little or no real long-run growth prospects
for employment or wage levels. The employment service should
have offices in the South to provide potential migrants with adequate
information on job opportunities and living conditions in other
parts of the country so that misguided moves may be substantially
decreased.[27]

Since the USES will almost certainly be the cornerstone in any
future national policy for manpower development, it has frequently
been suggested that it be federalized so that it will be more responsive to national objectives. Because national manpower priorities
have not yet been systematically determined it may be premature to
believe that the present federal-state structure can be dismantled
and replaced by a new structure. As Arnold Nemore and Garth
Mangum have said, "the federal-state Employment Service is a
cumbersome bureaucracy with a complex decision-making structure," but "its very size is inextricably linked to the system's value
in implementing national manpower policy. Duplicating its 2,000
local offices is inconceivable and another 30 years would be required
to duplicate its experience."[28] Nevertheless, they acknowledge that
even though local employment offices must be staffed by local
people who understand local needs, "A larger federal role would . . .
be useful in the interstate placement process and in serving labor
markets which overlap state boundaries."[29]

If the Employment Service is to become a comprehensive manpower agency serving both employers and workers more efficiently, it must function as an interarea clearing-house, relating worker availability to job opportunities. To become effective in this regard it needs to adopt modern methods of data collection, storage, and retrieval; it must make maximum use of the latest computer technology on a nationwide basis. Pilot studies already have demonstrated the feasibility of collecting job vacancy information from employers. The USES, in cooperation with its affiliated state employment service agencies and the Bureau of Labor Statistics, has conducted comprehensive job vacancy surveys in sixteen metropolitan areas representing a broad cross-section of American industry. In the aggregate, these areas account for about one-fourth of all nonfarm employment in the nation.

One of the most significant and conclusive results of the experimental program was the demonstration that valid job vacancy information by detailed occupation can be collected from a large sample of employing establishments. Approximately 80 per cent of the nearly 20,000 employers sampled responded to the survey questionnaires. As a result of additional experimentation in some areas, it was demonstrated that employers would also provide information on wage rates offered for the vacant jobs and on the number of vacancies for part-time or temporary jobs.[30]

The operational success that pilot studies have had with regard to definitions, sampling, and reporting still does not change the fact that job vacancy concepts and data do not play a large role in the operations of public or private employers. John Dunlop has argued that "Until these data are perfected and enter into internal organizational processes, the regular completion of questionnaires for outsiders will have limited meaning."[31] While job vacancy data are needed by occupational and regional categories, job titles are frequently not comparable among employers, especially across industry lines. Because there are still no analytically significant definitions to order and compare occupations and job classifications, Dunlop emphasizes that "manpower projections by the enterprise, internal labor markets, and occupational tables arranged by job content and job families constitute areas in which significant work is vital in order to enhance the meaning and measurement of job vacancies."[32]

On the supply side, a greater outreach effort must be made to test, counsel, and place disadvantaged workers, including those whose geographic location isolates them from job opportunities. In particular, a much more coordinated and comprehensive program of social services must be made available to the mobile poor in new job areas. The Employment Service does not have the resources to provide all of the services that workers and their families moving to new areas may need. It should, however, take the initiative in involving social welfare organizations in these kinds of activity. Despite allegations that mobility projects only "skim the cream" of the unemployed in lagging areas, there is evidence that mobility projects can reach the more "hard-core" cases. For example, a mobility project involving employment in New York showed that middle-aged workers can be satisfactorily relocated if supportive manpower and social services are provided. The average age of relocated workers in the New York project was 41.[33] In general, the mobility projects have shown that both willingness to move and job retention after moving have been higher among applicants who had been in low-wage jobs than among those who once held higher-paying jobs. This suggests greater program effectiveness for the poor, since those who once held higher-paying jobs may be more skilled and have more choices available.[34] Some of the larger projects also have begun to follow the approach suggested by the growth center discussion presented in the last chapter. That is, they have diverted migration away from large cities where an unemployed worker would arrive with little or no funds and no immediate employment prospects, and toward medium-sized cities where labor demand is strong and adjustment chances better.[35] This approach should be continued and expanded as a part of a national program that integrates regional and manpower policies.

Chapter 12

A Summary View

As the aggregate rate of growth of employment rises and remains relatively high there is a tendency for regional employment growth rates to become more uniform. The convergence of employment growth rates during periods of national prosperity is due more to changes in the competitive component of total employment change than to changes in the industry mix, which is generally moving closer to that of the industrialized states because of rural to urban population shifts and the concomitant movement from agricultural employment into non-agricultural jobs. Increased uniformity in regional income changes also results from rapid growth in aggregate economic activity. While regional income differences are diminishing, the rate of convergence is slow, and considerable absolute differences still remain among the states. In 1967, per capita personal income ranged from $1,895 in Mississippi to $3,865 in Connecticut.

Because urbanization is perhaps the dominant attribute of contemporary American social, economic, and political life, it is essential to consider spatial economic change and manpower problems within the context of the dynamics of urban growth. The growth of a region is closely linked to the growth of its cities. About two-thirds of the nation's population lives in SMSA's, and over three-fourths of the nation's population growth in this century is accounted for by the growth of SMSA's. Industrial and population concentration in SMSA's is greatest in the Northeast and North Central regions, but the highest rates of population growth in SMSA's are found in the West and South. Between 1950 and 1960, cities in the 10,000 to 100,000 population range grew more rapidly than either small or very large urban places, but many of the middle-sized places are close to a large city or within a large urban complex, rather than relatively independent entities dominating their own hinterlands. Income differences among SMSA's are tending to decrease, largely because of their increasingly diversified and similar industrial mixes.

Despite the rapid growth of SMSA's, many of the older central cities have had stagnant or declining populations. The postwar flight of people to the suburbs and the decentralization of economic activity within metropolitan areas has resulted in substantial segregation of people in terms of race, income, age, and economic opportunity. Especially difficult problems have been created by the migration of large numbers of southern Negroes seeking improved social and economic opportunities in the North. On the other hand, although the central city-suburb dichotomy is relevant to SMSA's that account for most of the total metropolitan population, the majority of smaller metropolitan areas of the South and West face similar problems in the suburbs and the central cities.

Despite relatively rapid growth in recent years, the South remains the nation's principal problem area. Per capita income in the Southeast increased more than threefold between 1948 and 1967, and its proportion of the national average increased from 70 percent to 77 percent, yet the absolute gap rose from $446 to $708. The South's economic development has been retarded by its specialization in relatively slow-growing sectors. The region's industry mix is becoming more like that of the rest of the nation, but its main employment increases continue to be in industries that are labor-intensive and pay relatively low wages. The South must increase its competitive gains in the more capital-intensive industries if its per capita income is to approach that of the nation as a whole. Because these industries have relatively high skill requirements it is imperative that there be greater investment in the South's human resources. The labor force in the South has a greater proportion of Negroes than the rest of the country, and, while the education and training of Negroes has been neglected in the nation as a whole, the southern Negro is worse off than Negroes in other regions in these regards. In addition, a higher proportion of whites in the South have low skill levels than do whites elsewhere. Underinvestment in human resources in the South has not only been the greatest impediment to the South's development, but it also has adversely affected the rest of the nation. When education is taken into account, the migration of people to and from the South has not, on balance, worked to the detriment of the South in terms of its human capital. Migration has, however, affected the rest of the nation unfavorably in relation to its existing educational distribution. For this reason the nation as a whole has a stake in the development of the South's human resources. A particular effort should be made to upgrade the health, education, and skills of southern Negroes since the human resources of southern Negroes are even less developed than those of the Negroes who have left the South.

In addition to the development of its human resources the economic progress of the South is dependent on its urbanization. If the South is to capture a greater share of rapidly growing, capital-intensive industries, it will have to generate more of the external economies that attract such industries, and these external economies are linked to urban growth. Although the South is still relatively underurbanized, its cities are growing more rapidly than those of the rest of the country. Moreover, whereas rural areas of the South continue to lose more well-educated people than they gain, the areas with large, growing metropolitan populations are net gainers of well-educated migrants from the rural South and the North. It may be expected that the urbanization of the South will be accompanied by a movement away from the traditional values and attitudes that have impeded the region's development and toward greater integration with the life of the nation as a whole. The South also has an opportunity to plan its urban growth so that many of the disagreeable aspects of northern cities may be avoided or minimized. The nation, then, has a vital interest in promoting the development of the South's human resources and the growth of urban areas in the South which are capable of providing new and attractive job opportunities to the region's people.

Since the future development of the South will be centered on its cities, those parts of the region that do not have vital metropolitan areas will continue to lag behind both regional and national income and employment growth rates. The lagging parts should squarely face the population migration question. Among the areas of the South where people should receive particular attention with respect to human resource investment and relocation assistance are most of Arkansas and Mississippi and the Southern Appalachians.

Though it is by no means a homogeneous region, Appalachia's employment structure tends to be heavily weighted with declining and slow-growing industries. The region's relative isolation, its neglect of its human resources, and its failure to develop rapidly growing metropolitan areas with attractive external economies have combined to discourage faster growing and better-paying industries from locating there. Many parts of Appalachia, and especially Central Appalachia, will continue to be hard pressed to provide decent job opportunities in the foreseeable future. The public works projects that are going into many of these areas may represent a misallocation of resources from an opportunity cost point of view, and they may do a disservice by building up false hopes among the people of the areas concerned.

The Appalachian Regional Development Act of 1965 was passed on the assumption that sufficient economic activity could be attracted to the region to give it a high and sustained rate of economic growth, and that employment opportunities approaching those in the rest of the nation could be achieved without significant outmigration. The Act placed primary emphasis on using public infrastructure investment to induce higher levels of private investment. Most of the original authorizations under the Act were for highway construction because it was felt that the region's greatest need was to be opened up to the more prosperous regions which surround it. Unfortunately, the relative advantages which Appalachia offers to private investment may be too small for the region to compete effectively with other regions, even with the projects that have been and will be provided for regional development purposes. Moreover, the original Appalachian Regional Development Act failed to recognize that the greatest need of Appalachia's people is for more investment in human resource development and manpower programs, including training for job opportunities outside the region and comprehensive relocation assistance programs.

Despite the claims of conservatives who wish to preserve the status quo and liberals who wish to preserve their notion of a world where the dulcimer and Elizabethan speech still proclaim the virtues of cultural pluralism, the people of even the poorer parts of Appalachia have much the same values and aspirations as other Americans. Moreover, many Appalachians are willing to move to areas where job opportunities are better, or at least they feel that their children should move. Unfortunately, underdeveloped human resources not only make Appalachia unattractive to growth industries, but they also make it difficult for many Appalachians to find employment outside of the region. If the nation as a whole has a stake in the human resources of the South, this is even more the case with respect to the hard-core poverty areas of Appalachia. The Appalachian Regional Commission has been well aware of the region's human resource deficiencies, and actual appropriations and expenditures under the Appalachian Regional Development Act have given more emphasis to human resource development than is indicated by the Act's original program authorizations. In addition, the Commission realizes that improving the quality of human resources may induce further outmigration, though it has no program to assist the moves of people leaving the region.

In the past, family members who have already migrated to cities outside the region have influenced the migration of their relatives still in the region; problems of adjustment to urban life of migrants from Appalachia have been greatly eased because of this process. In the future, however, migrants probably will be less influenced by previous choices of their families and more responsive to opportunities in the job market. In any event, their destinations need not be ghettos in large northern cities since jobs are available in intermediate areas. For example, employment opportunities are promising in the Lexington-Louisville-Cincinnati triangle and the Piedmont Crescent of North Carolina. Cities such as Baltimore, Washington, Norfolk, Richmond, and Atlanta could also be tied into planning for Appalachia, though every effort should be made to link Appalachia's workers to the growth of urban centers or complexes as close as possible to their places of origin. In general, Appalachia is a collection of hinterlands for urban centers outside the region, and the people in these hinterlands might be better off if more emphasis were placed on linking them to these centers and less emphasis were placed on trying to force-feed economic activity in the hinterlands. The latter approach is not only inefficient but too often ineffective.

There are places within Appalachia with growth potential and the Appalachian Regional Commission can play a valuable role in stimulating, guiding, and coordinating their development. Nevertheless, this does not necessarily imply that these places will transform the entire region, nor does it deny the necessity to link Appalachia to growth centers surrounding the region. The Appalachian highway program provides links to many of these centers, but the Commission views them primarily in terms of commuting for Appalachian residents or markets for Appalachian firms, rather than in terms of comprehensive labor mobility programs.

The Appalachian development program is especially instructive because it is supposed to serve as a model for the regional commissions that have been created for the Ozarks, the Coastal Plains, the Upper Great Lakes, the Four Corners, and New England. The last is an exceptional region because it includes a metropolitan area (Boston) which is a center for some of the fastest-growing sectors in the country, the state with the highest per capita income (Connecticut), and a relatively well-educated population even in its most lagging part (northern New England). The other regions are made up of areas that are relatively unattractive to industry and, with the exception of the Upper Great Lakes, areas that are badly in need of more investment in human resources. The new commissions have not been in existence long enough for them to establish program priorities. There are indications, nonetheless, that they are showing more interest in human resource development and manpower programs than was the case only a short time ago. Unfortunately, the new commissions are primarily geared to attracting economic activity to their respective regions, with no programs being undertaken to place unemployed and underemployed workers in jobs in other areas where opportunities are greater. Again, the New England region is an exception because it is comprised of both rapidly advancing and lagging areas. Indeed, it would be preferable if the other commissions would include relatively close urban growth centers as an integral part of their planning activities. More will be said on this point later.

The Economic Development Administration was created by the Public Works and Economic Development Act of 1965 to help areas characterized by substantial and persistent unemployment and relatively low income levels. There is a great deal of overlap between counties receiving EDA assistance and those included within the domains of the regional commissions. Although the commissions and EDA were created by the same legislation, there has been little coordination of effort among these agencies, primarily because each commission wants to function with a maximum degree of independence. As in the cases of the Appalachian Regional Commission and its own predecessor, the Area Redevelopment Administration, EDA's legislative mandate assumes that what the people of lagging regions most need is improved public works facilities, which in turn will induce more private investment and create more jobs. Insofar as EDA has followed any overall strategy, it has been based on the theme of "worst first." Under this approach expenditure priorities favor areas where growth responses are the least evident.

The worst-first policy involves a number of difficulties. The multicounty districts that have been found to promote more rational planning in lagging areas are required to prepare Overall Economic Development Programs which describe the problems of their respective districts and propose solutions. However, EDA admits that better-off districts tend to submit better OEDP's and more attractive projects. Still, the worst-off areas know that they will receive top priority no matter how minimal their planning efforts have been. In fact, the quality of most OEDP's leaves much to be desired, and Washington provides little incentive to improve the situation. The worst-first policy also runs counter to EDA's own economic development center policy. These centers are communities or localized areas with fewer than 250,000 persons where, hopefully, resources can be concentrated to create more jobs and higher incomes for the people of the surrounding area. Thus, the centers are supposed to have high growth potential and would not be likely to qualify for aid under the worst-first criterion. On the other hand, even if EDA's "growth center" approach was not contradicted by worst-first considerations, the centers actually chosen by the agency have been for the most part too small to have any real impact on their surrounding hinterlands. The major difficulty here is that EDA's legislation precludes the agency's operating in areas which are neither congested urban agglomerations nor small cities and towns that are part of or in close proximity to lagging areas. The excluded intermediate areas have urban growth centers which, under a comprehensive regional policy, probably could absorb more migrants more efficiently than the EDA growth centers, especially if they too benefited from federal aid aimed at helping migrants from lagging areas to find employment. Finally, if the difficulties of rural migrants to large metropolitan areas are largely a function of lack of education and job skills, as EDA has correctly maintained, it should also follow that the migration of these people to smaller growth centers would pose similar problems. Yet so long as policy for lagging regions continues to emphasize public works projects, the pressing needs of the people in these regions for more investment in human resources and for expanded manpower programs will continue to be neglected.

Among the people who particularly need greater investment in human resources are the Mexican Americans and the Indians. While considerable attention has been given to programs designed to further the social and economic advancement of the Negro, relatively little attention has been devoted to the often equally severe problems of these minorities. The geographic concentration of the Mexican Americans in the Southwest and the geographic isolation of the Indians on reservations have tended to make the nation as a whole unaware of their problems and therefore relatively unresponsive to them. In addition, the conservative leadership of both the Mexican Americans and the Indians has tended to play up the attachment of their people to traditional values and their native soil. Too often this defensive response to a larger urban-industrial society has only served to deny the people in question their potential share in the fruits of the larger society's economic progress. The appeal of the traditional way of life has had especially negative consequences for the development of the human resources of the groups in question. The traditional values of these groups tend to play down the importance of education and to foster short time-horizons that leave the individual's long run welfare to forces beyond his control. Programs aimed at upgrading the human resources of minority groups must include an understanding and appreciation of these groups' traditions and values, but they must also recognize the necessity of preparing individuals from these groups for life in the larger society if this is the life the people wish to choose. At present too many of these persons simply have no choice. For those individuals who do wish to participate in the larger society and to take advantage of the job opportunities which it offers to those with the necessary skills and training to take advantage of them, it is essential that the migration issue be squarely faced.

The widespread assumption that Indians are not suited to life off the reservations was reinforced by the failure of the relocation policy of the 1950's, which moved a large number of Indians directly from reservations to cities, without adequate preparation and training. In consequence, efforts to aid Indian populations have tended to take the form of programs to attract industry to the reservations. Despite some progress in this regard, Indian reservations have even fewer attributes than most lagging regions that would make them attractive to industry. On the other hand, although their responses will vary from tribe to tribe, Indians are not so reluctant to leave the reservations or as unable to adapt to urban life as many believe. However, they do need comprehensive programs to help them prepare for life and work off the reservations. There is a direct relationship between the amount of training and comprehensive assistance given to the Indian and his family and both his income after relocating and his success at adapting to his new environment. Moreover, the cost per job obtained by relocation programs is less than the cost per job created by attempts to attract industry to the reservations.

There is clear evidence that the quality and quantity of education and training received by the Mexican American population needs substantial upgrading, and that increased education pays off for them in terms of concrete economic gains. The greatest difficulties for Mexican Americans are encountered in south Texas, where educational levels are low and where pressures from migration and commuting from Mexico tend to keep wages and employment opportunities depressed. Migration to better opportunities elsewhere, particularly in California, where discrimination is less a problem, is one means by which many Mexican Americans from south Texas have achieved some measure of progress. However, so long as migrants and commuters from Mexico continue to flow into south Texas, wages will remain low and unemployment rates will remain high.

With the exception of cheap labor, south Texas offers so few locational advantages to firms that employment opportunities would not be promising in the area in any event. Moreover, any significant increase in agricultural wages would increase mechanization and increase unemployment. The essential preconditions for any effective manpower program in south Texas are restrictions on the commuting of "green carders" and on migration. All indications are that Mexicans will continue to move to the border in large numbers, and that many will seek jobs in the United States or in American plants attracted to the Mexican side of the border by the

Mexican government's Border Industrial Development Program. The tendency for Congress to introduce greater restrictions to protect Mexican American workers should take the form of a gradual tightening to permit the Mexican population to adjust to the new situation with a minimum of friction. Meanwhile, adequate job training is needed for the Mexican Americans who will still be confronted with limited opportunities in south Texas, as well as in other areas of the Southwest. Comprehensive relocation programs, which already have proven to be feasible and efficient in matching workers from south Texas with jobs in industrial centers to the north, should be greatly expanded and made available to those who wish to leave the area.

In general, it is obvious that regional policy in the United States has been formulated and implemented on the assumption that it is possible to attract sufficient industry to lagging, and for the most part rural, regions of the country to give residents of these regions economic opportunities comparable to those enjoyed by other Americans. Moreover, most proposals concerning future regional policy continue to stress this theme, as is apparent from recommendations of the Department of Agriculture, the Manpower Report of the President for 1968, the President's National Advisory Commission on Rural Poverty, and the writings of some scholars. On the other hand, the experience of other countries which have been trying for longer than the United States to stimulate the growth of large lagging regions indicates that such force-feeding has generally been unsuccessful. The cheap land and low tax rates of lagging rural regions may be more than offset by low levels of services. Labor may be plentiful in such areas but it may prove costly to adapt relatively untrained and unskilled workers to firms' needs. Moreover, there are few contacts with other producers, suppliers, and those who provide auxiliary business services. The local market may not be significant and firms often prefer to locate near competitors rather than at a distance. Bad connections with long distance traffic may mean higher transportation costs and more time in transit, though these problems have become less important than in the past. The cultural and educational facilities of rural areas also tend to be relatively undeveloped. Finally, there is often a great deal of mistrust of industrialization in rural areas, including lack of co-operation from local leaders who do not wish to change the status quo.

Recent American and foreign evidence on greater equality in the geographical distribution of manufacturing does not indicate any corresponding lessening of regional income differences or any rela-tively greater attractiveness of small towns or rural areas. Recent growth in total national employment has primarily been accounted for by expanding tertiary activities, which have been located for the most part in metropolitan areas. Those industries that have tended to leave metropolitan areas have been characterized by relative stag-nation or decline; they frequently seek cheap labor in areas with surplus agricultural populations. Rapidly expanding sectors, in con-trast, have favored metropolitan areas because of their numerous external economies.

This is not to say that the continuing expansion of large metro-politan areas is a desirable phenomenon. Questions of efficient city sizes are difficult to deal with because of the impossibility of measur-ing adequately the external economies and diseconomies of metro-politan growth. There are a number of students of this problem who maintain that there is no evidence that even the largest metropoli-tan areas are too big, in the sense that marginal costs exceed mar-ginal productivity. These arguments generally are based on a consideration of the costs and benefits to firms. However, external diseconomies which result from congestion—for example, traffic congestion, inadequate parks and recreation facilities, slum neighbor-hoods, and air pollution—are often not internalized by private firms; or if they are, they are not of a magnitude sufficient to offset the external economies of agglomeration. Thus, firms will continue to locate in areas where the relationship between external disecono-mies and external economies makes the net social product less than it would be in an alternative location.

The failure of the market mechanism to stem the growth of large metropolitan agglomerations suggests that public policy measures might be introduced to retard their growth and to prevent other cities from expanding to a point where they too become overconcentrated in terms of social costs and benefits. Taxation and credit policy as well as land use controls could be used to limit private investment in congested metropolitan areas. From a political viewpoint, however, a more feasible alternative might be to encourage private capital to locate in other areas. Public overhead investment and subsidies in one form or another could be used toward this end. Such tools have been used by regional development agencies, but they have usually been applied to promote economic growth in rural areas and small towns, and thus they have been not only economically inefficient, but too frequently ineffective. Of course, there may be some locations in rural areas with promising industrial potential; in general, though, the most efficient use of public funds would be to encourage the growth of medium-sized cities, especially those that have already given some real evidence of possessing growth characteristics. In these centers public funds may be integrated with actual or potential external economies to produce rapid growth with a minimum of external diseconomies of congestion. Although such centers do not "need" any government subsidy, it is easier to accelerate their growth than it would be to accelerate growth in a lagging region.

The type of growth center policy proposed here contradicts both those who claim that large metropolitan areas are not too big, and those who claim that the only alternative to force-feeding the growth of rural areas is for rural people to migrate to metropolitan ghettos. Such evidence as we have concerning both public locational preferences and efficient city sizes suggests that a growth center policy could build on rapidly expanding cities in the 250,000 to 750,000 range, though wider limits should be considered for the sake of flexibility.

It should be emphasized that not every rapidly growing city within this range would be eligible for designation as a federally assisted growth center. Only those cities that could be expected to benefit a significant number of persons from lagging regions (and the unemployed and underemployed within the center) would be eligible for designation. Thus, growth centers would have to be selected on the basis of study of commuting and migration data, as well as data on employment growth. A growth center policy would not reinforce existing migration patterns that represent movement from rural areas to metropolitan ghettos. However, migration and commuting studies would give valuable insights into the migration streams linking lagging rural areas to rapidly growing, intermediate-sized cities, streams that could be reinforced by a growth center policy. This in turn implies that education and training programs in lagging areas be geared to employment opportunities in growth centers. Those who benefit from such programs will be under no compulsion to move, but at least they will have a choice, something that too many of our citizens now lack.

A national regional policy should attempt to help areas with problems arising from outmigration to attain new equilibria with a minimum of friction. People in these areas, such as older workers whose prospects for either local employment or retraining and migration are dim, might be aided by the nation as a whole, though here we are talking about welfare rather than economic development policy. In any event, the principal thrust of public policy in lagging regions should still be in the direction of active manpower and human resource programs.

The need for comprehensive relocation assistance for workers and their families has been urged by numerous students of manpower problems. The feasibility of such programs has been amply demonstrated by both European experience and labor mobility pilot projects in the United States. Because the United States Employment Service will almost certainly be the cornerstone in any national program for comprehensive relocation assistance, it is necessary that it function as an interarea clearing-house, relating job opportunities to workers with relevant skills and training. To become effective in this regard, it must make use of the latest computer technology for data collection, storage, and retrieval on a nationwide basis. Experimental programs have shown that useful job vacancy data can be collected from employers, though there is still a need for more analytically significant definitions to order and compare occupations and job classifications. On the supply side, a greater outreach effort must be made to test, counsel, and place disadvantaged workers, including those whose geographic location has isolated them from job opportunities. In particular, a much more coordinated and comprehensive program of social services must be made available to relocatees in receiving areas. The Employment Service does not have the resources to provide all of the services that workers and their families moving to new areas may need, but it should take the initiative in involving social welfare agencies in these kinds of activity.

Some of the larger labor mobility demonstration projects have shown that it is possible to divert migration away from large cities where an unemployed worker would arrive with little or no funds and no immediate employment prospects, and toward medium-sized cities where the demand for labor is strong and chances for adjustment are better. For those persons who have already moved to metropolitan central cities where there is a lack of available jobs, a growth center policy, including a national system of job information, could provide an alternative opportunity for employment. However, for minority-group ghetto dwellers in particular, there are job opportunities available in metropolitan areas. The problem is that minority groups have been denied these opportunities, as much because of housing discrimination as because of employment discrimination. There is clear evidence that Negroes are not concentrated in central cities because they are poor, but because they cannot obtain housing in the suburbs, where jobs are available. Residents of urban ghettos, like those of lagging rural areas, are badly in need of better education, job training, and generally expanded investment in human resources, but they also need better access to suburban employment sites. Among the means that can be employed toward this end are improved transportation between the ghetto and suburban jobs, expansion of low-income housing outside of the ghetto, vigorous enforcement of open housing statutes, and rent subsidies. Policies which are based on refurbishing the ghetto, and which therefore assume the permanence of the ghetto, will not resolve the employment problems of our big cities. Rather what is called for is a change in the structure of the cities.

From the foregoing analysis it is evident that rural and urban problems, which continue to be dealt with in piecemeal fashion, need to be treated within an integrated framework. It would be desirable and feasible to establish a regional policy agency at the national level to coordinate and watch over the formulation and implementation of comprehensive regional policy. Such an agency should be attached to the White House and be independent of any Cabinet member. EDA, or some equivalent agency within the Commerce Department, could have principal responsibility for economic infrastructure investment and business-oriented programs in growth centers, though greater emphasis should be given to intermediate-sized cities and less to the smaller "development centers" on which the agency now concentrates. The principal responsibility for lagging areas should be given to an agency, or set of agencies, which have manpower and human resource development programs as their principal concern. The most likely candidates would be the Department of Labor, the Office of Economic Opportunity, and the Department of Health, Education, and Welfare. The United States Employment Service and the respective state systems should provide an effective clearing-house function at the regional and national, as well as state and local, levels. The Employment Service should also coordinate comprehensive relocation programs. In any case it is important that the overall coordination of regional policy be entrusted to a truly independent agency. To place this function in any department would create the obvious danger that it would give major attention to its own objectives and programs and then try to force—whether consciously or unconsciously—the accommodation of other departments' programs to its own.

A large and growing number of persons—Democrats and Republicans, liberals and conservatives—recognize that federal administration of billions of dollars for the War on Poverty is sprawling, inefficient, and often chaotic. There is no place in the federal government where one can go to obtain a comprehensive view of federal antipoverty programs. Congress does not have sufficient information to evaluate the relative effectiveness of various programs, and the executive branch does not even have enough information to find overlapping and duplication. In lagging areas which are the object of federal aid, it is possible for a community leader to serve simultaneously on at least five local committees or councils that are the local links with federal agencies. The Appalachian Regional Commission, OEO, EDA, HUD, and HEW all have them, and a late-starting Department of Agriculture is now attempting to get into the act.

The alternative to the disunity of the present federal complex is to decentralize assistance programs. This explains the recent popularity of revenue-sharing proposals that would turn over federal money to the states, and in some versions, to the cities, with no strings attached as to how the funds should be spent. The principal difficulty with this approach is that many state and local governments have not demonstrated that they are capable of dealing with economic and social problems. It is possible, however, through the vehicle of regional commissions, to have state and local officials and leaders prepare coherent and comprehensive programs that would be federally financed but to preserve a federal veto over projects which are contrary to efficient resource allocation from a national perspective. It would be necessary to divide the entire country into multi-state regions[1] (though they would not have to follow existing state boundaries). Moreover, the present regional commissions, with the exception of that for New England, should be redefined to encompass both lagging areas and growth centers,[2] as defined earlier, in contrast to the present policy of defining regions which are made up almost entirely of lagging areas. Only then will it be possible to relate problems of lagging areas and opportunities in genuine growth centers within a common framework.

So long as national policy succeeds in maintaining a rate of aggregate growth sufficient to guarantee reasonably full employment, I believe that a growth center strategy can be successfully integrated with manpower and relocation programs. This is not to say that programs to help develop rural areas or to improve conditions in our large cities should be discontinued; I am not advocating putting all of our financial aids into one policy basket. I have stressed the possibilities inherent in an intermediate-sized growth center approach because I believe that they have been greatly neglected in favor of alternatives which frequently have been less satisfactory in terms of public preferences and economic efficiency. Of course, implementation of the growth center strategy proposed here would no doubt raise a number of problems. The matching of training in lagging areas to job opportunities in growth centers would no doubt involve measurement difficulties. It might also be difficult to avoid giving subsidies to relocatees who would have moved to the growth center in any case, or to firms which might have expanded their operations and hired a substantial number of lagging-region residents even in the absence of federal aid. Housing bottlenecks might exist in the growth centers. Another potential problem is that the kinds of firms most likely to locate in growth centers may not be as responsive to subsidies as would be firms seeking cheap labor and subsidies in rural areas. Despite these difficulties, I believe that the strategy developed in this study opens new possibilities for dealing more rationally with problems of rural-urban transition and the restructuring of our large metropolitan areas, to create efficiently more equal opportunities for all of our citizens.

DEPARTMENT OF LABOR REGIONS

New England
  Maine
  New Hampshire
  Vermont
  Massachusetts
  Rhode Island
  Connecticut

Middle Atlantic
  New York
  New Jersey
  Pennsylvania

East North Central
  Ohio
  Indiana
  Illinois
  Michigan
  Wisconsin

West North Central
  Minnesota
  Iowa
  Missouri
  North Dakota
  South Dakota
  Nebraska
  Kansas

South Atlantic
  Delaware
  Maryland
  District of Columbia
  Virginia
  West Virginia
  North Carolina
  South Carolina
  Georgia
  Florida

East South Central
  Kentucky
  Tennessee
  Alabama
  Mississippi

West South Central
  Arkansas
  Louisiana
  Oklahoma
  Texas

Mountain
  Montana
  Idaho
  Wyoming
  Colorado
  New Mexico
  Arizona
  Utah
  Nevada

Pacific
  Washington
  Oregon
  California
  Alaska
  Hawaii

OFFICE OF BUSINESS ECONOMICS REGIONS

New England
Maine
New Hampshire
Vermont
Massachusetts
Rhode Island
Connecticut

Mideast
New York
New Jersey
Pennsylvania
Delaware
Maryland
District of Columbia

Great Lakes
Michigan
Ohio
Indiana
Illinois
Wisconsin

Plains
Minnesota
Iowa
Missouri
North Dakota
South Dakota
Nebraska
Kansas

Southeast
Virginia
West Virginia
Kentucky
Tennessee
North Carolina
South Carolina
Georgia
Florida
Alabama
Mississippi
Louisiana
Arkansas

Southwest
Oklahoma
Texas
New Mexico
Arizona

Rocky Mountain
Montana
Idaho
Wyoming
Colorado
Utah

Far West
Washington
Oregon
Nevada
California

DESIGN OF MOBILITY DEMONSTRATION PROJECTS IN VARIOUS STATE EMPLOYMENT SERVICES

State Conducting Project	Supply Areas	Demand Areas	Project Population	Special Notes
California	Sacramento, 8 smaller areas in north California	in state and nearby states	laid-off aerospace workers and unemployed workers in smaller areas	experimenting with budgeted allowances depending on need
Delaware*	entire state, nearby states	New Castle County (Washington)	selectees from unemployed who indicate interest in moving reached by Employment Service	primarily a "demand area" project seeking workers for labor-short city
Georgia*	entire state, nearby states	in state, nearby states	selectees from unemployed who indicate interest in moving reached by Employment Service	partly a "demand area" project seeking workers for labor-short city
Illinois*	entire state, major inner-city ghetto areas	major industrial centers in state	selectees from unemployed who indicate interest in moving reached by Employment Service	focus on unemployed in ghetto areas, welfare recipients
Iowa	12 county rural area; south central Iowa	urban areas in same 12 county area	rural disadvantaged	cooperating with Concentrated Employment Program centers and Industrial Development Council

APPENDIX B—*Continued*

State Conducting Project	Supply Areas	Demand Areas	Project Population	Special Notes
Kentucky*	rural counties and Appalachian areas	Lexington, Louisville	selectees from unemployed who indicate interest in moving reached by Employment Service	particular efforts directed to youth and welfare recipients
Maryland*	western and southern largely rural counties	Baltimore, labor-short areas near Washington, D.C.	selectees from unemployed who indicate interest in moving reached by Employment Service	
Michigan*	entire state, other states	Wayne, Macomb, Oakland counties	selectees from unemployed who indicate interest in moving reached by Employment Service	primarily a "demand area" project seeking workers for labor-short areas
Mississippi*	entire state	in state, nearby states	selectees from unemployed who indicate interest in moving reached by Employment Service	emphasizes movement of Concentrated Employment Program applicants
Missouri	Bootheel, Ozark areas in southern Missouri	St. Louis, western Missouri	Displaced farm workers, other rural residents	primarily from erratic farm work to steady farm jobs; special "hire days" bringing farmers and workers together in central location

APPENDIX B—Continued

State Conducting Project	Supply Areas	Demand Areas	Project Population	Special Notes
Montana	rural areas of entire state	cities in Montana, nearby states	off-reservation Indians, other disadvantaged	special outreach to isolated rural areas; cooperation with Bureau of Indian Affairs on resettling of Indians
New York*	entire state, major inner-city ghetto areas	in state, nearby states	selectees from unemployed who indicate interest in moving reached by Employment Service	special experimentation with mobility aid for residents of high-unemployed ghetto areas
Pennsylvania*	Altoona, Johnstown	in state, nearby states	selectees from unemployed who indicate interest in moving reached by Employment Service	
Texas	Rio Grande Valley, San Antonio, Corpus Christi, Laredo, other Mexican border areas	Dallas–Fort Worth, Houston, Beaumont, Port Arthur	Mexican American migrants	relocatees are receiving basic education and skill training; large proportion moving to MDTA on-the-job training as aircraft assemblers at Ling-Temco-Vought
Virginia*	Southwest (Appalachian) area of state	Newport News, Radford, other in-state areas	selectees from unemployed who indicate interest in moving reached by Employment Service	

Appendix B—*Continued*

State Conducting Project	Supply Areas	Project Population	Special Notes
Washington	entire state, other western states	unemployed workers in high-unemployment areas	Project based on labor-shortage areas is drawing from "surplus labor" areas; extensive settling-in assistance provided to newcomers to area through contract with Travelers Aid Society
West Virginia*	southern (Appalachian) areas of state	selectees from unemployed who indicate interest in moving reached by Employment Service	concentrates on movement in groups to major employers in selected labor-short cities
Wisconsin*	entire state	selectees from unemployed who indicate interest in moving reached by Employment Service	concentrates on rural moves to labor-short areas

* Part of linked "interregional program" developing guides to interstate coordination of job-vacancy information and mobility assistance; contract with Travelers Aid Society provides for pre-move orientation and settling-in social services in most areas of concentrated mobility activity.

Source: *Moving To Work* (Washington, D.C.: Labor Mobility Services Unit, United States Employment Service, 1968).

Selected Bibliography

BOOKS

AFL-CIO Platform Proposals. Washington, D.C.: AFL-CIO, 1968.

Beaujeu-Garnier, J., and G. Chabot. *Urban Geography.* New York: John Wiley and Sons, 1967.

Bishop, C. E. *Farm Labor in the United States.* New York: Columbia University Press, 1967.

Blau, Peter M., and Otis Dudley Duncan. *The American Occupational Structure.* New York: John Wiley and Sons, 1967.

Borts, George, and Jerome L. Stein. *Economic Growth in a Free Market.* New York: Columbia University Press, 1964.

Bowman, Mary Jean, and W. Warren Haynes. *Resources and People in East Kentucky.* Baltimore: The Johns Hopkins Press, 1963.

Brophy, William A., and Sophie D. Aberle. *The Indian: America's Unfinished Business.* Norman, Okla.: University of Oklahoma Press, 1966.

Cassell, Frank H. *The Public Employment Service: Organization in Change.* Ann Arbor, Mich.: Academic Publications, 1968.

Chapin, F. Stuart, and Shirley F. Weiss. *Urban Growth Dynamics in a Regional Cluster of Cities.* New York: John Wiley and Sons, 1962.

Cities. New York: Alfred Knopf, 1965.

Clawson, Marion. *Policy Directions for U. S. Agriculture.* Baltimore: The Johns Hopkins Press, 1968.

Davis, Lloyd, ed. *The Public University in Its Second Century.* Morgantown, W. Va.: West Virginia Center for Appalachian Studies and Development, 1967.

Denison, Edward. *The Sources of Economic Growth in the United States and the Alternatives Before Us.* New York: Committee for Economic Development, 1962.

Eldridge, H. Wentworth. *Taming Megalopolis.* Garden City, N.Y.: Doubleday Anchor Books, 1967.

Fogel, Walter. *Mexican Americans in Southwest Labor Markets.* Los Angeles: U.C.L.A. Graduate School of Business Administration,

Mexican-American Study Project, Advance Report No. 10, October, 1967.

Ford, Thomas R., ed. *The Southern Appalachian Region.* Lexington, Ky.: University of Kentucky Press, 1962.

Friedmann, John. *Regional Development Policy: A Case Study of Venezuela.* Cambridge, Mass.: The M.I.T. Press, 1966.

Fuchs, Victor. *Changes in the Location of Manufacturing in the United States Since 1929.* New Haven, Conn.: Yale University Press, 1962.

Ganz, Alexander. *Emerging Patterns of Urban Growth and Travel.* Cambridge, Mass.: M.I.T. Department of City and Regional Planning, 1968.

Ginzberg, Eli. *Manpower Agenda for America.* New York: McGraw-Hill Book Co., 1968.

Ginzberg, Eli. *The Development of Human Resources.* New York: McGraw-Hill Book Co., 1966.

Gonzalez, Nancie L. *The Spanish Americans of New Mexico: A Distinctive Heritage.* Los Angeles: U.C.L.A. Graduate School of Business Administration, Mexican-American Study Project, Advance Report No. 9, September, 1967.

Gordon, Robert Aaron. *Toward a Manpower Policy.* New York: John Wiley and Sons, 1967.

Grebler, Leo. *Mexican Immigration to the United States.* Los Angeles: U.C.L.A. Graduate School of Business Administration, Mexican-American Study Project, Advance Report No. 2, January, 1967.

Greenhut, Melvin L., and W. Tate Whitman, eds. *Essays in Southern Economic Development.* Chapel Hill, N.C.: University of North Carolina Press, 1964.

Hansen, Niles M. *French Regional Planning.* Bloomington, Ind.: Indiana University Press, 1968.

Heller, Celia S. *Mexican American Youth: Forgotten Youth at the Crossroads.* New York: Random House, 1966.

Higbee, Edward. *The Squeeze: Cities Without Space.* New York: William Morrow, 1960.

Higgins, Benjamin. *Economic Development,* revised edition. New York: W. W. Norton and Co., 1968.

Hough, Henry W. *Development of Indian Resources.* Denver: World Press, 1967.

International Differences in Factors Affecting Labour Mobility. Geneva, Switzerland: International Labour Office, 1965.

Jakubauskas, Edward B., and C. Phillip Baumel, eds. *Human Resources Development.* Ames, Iowa: Iowa State University Press, 1967.

Jarrett, Henry, ed. *Environmental Quality in a Growing Economy*. Baltimore: The Johns Hopkins Press, 1966.

Krier, H. *Rural Manpower and Industrial Development*. Paris: Organization for Economic Cooperation and Development, 1961.

Lansing, John B. *Residential Location and Urban Mobility: The Second Wave of Interviews*. Ann Arbor, Mich.: University of Michigan Survey Research Center, 1966.

Lansing, John, and Eva Mueller. *The Geographic Mobility of Labor*. Ann Arbor, Mich.: University of Michigan Survey Research Center, 1967.

Levitan, Sar A. *Federal Aid to Depressed Areas*. Baltimore: The Johns Hopkins Press, 1964.

Maddox, James G., E. E. Liebhafsky, Vivian W. Henderson, and Herbert M. Manlin. *The Advancing South*. New York: The Twentieth Century Fund, 1967.

Madsen, William. *The Mexican-Americans of South Texas*. New York: Holt, Rinehart and Winston, 1964.

Mangum, Garth L. *Reorienting Vocational Education*. Ann Arbor, Mich.: Institute of Labor and Industrial Relations, 1968.

Mangum, Garth L., ed. *The Manpower Revolution*. Garden City, N.Y.: Doubleday Anchor Books, 1966.

McKinney, John C., and Edgar T. Thompson, eds. *The South in Continuity and Change*. Durham, N.C.: Duke University Press, 1965.

Meyer, J. R., J. F. Kain and M. Wohl. *The Urban Transportation Problem*. Cambridge, Mass.: Harvard University Press, 1965.

Mittelbach, Frank G., Joan W. Moore, and Ronald McDaniel. *Inter-Marriage of Mexican Americans*. Los Angeles: U.C.L.A. Graduate School of Business Administration, Mexican-American Study Project, Advance Report No. 6, November, 1966.

Moore, Joan W. *Mexican-Americans: Problems and Prospects*. Madison, Wis.: Institute for Research on Poverty, 1967.

National Bureau of Economic Research. *The Measurement and Interpretation of Job Vacancy Statistics*. New York: Columbia University Press, 1966.

Nemore, Arnold E., and Garth L. Mangum. *Reorienting the Federal-State Employment Service.* Ann Arbor, Mich.: Institute of Labor and Industrial Relations, May, 1968.

Neutze, G. M. *Economic Policy and the Size of Cities*. New York: Augustus M. Kelley, 1967.

Nicholls, William H. *Southern Tradition and Regional Progress*. Chapel Hill, N.C.: University of North Carolina Press, 1960.

Papers and Proceedings of the International Symposium on Regional Development. Hakone, Japan: Japan Center for Area Development Research, 1967.

Perloff, Harvey S., and Lowden Wingo, Jr. *Issues in Urban Economics.* Baltimore: The Johns Hopkins Press, 1968.

Perloff, Harvey S., and Vera Dodds. *How a Region Grows.* New York: Committee for Economic Development, 1963.

Ross, Arthur M. *Unemployment and the American Economy.* New York: John Wiley and Sons, 1964.

Schachter, Gustav. *The Italian South.* New York: Random House, 1965.

Schmid, A. Allan. *Converting Land from Rural to Urban Uses.* Baltimore: The Johns Hopkins Press, 1968.

Siegal, Irving M., ed. *Manpower Tomorrow: Prospects and Priorities.* New York: Augustus M. Kelley, 1967.

Somers, Gerald G. *Retraining the Unemployed.* Madison, Wis.: University of Wisconsin Press, 1968.

Statistiques et indicateurs des régions françaises. Paris: Imprimerie Nationale, 1968.

Sutton, Willis A., Jr., and Jerry Russell. *The Social Dimensions of Kentucky Counties.* Lexington, Ky.: Bureau of Community Service, University of Kentucky, 1964.

Thompson, Wilbur R. *A Preface to Urban Economics.* Baltimore: The Johns Hopkins Press, 1965.

University of Wisconsin Industrial Relations Research Institute. *Retraining and Migration as Factors in Regional Economic Development.* Madison, Wis.: University of Wisconsin Industrial Relations Research Institute, 1966.

Vance, Rupert B. *Human Geography of the South.* Chapel Hill, N.C.: University of North Carolina Press, 1932.

Vernon, Raymond. *The Changing Economic Function of the Central City.* New York: Committee for Economic Development, 1959.

Warner, S. B., Jr. *Planning for a Nation of Cities.* Cambridge, Mass.: The M.I.T. Press, 1966.

Weller, Jack E. *Yesterday's People.* Lexington, Ky.: University of Kentucky Press, 1966.

Whitlock, James G., and Billy J. Williams. *Jobs and Training for Southern Youth.* Nashville, Tenn.: George Peabody College, 1963.

Will, Robert E., and Harold G. Vatter. *Poverty in Affluence.* New York: Harcourt, Brace and World, 1965.

Wright, Dale. *They Harvest Despair.* Boston: Beacon Press, 1965.

Yavitz, Boris, and Thomas M. Stanback, Jr. *Electronic Data Processing in New York City.* New York: Columbia University Press, 1967.

PERIODICALS AND NEWSPAPERS

Alonso, William. "Urban and Regional Imbalances in Economic Development." *Economic Development and Cultural Change,* Vol. 17, No. 1 (October, 1968).

Ashby, Lowell D. "The Shift and Share Analysis: A Reply." *Southern Economic Journal,* Vol. 34, No. 3 (January, 1968).

Aydalot, Philippe. "Note sur les économies externes et quelques notions connexes." *Revue économique* (November, 1965).

Berry, Brian J. L. "A Summary —Spatial Organization and Levels of Welfare: Degree of Metropolitan Labor Market Participation as a Variable in Economic Development." *EDA Research Review,* June, 1968.

Bishop, C. E. "City and Countryside: An Interdependent Future." *Appalachia,* Vol. 1, No. 8 (April, 1968).

Borts, George H. "The Equalization of Returns and Regional Economic Growth." *American Economic Review,* Vol. 50, No. 2 (June, 1960).

Brazer, Marjorie Cahn. "Economic and Social Disparities Between Central Cities and Their Suburbs." *Land Economics,* Vol. 43, No. 3 (August, 1967).

Bretzfelder, Robert B. "Regional Changes in Personal Income." *Survey of Current Business,* Vol. 48, No. 4 (April, 1968).

Briggs, Vernon M. "Manpower Programs and Regional Development." *Monthly Labor Review,* Vol. 91, No. 3 (March, 1968).

Brown, James S., Harry K. Schwarzweller, and Joseph J. Mangalam. "Kentucky Mountain Migration and the Stem-Family: An American Variation on a Theme by LePlay." *Rural Sociology,* Vol. 28, No. 1 (March, 1963).

Darwent, David F. *Growth Pole and Growth Center Concepts: A Review, Evaluation and Bibliography.* Berkeley, Calif.: University of California Center for Planning and Development Research, Working Paper No. 89, October, 1968.

Davis, Ross D. "A Look at Rural America." *Economic Development,* Vol. 4, No. 8 (August, 1967).

Davis, Ross D. "Economic Development Program Scores Substantial Gains in First Two Years." *Economic Development,* Vol. 4, No. 9 (September, 1967).

Davis, Ross D. "EDA Sets 'Worst First' Policy on Use of Funds." *Economic Development,* Vol. 4, No. 6 (June, 1967).

Davis, Ross D. "The New Approach to Solving Urban Unemployment." *Economic Development,* Vol. 4, No. 11 (November, 1967).

Fein, Rashi. "Educational Patterns in Southern Migration." *Southern Economic Journal,* Vol. 32, No. 1, Part 2 (July, 1965).

Fogel, Walter. "The Effect of Low Educational Attainment on Incomes: A Comparative Study of Selected Ethnic Groups." *Journal of Human Resources,* Vol. 1, No. 2 (Fall, 1966).

Freedman, Audrey, "Labor Mobility Projects for the Unemployed." *Monthly Labor Review,* Vol. 91, No. 6 (June, 1968).

Friedmann, John R. P. "The Concept of a Planning Region." *Land Economics,* Vol. 32, No. 1 (February, 1956).

Fuchs, Victor. *Differentials in Hourly Earnings by Region and City Size, 1959.* New York: National Bureau of Economic Research Occasional Paper No. 101, 1967.

Fuchs, Victor. *The Growing Importance of the Service Industries.* New York: National Bureau of Economic Research Occasional Paper No. 96, 1965.

Gallaway, Lowell E. "Labor Mobility, Resource Allocation, and Structural Unemployment." *American Economic Review,* Vol. 53, No. 4 (September, 1963).

Girard, Alain, and Henri Bastide. "Les problèmes démographiques devant l'opinion." *Population,* Vol. 15 (April–May, 1960).

Hansen, Niles M. "Municipal Investment Requirements in a Growing Agglomeration." *Land Economics,* Vol. 41, No. 1 (February, 1965).

Hansen, Niles M. "The Structure and Determinants of Local Public Investment Expenditures." *Review of Economics and Statistics,* Vol. 47, No. 2 (May, 1965).

Hansen, Niles M. "Unbalanced Growth and Regional Development." *Western Economic Journal,* Vol. 4, No. 1 (Fall, 1965).

Hoover, Edgar M. "Some Old and New Issues in Regional Development." University of Pittsburgh Center for Regional Economic Studies Occasional Paper No. 5, 1967.

Houston, David B. "The Shift and Share Analysis of Regional Growth: A Critique." *Southern Economic Journal,* Vol. 33, No. 4 (April, 1967).

Iden, George. "Unemployment Classification of Major Labor Areas, 1950–65." *Journal of Human Resources,* Vol. 2, No. 3 (Summer, 1967).

Kain, John F. "Housing Segregation, Negro Employment, and Metro-politan Decentralization." *Quarterly Journal of Economics,* Vol. 82, No. 2 (May, 1968).

Kain, John F. "Postwar Changes in Land Use in the American City." Harvard University Program on Regional and Urban Economics Discussion Paper No. 24 (November, 1967).

Kain, John F., and Joseph J. Persky. "Alternatives to the Gilded Ghetto." Harvard University Program on Regional and Urban Economics Discussion Paper No. 21, February, 1968.

Kain, John F., and Joseph J. Persky. "The Ghetto, the Metropolis and the Nation." Harvard University Program on Regional and Urban Economics Discussion Paper No. 30, March, 1968.

Kain, John F., and Joseph J. Persky. "The North's Stake in Southern Rural Poverty." Harvard University Program on Regional and Urban Economics Discussion Paper No. 18, May, 1967.

Kaldor, Donald R., and William E. Saupe. "Estimates and Projections of an Income-Efficient Commercial-Farm Industry in the North Central States." *Journal of Farm Economics,* Vol. 48, No. 3, Part 1 (August, 1966).

Krass, Elaine M., Claire Peterson, and Lyle W. Shannon. "Mexican-Americans and Negroes in a Northern Industrial Community." *Southwestern Social Science Quarterly,* Vol. 47, No. 3 (December, 1966).

Laber, Gene. "Unemployment Classification of Major Labor Areas, 1950–65: A Comment." *Journal of Human Resources,* Vol. 3, No. 4 (Fall, 1968).

Lee, Joe Won. "Dimensions of U. S. Metropolitan Change." *Looking Ahead.* Washington, D.C.: National Planning Association, June, 1967.

Liebhafsky, E. E. "Migration and the Labor Force: Prospects." *Monthly Labor Review,* Vol. 91, No. 3 (March, 1968).

Lindley, Jonathan. "The Economic Environment and Urban Development." Paper presented to the Eighth Annual Conference, Center for Economic Projections, National Planning Association, April 28, 1967.

Lindley, Jonathan, James W. Walker, and William J. Dircks. "Changes in Location of Employment and Opportunity: Implications for National Policy." Paper given at the Conference on the rural to Urban Population Shift—A National Problem, Oklahoma State University, Stillwater, Oklahoma, May 17, 1968.

Louisville Courier-Journal.

Lurie, Melvin, and Elton Rayack. "Racial Differences in Migration and Job Search: A Case Study." *Southern Economic Journal,* Vol. 23, No. 1 (July, 1966).

Miernyk, William H. "Appalachia's Economic Future." *Appalachia,* Vol. 1, No. 10 (June–July, 1968).

Newman, Dorothy K. "The Decentralization of Jobs." *Monthly Labor Review,* Vol. 90, No. 5 (May, 1967).

Newman, Dorothy K. "The Negro's Journey to the City—Part 2." *Monthly Labor Review,* Vol. 88, No. 6 (June, 1965).

Newman, Monroe. "Urban Services and Future Growth—A Challenge to Appalachia." *Appalachia,* Vol. 1, No. 6 (February, 1968).

New York Times.

Olsen, Erling. "Erhvervslivets Lokalisering." *Nationaløkonomisk Tidsskrift* [Denmark], Nos. 1–2 (1965).

Parker, John E., and Lois B. Shaw. "Labor Force Participation Within Metropolitan Areas." *Southern Economic Journal,* Vol. 34, No. 4 (April, 1968).

Parr, John B. "Outmigration and the Depressed Area Problem." *Land Economics,* Vol. 42, No. 2 (May, 1966).

Price, John A. "The Migration and Adaptation of American Indians to Los Angeles." *Human Organization,* Vol. 27, No. 2 (Summer, 1968).

Schultz, Theodore. "Investment in Human Capital." *American Economic Review,* Vol. 51, No. 1 (March, 1961).

Schwarzweller, Harry K. *Career Placement and Economic Life Chances of Young Men from Eastern Kentucky.* University of Kentucky Agricultural Experiment Station Bulletin No. 686, January, 1964.

Schwarzweller, Harry K. *Sociocultural Origins and Migration Patterns of Young Men from Eastern Kentucky.* University of Kentucky Agricultural Experiment Station Bulletin No. 685, December, 1963.

Shyrock, Henry S., and Charles B. Nam. "Educational Selectivity of Inter-regional Migration." *Social Forces,* Vol. 43, No. 3 (March, 1965).

Smith, Robert W. "Employment and Economic Growth: Southwest." *Monthly Labor Review,* Vol. 91, No. 3 (March, 1968).

Somers, Gerald G. "The Returns to Geographic Mobility: A Symposium." *Journal of Human Resources,* Vol. 2, No. 4 (Fall, 1967).

Sorkin, Alan L. "American Indians Industrialize to Combat Poverty." *Monthly Labor Review,* Vol. 92, No. 3 (March, 1969).

Stober, William J. "Employment and Income Growth: Southeast." *Monthly Labor Review,* Vol. 91, No. 3 (March, 1968).

Suval, Elizabeth M., and C. Horace Hamilton. "Some New Evidence on

Educational Selectivity in Migration to and from the South." *Social Forces,* Vol. 43, No. 4 (May, 1965).

Tyner, Fred H., and Luther G. Tweeten. "Optimum Resource Allocation in U.S. Agriculture." *Journal of Farm Economics,* Vol. 48, No. 3, Part 1 (August, 1966).

Via, Emory F. "Discrimination, Integration, and Job Equality." *Monthly Labor Review,* Vol. 91, No. 3 (March, 1968).

Wall Street Journal.

Weisbrod, Burton. "Investing in Human Capital." *Journal of Human Resources,* Vol. 1, No. 1 (Summer, 1966).

Whitlock, James W. "Changing Elementary and Secondary Education." *Monthly Labor Review,* Vol. 91, No. 3 (March, 1968).

Widner, Ralph R. "The First Three Years of the Appalachian Program: An Evaluation." *Appalachia,* Vol. 1, No. 11 (August, 1968).

GOVERNMENT PUBLICATIONS

Where no publisher is specified the entry was published by the agency in question or the Government Printing Office. Some articles in periodicals published by government agencies are listed in the previous section.

Advisory Commission on Intergovernmental Relations. *Urban and Rural America: Policies for Future Growth,* 1968.

Appalachian Regional Commission Annual Report, 1967.

Appalachian Regional Commission Annual Report, 1968.

Appalachian Regional Commission. *Capitalizing on New Development Along the Baltimore-Cincinnati Appalachian Development Highway,* 1968.

Appalachian Regional Commission. *Preliminary Analysis for Development of Central Appalachia,* 1968.

Appalachian Regional Commission. *State and Regional Development Plans in Appalachia, 1968.*

Ashby, Lowell D. "Regional Change in a National Setting." U.S. Department of Commerce Staff Working Paper in Economics and Statistics, No. 7, April, 1964.

Bird, Alan R., and John L. McCoy. *White Americans in Rural Poverty.* U.S. Department of Agriculture Economic Research Service, Agricultural Economics Report No. 124, 1967.

Bureau of Indian Affairs. "A Followup Study of 1963 Recipients of the

Services of the Employment Assistance Program, Bureau of Indian Affairs," 1966.

Bureau of Indian Affairs. *Answers to Your Questions About American Indians,* 1968.

Bureau of Indian Affairs. *Indian Affairs, 1967.*

Bureau of Labor Statistics Reports.

Bureau of the Census. *Current Population Reports.*

Coastal Plains Regional Commission. *Coastal Plains Economic Development Region,* 1968.

Department of Agriculture. *Communities of Tomorrow, Agriculture 2000,* 1968.

Department of Labor, Manpower Administration. *Manpower Daily Reporter.*

Department of the Interior. "Indians: Job Training and Placement Studies." Issue Support Paper No. 70–1, 1968.

Duskin, Gerald L., and Ronald L. Moomaw. "Economic Development Centers: A Review." EDA Office of Economic Research Staff Paper, 1967.

Economic Development Administration Annual Report, 1967.

Economic Development Administration. *EDA Handbook, 1968.*

Economic Development Administration. *Industrial Location as a Factor in Regional Economic Development, 1967.*

Economic Development Administration Progress Report, 1968.

Economic Development Administration. *Regional Economic Development in the United States, 1967.*

Economic Report of the President, 1969.

Joint Economic Committee, Congress of the United States. *Federal Programs for the Development of Human Resources,* Vol. 1. 90th Congress, 2nd session, 1968.

Joint Economic Committee, Congress of the United States. *Job Vacancy Statistics.* 89th Congress, 2nd session, 1966.

Joint Economic Committee, Congress of the United States. *Programs for Relocating Workers Used by Governments of Selected Countries,* 1966.

Joint Economic Committee, Congress of the United States. *The 1968 Economic Report of the President.* Hearings, Part 1, 90th Congress, 2nd session, 1968.

Joint Economic Committee, Congress of the United States. *Urban America: Goals and Problems.* 90th Congress, 1st session, 1967.

Jordan, Max F., and Lloyd D. Bender. *An Economic Survey of the*

Ozark Region. Department of Agriculture Economic Research Service, Agricultural Economic Report No. 97, 1966.

Labor Mobility Services Unit, United States Employment Service. *Moving To Work,* 1968.

Manpower Report of the President, 1967.

Manpower Report of the President, 1968.

Ozarks Regional Commission. *Ozarks Region,* no date.

President's Appalachian Regional Commission. *Appalachia,* 1964.

President's National Advisory Commission on Rural Poverty. *Rural Poverty in the United States,* 1968.

President's National Advisory Commission on Rural Poverty. *The People Left Behind,* 1967.

Rapton, Avra. *Domestic Migratory Farmworkers.* U.S. Department of Agriculture Economic Research Service, Agricultural Economics Report No. 121, 1967.

Rothman, Elizabeth. "Manpower and Education in the Upper Great Lakes Region." Washington, D.C.: Upper Great Lakes Regional Commission, no date.

Statement of the Governor of Virginia (The Honorable Mills E. Godwin, Jr.) to the Subcommittee on Regional Development of the Committee on Public Works, United States Senate, March, 1969.

Statement of William M. McCandless, Federal Co-chairman, Ozarks Regional Commission, before the Special Subcommittee of the Senate Committee on Public Works, September 26, 1967.

The Mexican American. Cabinet Committee Hearings on Mexican American Affairs, El Paso, Texas, October 26–28, 1967; 1968.

United States Department of Commerce News.

United States Senate, Subcommittee of the Committee on Appropriations. *Department of Agriculture and Related Agencies Appropriations for Fiscal Year 1968, Part 4, Farm Labor in a Changing Agriculture.* Hearings, 90th Congress, 1st session, Washington, D.C., 1967.

Upper Great Lakes Regional Commission. "Strategy for Development," 1968.

Notes

Chapter 1

1. Walter W. Heller, "The Case for Aggregate Demand," in Garth L. Mangum, ed., *The Manpower Revolution* (Garden City, N.Y.: Doubleday Anchor Books, 1966), p. 127.

2. John R. P. Friedmann, "The Concept of a Planning Region," *Land Economics,* Vol. 32, No. 1 (February, 1956), pp. 2–3.

3. Originally the term "external economies" was used to describe the cost reductions experienced by individual firms in a growing industry. The relevant economies (service facilities, specialized education, etc.) were external to the firm but internal to the industry. "More recently, the term has been used to describe any economies of operation which are 'external' to a firm but result from the prior establishment of other firms, whether these firms are within the industry or not. Thus the term would apply to services or facilities which exist outside the firm, which serve to reduce its operating costs, and which are available because other economic activities have already brought them into being. It is conceptually useful to say that external economies so conceived are *external* to the *firm,* but *internal* to the *region.*" Boris Yavitz and Thomas M. Stanback, Jr., *Electronic Data Processing in New York City* (New York: Columbia University Press, 1967), p. 12.

4. The arguments which are briefly outlined here are developed in more detail in Niles M. Hansen, *French Regional Planning* (Bloomington: Indiana University Press, 1968), Chapter 1; and "Unbalanced Growth and Regional Development," *Western Economic Journal,* Vol. 4, No. 1(Fall, 1965), pp. 3–14.

Chapter 2

1. Lowell D. Ashby, "Regional Change in a National Setting," U.S. Department of Commerce Staff Working Paper in Economics and Statistics, No. 7, April, 1964, p. 13.

2. George H. Borts and Jerome L. Stein, *Economic Growth in a Free Market* (New York: Columbia University Press, 1964), p. 46.

3. James G. Maddox, with E. E. Liebhafsky, Vivian W. Henderson, and Herbert M. Manlin, *The Advancing South* (New York: The Twentieth Century Fund, 1967), pp. 53–63; William J. Stober, "Employment and Income Growth: Southeast," *Monthly Labor Review,* Vol. 91, No. 3 (March, 1968), p. 19.

4. Robert B. Bretzfelder, "Regional Changes in Personal Income," *Survey of Current Business,* Vol. 48, No. 4 (April, 1968), pp. 9–12.

5. Ibid., pp. 14–15.

6. Ibid., p. 28.

7. Marion Clawson, "Preface," in A. Allan Schmid, *Converting Land From Rural to Urban Uses* (Baltimore: The Johns Hopkins Press, 1968), p. v.

8. Joe Won Lee, "Dimensions of U.S. Metropolitan Change," *Looking Ahead* (Washington, D.C.: National Planning Association, June, 1967), p. 2.

9. *Current Population Reports* (Washington, D.C.: U.S. Department of Commerce, Bureau of the Census, December 16, 1966), Series P–20, No. 157.

10. *Manpower Report of the President, 1968* (Washington, D.C.: Government Printing Office, 1968), p. 132.

11. *United States Department of Commerce News* (Office of Business Economics), for release August 26, 1968, pp. 2–3.

12. Ibid., p. 3.

13. Ibid.

14. Ibid.

15. Wilbur R. Thompson, *A Preface to Urban Economics* (Baltimore: The Johns Hopkins Press, 1968), p. 193.

16. Alexander Ganz, *Emerging Patterns of Urban Growth and Travel,* M.I.T. Project Transport Report 68–1, M.I.T. Department of City and Regional Planning, January, 1968, p. 156.

17. *Manpower Report of the President, 1967* (Washington, D.C.: Government Printing Office, 1967), p. 73.

18. "Slums and Poverty," in Robert E. Will and Harold G. Vatter, *Poverty in Affluence* (New York: Harcourt, Brace and World, 1965), pp. 95–6.

19. *Manpower Report of the President, 1967,* pp. 74–5. The "subemployment" concept and index include:
1. People classed as unemployed, since they were jobless and looking for work during the survey week;
2. Those working only part time though they wanted full-time work;
3. Heads of households under 65 years of age who earn less than $60 a

week though working full time; also individuals under 65, not heads of households, who earn less than $56 a week on a full-time job (the equivalent of $1.40 an hour for a 40-hour week);

4. Half the number of "nonparticipants" among men aged 20 to 64 (on the assumption that the other half are not potential workers, chiefly because of physical or mental disabilities or severe personal problems); and

5. An estimate of the male "undercount" group (based on the assumption that the number of men in the area should bear the same relation to the number of women that exists in the population generally; also that half of the unfound men are in the four groups of subemployed people just listed—the others being either employed or not potential workers).

20. Ibid., p. 87.

21. J. R. Meyer, J. F. Kain, and M. Wohl, *The Urban Transportation Problem* (Cambridge, Mass.: Harvard University Press, 1965), Chapters 1 and 2. John B. Lansing, *Residential Location and Urban Mobility: The Second Wave of Interviews* (Ann Arbor: University of Michigan Survey Research Center, 1966).

22. Dorothy K. Newman, "The Decentralization of Jobs," *Monthly Labor Review,* Vol. 90, No. 5 (May, 1967), pp. 9–13.

23. Marjorie Cahn Brazer, "Economic and Social Disparities Between Central Cities and their Suburbs," *Land Economics,* Vol. 43, No. 3 (August, 1967), p. 300.

24. Ibid.

25. *Manpower Report of the President, 1968,* p. 136.

26. United States Senate, Subcommittee of the Committee on Appropriations, *Department of Agriculture and Related Agencies Appropriations for Fiscal Year 1968, Part 4, Farm Labor in a Changing Agriculture,* Hearings, 90th Cong., 1st sess., Washington, D.C., 1967, p. viii.

27. Varden Fuller, "Farm Manpower Policy," in C. E. Bishop, ed., *Farm Labor in the United States* (New York: Columbia University Press, 1967), pp. 97–8.

28. *Department of Agriculture and Related Agencies . . . ,* p. viii.

29. *Manpower Report of the President, 1968,* p. 136.

30. *Department of Agriculture and Related Agencies . . . ,* p. ix.

31. *Manpower Report of the President, 1968,* p. 136.

32. Fred H. Tyner and Luther G. Tweeten, "Optimum Resource Allocation in U.S. Agriculture," *Journal of Farm Economics,* Vol. 48, No. 3, Part I (August, 1966), p. 629.

33. Donald R. Kaldor and William E. Saupe, "Estimates and Projections of an Income-Efficient Commercial-Farm Industry in the North Central States," *Journal of Farm Economics,* Vol. 48, No. 3, Part I, (August, 1966), pp. 578–96.

34. Eber Eldridge, "Trends Related to Agricultural Employment," in Edward B. Jakubauskas and C. Phillip Baumel, eds., *Human Resources Development* (Ames, Iowa: Iowa State University Press, 1967), p. 74.

35. *The People Left Behind* (Washington, D.C.: Government Printing Office, 1967), p. 3.

36. Alan R. Bird and John L. McCoy, *White Americans in Rural Poverty,* U.S. Department of Agriculture Economic Research Service, Agricultural Economics Report No. 124 (Washington, D.C.: Government Printing Office, 1967), p. 15.

37. Ibid. See also *The People Left Behind,* p. 8.

38. *The People Left Behind,* p. 93.

39. Avra Rapton, *Domestic Migratory Farmworkers,* U.S. Department of Agriculture Economic Research Service, Agricultural Economics Report No. 121 (Washington, D.C.: Government Printing Office, 1967).

40. Dale Wright, *They Harvest Despair* (Boston: Beacon Press, 1965), p. 126.

Chapter 3

1. Of these eleven sectors, four grew at rates less than the national rate and seven had actual decreases in employment. The first group includes forestry, fisheries, and logging; petroleum and coal products manufacturing; furniture, fixtures, and miscellaneous wood manufacturing; and transportation, communications, and public utilities. The second group includes agriculture; mining, textile mill products; personal services; tobacco products manufacturing; leather and leather products manufacturing; and sawmills and planing mills. See James G. Maddox, with E. E. Liebhafsky, Vivian W. Henderson, and Herbert M. Hamlin, *The Advancing South* (New York: The Twentieth Century Fund, 1967), pp. 53–9.

2. Ibid., pp. 55–9.

3. Ibid., p. 63. The states in question are Kentucky, Tennessee, North Carolina, South Carolina, Georgia, Alabama, Mississippi, Louisiana, Arkansas, Oklahoma, Virginia, Texas, and Florida.

4. Ibid., pp. 69–70.

5. Ibid., p. 72.

6. William J. Stober, "Employment and Economic Growth: Southeast," *Monthly Labor Review,* Vol. 91, No. 3 (March, 1968), p. 19.

7. James M. Henderson, "Some General Aspects of Recent Regional Development," in Melvin L. Greenhut and W. Tate Whitman, eds., *Essays in Southern Economic Development* (Chapel Hill, N.C.: University of North Carolina Press, 1964), p. 186. Victor R. Fuchs, *Changes in the Location of Manufacturing Since 1929* (New Haven, Conn.: Yale University Press, 1962), p. 205.

8. Maddox et al., p. 72.

9. Ibid., p. 73.

10. Stober, pp. 22–3.

11. David B. Houston, "The Shift and Share Analysis of Regional Growth: A Critique," *Southern Economic Journal,* Vol. 33, No. 4 (April, 1967), pp. 577–81; Lowell D. Ashby, "The Shift and Share Analysis: A Reply," *Southern Economic Journal,* Vol. 34, No. 3 (January, 1968), pp. 423–5.

12. Theodore W. Schultz, "National Employment, Skills, and Earnings of Farm Labor," in C. E. Bishop, ed., *Farm Labor in the United States* (New York: Columbia University Press, 1967), p. 68.

13. Vernon M. Briggs, Jr., "Manpower Programs and Regional Development," *Monthly Labor Review,* Vol. 91, No. 3 (March, 1968), p. 60.

14. Joseph J. Spengler, "Southern Economic Trends and Prospects," in John C. McKinney and Edgar T. Thompson, eds., *The South in Continuity and Change* (Durham, N.C.: Duke University Press, 1965), p. 117.

15. Maddox et al., p. 79.

16. John F. Kain and Joseph J. Persky, "The North's Stake in Southern Rural Poverty," Harvard University Program on Regional and Urban Economics Discussion Paper No. 18, May, 1967, p. 45.

17. Maddox et al., pp. 14–5.

18. Eli Ginzberg, *Manpower Agenda for America* (New York: McGraw-Hill Book Co., 1968), p. 66.

19. James W. Whitlock, "Changing Elementary and Secondary Education," *Monthly Labor Review,* Vol. 91, No. 3 (March, 1968), pp. 41–2.

20. Ibid., p. 39.

21. Kain and Persky, pp. 50–1.

22. Whitlock, p. 39.

23. Ibid., p. 40.

24. Ibid., pp. 39–43.

25. Ibid., p. 41.

26. James W. Whitlock and Billy J. Williams, *Jobs and Training for Southern Youth* (Nashville, Tenn.: George Peabody College, 1963), p. 24.

27. Ginzberg, p. 64.

28. Whitlock, p. 42.

29. William H. Nicholls, *Southern Tradition and Regional Progress* (Chapel Hill, N.C.: University of North Carolina Press, 1960).

30. Ginzberg, p. 63.

31. Ibid., p. 64.

32. E. E. Liebhafsky, "Migration and the Labor Force: Prospects," *Monthly Labor Review*, Vol. 91, No. 3 (March, 1968), p. 11.

33. John L. Fulmer, "Trends in Population and Employment in the South from 1930 to 1960 and Their Economic Significance," in Greenhut and Whitman, eds., pp. 227–8.

34. James M. Henderson, "Some General Aspects of Recent Regional Development," in Ibid., pp. 177–80.

35. Leonard Reissman, "Urbanization in the South," in McKinney and Thompson, eds., pp. 96–7.

36. Ibid., p. 100.

37. Kain and Persky, p. 79.

38. Victor R. Fuchs, *Differentials in Hourly Earnings by Region and City Size, 1959,* National Bureau of Economic Research Occasional Paper No. 101 (New York: National Bureau of Economic Research, 1967).

39. Kain and Persky, p. 85.

40. Rupert B. Vance, *Human Geography of the South* (Chapel Hill, N.C.: University of North Carolina Press, 1932), p. 507.

41. Spengler, pp. 106–7.

42. Reissman, p. 86.

43. C. Horace Hamilton, "Continuity and Change in Southern Migration," in McKinney and Thompson, eds., pp. 61–2.

44. Rashi Fein, "Educational Patterns in Southern Migration," *Southern Economic Journal,* Vol. 32, No. 1, Part 2 (July, 1965), pp. 119–24.

45. Ibid., p. 124. For similar findings, see Henry S. Shyrock and Charles B. Nam, "Educational Selectivity of Inter-regional Migration," *Social Forces,* Vol. 43, No. 3 (March, 1965), pp. 299–310.

46. Elizabeth M. Suval and C. Horace Hamilton, "Some New Evidence on Educational Selectivity in Migration to and from the South," *Social Forces,* Vol. 43, No. 4 (May, 1965), pp. 536–47.

47. Kain and Persky, pp. 14–5.

48. Burton Weisbrod, "Investing in Human Capital," *Journal of Human Resources,* Vol. 1, No. 1 (Summer, 1966), pp. 15–6.

49. Kain and Persky, pp. 20–4.

50. Ibid.

51. John F. Kain and Joseph J. Persky, "Alternatives to the Guilded Ghetto," Harvard University Program on Regional and Urban Economics Discussion Paper No. 21 (February, 1968), p. 16.

52. John F. Kain and Joseph J. Persky, "The Ghetto, the Metropolis and the Nation," Harvard University Program on Regional and Urban Economics Discussion Paper No. 30 (March, 1968), pp. 18–9.

53. Kain and Persky, "The North's Stake in Southern Rural Poverty," p. 71.

54. "Recent Trends in Social and Economic Conditions of Negroes in the United States," *Current Population Reports, Series P–23,* No. 26 and *BLS Report* No. 347 (Washington, D.C.: Government Printing Office, July, 1968), p. 4.

55. Kain and Persky, "Alternatives to the Gilded Ghetto," p. 16.

56. *Chicago Tribune,* May 8, 1969, as reproduced in U.S. Department of Labor, Manpower Administration, *The Manpower Daily Reporter,* May 8, 1969, p. 1.

Chapter 4

1. U.S. Department of Commerce, Economic Development Administration, *Regional Economic Development in the United States,* Part 2, Section VII (Washington, D.C.: Government Printing Office, 1967), pp. 3–8.

2. Savings data are from President's Appalachian Regional Commission, *Appalachia* (Washington, D.C.: Government Printing Office, 1964). Other data were supplied by the Appalachian Regional Commission.

3. U.S. Department of Commerce, p. 6.

4. Monroe Newman, "Urban Services and Future Growth—A Challenge to Appalachia," *Appalachia,* Vol. 1, No. 6 (February, 1968), pp. 18–9.

5. James S. Brown and George A. Hillery, Jr., "The Great Migration, 1940–1960," in Thomas R. Ford, ed., *The Southern Appalachian Region* (Lexington, Ky.: University of Kentucky Press, 1962), p. 73.

6. Newman, p. 19.

7. Ibid.

8. Benjamin Chinitz, "Economic Development in Appalachia: The Role of the University," in Lloyd Davis, ed., *The Public University in Its Second Century* (Morgantown, W.Va.: West Virginia Center for Appalachian Studies and Development, 1967), pp. 47–8.

9. William H. Miernyk, "Appalachia's Economic Future," *Appalachia*, Vol. 1, No. 10 (June–July, 1968), p. 19.

10. Rupert B. Vance, "The Region's Future: A National Challenge," in Ford, p. 296.

11. Data supplied by the Appalachian Regional Commission.

12. *Appalachian Regional Commission Annual Report, 1967* (Washington, D.C.: Appalachian Regional Commission, 1968), p. 31.

13. William Greider, "Congress Told of Job Training Waiting Lists," *Louisville Courier-Journal*, May 15, 1968, p. 1.

14. Ibid.

15. Ford, p. 32.

16. Ibid., p. 17.

17. Ibid.

18. Paul Janensch, "U.S. to Attack East Kentucky 'Health Gap'," *Louisville Courier-Journal*, November 30, 1967, p. 1.

19. *Appalachian Regional Commission Annual Report, 1967*, p. 34.

20. United States Public Law 89–4, Appalachian Regional Development Act of 1965, 89th Congress, March 9, 1965.

21. U.S. Department of Commerce, Economic Development Administration, *Annual Report, 1967* (Washington, D.C.: Government Printing Office, 1967), pp. 29, 101.

22. *Appalachian Regional Commission Annual Report, 1968* (Washington, D.C.: Appalachian Regional Commission, 1968), p. 29.

23. Statement to the author, March, 1969.

24. *State and Regional Development Plans in Appalachia, 1968* (Washington, D.C.: Appalachian Regional Commission, 1968), p. 9.

25. Statement of the Governor of Virginia (The Honorable Mills E. Godwin, Jr.) to the Subcommittee on Regional Development of the Committee on Public Works, United States Senate, March, 1969.

26. *Appalachian Regional Commission Annual Report, 1968*, pp. 8–9; *State and Regional Development Plans in Appalachia, 1968*, p. 25; *Capitalizing on New Development Along the Baltimore-Cincinnati Appalachian Development Highway* (Washington, D.C.: Appalachian Regional Commission, 1968), p. 1.

27. Robert Coles, "The Mind of Appalachia," in Davis, ed., p. 12.

28. Harry K. Schwarzweller, *Career Placement and Economic Life Chances of Young Men from Eastern Kentucky*, University of Ken-

tucky Agricultural Experiment Station Bulletin No. 686, January, 1964, pp. 8–9.

29. Thomas R. Ford, "The Passing of Provincialism," in Ford, ed., p. 18.

30. J. Earl Williams, "Retraining in Tennessee," in Gerald G. Somers, ed., *Retraining the Unemployed* (Madison, Wis.: University of Wisconsin Press, 1968), p. 182.

31. Harry K. Schwarzweller, *Sociocultural Origins and Migration Patterns of Young Men from Eastern Kentucky,* University of Kentucky Agricultural Experiment Station Bulletin No. 685, December, 1963, p. 27.

32. Jack E. Weller, *Yesterday's People* (Lexington, Ky.: University of Kentucky Press, 1966), p. 139.

33. John F. Kain and Joseph J. Persky, "The North's Stake in Southern Rural Poverty," Harvard University Program on Regional and Urban Economics Discussion Paper No. 18, May, 1967, p. 15.

34. James S. Brown, Harry K. Schwarzweller, and Joseph J. Mangalam, "Kentucky Mountain Migration and the Stem-Family: An American Variation on a Theme by LePlay," *Rural Sociology,* Vol, 28, No. 1 (March, 1963), pp. 48–69.

35. James S. Brown, "Population and Migration Changes in Appalachia," Paper given at the Rural Appalachia in Transition Conference, University of West Virginia, October 18, 1967, pp. 26–9. This paper will appear in a book edited by John Photiadis and Fred Zeller.

36. *Appalachian Regional Commission Annual Report, 1967,* pp. 7–9.

37. *Preliminary Analysis for Development of Central Appalachia,* Appalachian Regional Commission Research Report No. 8, Washington, D.C., 1968, Appendix, p. 13.

38. Ibid., p. III–8A.

39. The data for the regression analyses in this section are taken from Willis A. Sutton, Jr., and Jerry Russell, *The Social Dimensions of Kentucky Counties* (Lexington, Ky.: Bureau of Community Service, University of Kentucky, September, 1964).

40. Mary Jean Bowman and W. Warren Haynes, *Resources and People in East Kentucky* (Baltimore: Johns Hopkins Press, 1963), p. 280.

41. Ibid., p. 281.

42. See, for example, Niles M. Hansen, "The Structure and Determinants of Local Public Investment Expenditures," *Review of Economics and Statistics,* Vol. 47, No. 2 (May, 1965), pp. 150–62; "Mu-

nicipal Investment Requirements in a Growing Agglomeration," *Land Economics*, Vol. 41, No. 1 (February, 1965), pp. 49–56; and *French Regional Planning* (Bloomington, Ind.: Indiana University Press, 1968).

43. Bowman and Haynes, p. 266.

44. Brown and Hillery, pp. 59–61.

45. U.S. Bureau of the Census, *Current Population Reports*, Series P–25, No. 415, "Projections of the Population of Metropolitan Areas, 1975," (Washington, D.C.: Government Printing Office, 1969), pp. 16–18.

46. Brown and Hillery, p. 71.

47. Ibid., p. 77.

48. See F. Stuart Chapin and Shirley F. Weiss, eds., *Urban Growth Dynamics in a Regional Cluster of Cities* (New York: John Wiley and Sons, 1962). This study is focused on the Piedmont Crescent.

49. C. E. Bishop, "City and Countryside: An Interdependent Future," *Appalachia*, Vol. 1, No. 8 (April, 1968), p. 11.

50. Ibid.

51. Brown and Hillery, p. 76.

52. Ralph R. Widner, "The First Three Years of the Appalachian Program: An Evaluation," *Appalachia*, Vol. 1, No. 11 (August, 1968), p. 19.

53. *Appalachian Regional Commission Annual Report, 1968*, pp. 24–25; *State and Regional Development Plans in Appalachia, 1968*, p. 12.

54. John W. Dyckman, "The Public and Private Rationale for a National Urban Policy," in S. B. Warner, Jr., ed., *Planning for a Nation of Cities* (Cambridge: The M.I.T. Press, 1966), p. 28.

Chapter 5

1. Public Law 90–103, Public Works and Economic Development Act of 1965, as Amended, October 11, 1967, Title V, Sec. 501.

2. Economic Development Administration, *Regional Economic Development in the United States*, Part 2 (Washington, D.C.: Government Printing Office, 1967), Section VI, p. 5.

3. Public Law 90–103, Title V, Sec. 504.

4. Ibid., Sec. 509.

5. *Ozarks Region* (Washington, D.C.: Ozarks Regional Commission, no date), pp. 9–11.

6. Marion Clawson, *Policy Directions for U.S. Agriculture* (Baltimore, Md.: Johns Hopkins Press, 1968), p. 21.

7. *Manpower Report of the President, 1968* (Washington, D.C.:

Government Printing Office, 1968), pp. 140–41; *Regional Economic Development in the United States,* Section VII, p. 21; *Ozarks Region,* p. 11.

8. *Ozarks Region,* pp. 1–2, 25–7.

9. Max F. Jordan and Lloyd D. Bender, *An Economic Survey of the Ozark Region,* Department of Agriculture Economic Research Service, Agricultural Economic Report No. 97 (Washington, D.C.: Government Printing Office, 1966), pp. vi, 10.

10. Ibid, p. vi.

11. Ibid., p. 64.

12. Statement of William M. McCandless, Federal Co-chairman, Ozarks Regional Commission, before the Special Subcommittee of the Senate Committee on Public Works, September 26, 1967. See also "Ozarks Commission Acts to Close Income Gap," *Economic Development,* Vol. 5, No. 8 (August, 1968), p. 1.

13. Bert L. Campbell, "Project Ozarka Hopes to Change Way of Life," *Louisville Courier-Journal,* December 25, 1967, p. C 11.

14. Statement of William M. McCandless, p. 9.

15. Ibid., p. 10.

16. Campbell, p. C 11.

17. Statement of William M. McCandless, p. 12.

18. Ibid., p. 13.

19. Ibid., pp. 14–5; *Ozarks Region,* pp. 19–20.

20. "Strategy for Development," Preliminary Report Oriented to Program of Supplemental Grants (Washington, D.C.: Upper Great Lakes Regional Commission, January, 1968), pp. 1–5.

21. Ibid., p. 4.

22. Ibid., p. 2; *Regional Economic Development in the United States,* Section VII, p. 35.

23. "Strategy for Development," pp. 3–5.

24. Ibid., pp. 23–5.

25. Ibid., pp. 25–6.

26. Ibid., p. 35.

27. *Regional Economic Development in the United States,* Section VII, p. 39.

28. Ibid., Section VII, p. 40.

29. Ibid., Section VII, pp. 38–9.

30. This report, "Manpower and Education in the Upper Great Lakes Region," by Elizabeth Rothman, is the basis for the remainder of this section.

31. This section is based on *Coastal Plains Economic Development*

Region, A Report on the Initial Action Planning Program of the Coastal Plains Regional Commission (Washington, D.C.: Coastal Plains Regional Commission, 1968); and on discussions with members of the Commission staff.

32. This section is based on *Regional Economic Development in the United States,* Section VII, pp. 25–32; and on discussions with members of the Commission staff.

33. The information in this section is based on preliminary reports of the Four Corners Regional Commission.

Chapter 6

1. Economic Development Administration, *Regional Economic Development in the United States,* Part 2 (Washington, D.C.: Government Printing Office, 1967), Section V, pp. 4–5. For a comprehensive critique of the ARA program see Sar A. Levitan, *Federal Aid to Depressed Areas* (Baltimore: Johns Hopkins Press, 1964).

2. U.S. Department of Commerce, Economic Development Administration, *EDA Handbook* (Washington, D.C.: Government Printing Office, 1968), p. 2.

3. Ibid., pp. 2–3.

4. Ibid., pp. 16–7.

5. Ibid., p. 17.

6. Ibid., p. 18.

7. Ibid., p. 19.

8. *1968 Progress Report of the Economic Development Administration* (Washington, D.C.: Government Printing Office, 1968), pp. 21, 128.

9. Ross D. Davis, "EDA Sets 'Worst First' Policy on Use of Funds," *Economic Development,* Vol. 4, No. 6 (June, 1967), pp. 1, 4.

10. *Economic Development Administration Annual Report, 1967* (Washington, D.C.: Government Printing Office, 1967), pp. 22–3.

11. Ibid., p. 23.

12. Ibid.

13. See Howard J. Samuels' statement on "Economic Development and the Problem of Rural-Urban Balance," in Joint Economic Committee, *The 1968 Economic Report of the President,* Hearings, Part 1, 90th Congress, 2nd session (Washington, D.C.: Government Printing Office, 1968), pp. 152–3. See also Ross D. Davis, "The New Approach to Solving Urban Unemployment," *Economic Development,* Vol. 4, No. 11 (November, 1967), p. 2.

14. Gerald L. Duskin and Ronald L. Moomaw, "Economic Development Centers: A Review," EDA Office of Economic Research Staff Paper, August, 1967, p. 7.

15. Brian J. L. Berry, "A Summary—Spatial Organization and Levels of Welfare: Degree of Metropolitan Labor Market Participation as a Variable in Economic Development," *Research Review* (June, 1968), pp. 1–6.

16. Ibid., p. 6.

17. Ibid.

18. Ibid.

19. These figures are computed from data supplied by EDA.

20. *Economic Development*, Vol. 4, No. 6 (June, 1967), p. 10.

21. Ross D. Davis, "A Look at Rural America," *Economic Development*, Vol. 4, No. 8 (August, 1967), p. 2.

22. Ross D. Davis, "Economic Development Program Scores Substantial Gains in First Two Years," *Economic Development*, Vol. 4, No. 9 (September, 1967), p. 3.

23. Edward Denison, *The Sources of Economic Growth in the United States and the Alternatives Before Us* (New York: Committee for Economic Development, 1962), p. 74.

24. Theodore Schultz, "Investment in Human Capital," *American Economic Review*, Vol. 51, No. 1 (March, 1961), p. 1.

25. George Iden, "Unemployment Classification of Major Labor Areas, 1950–65," *Journal of Human Resources*, Vol. 2, No. 3 (Summer, 1967), p. 391.

26. Gene Laber, "Unemployment Classification of Major Labor Areas, 1950–65: A Comment," *Journal of Human Resources*, Vol. 3, No. 4 (Fall, 1968), pp. 515–9.

Chapter 7

1. U.S. Department of the Interior, Bureau of Indian Affairs, *Answers to Your Questions About American Indians* (Washington, D.C.: Government Printing Office, 1968), pp. 2–3.

2. Ibid., p. 2.

3. Herbert E. Striner, "Toward a Fundamental Program for the Training, Employment and Economic Equality of the American Indian," in Joint Economic Committee, *Federal Programs for the Development of Human Resources*, Vol. 1, 90th Congress, 2nd Session (Washington, D.C.: Government Printing Office, 1968), p. 294.

4. *Answers to Your Questions . . . , p. 15.*

5. Ibid., pp. 15–6.
6. William A. Brophy and Sophie D. Aberle, *The Indian: America's Unfinished Business* (Norman, Okla.: University of Oklahoma Press, 1966), p. 4.
7. Striner, p. 296.
8. Brophy and Aberle, p. 63.
9. Striner, p. 298.
10. United States Department of Labor, *Manpower Report of the President, 1967* (Washington, D.C.: Government Printing Office, 1967), p. 63.
11. President's National Advisory Commission on Rural Poverty, *The People Left Behind* (Washington, D.C.: Government Printing Office, 1967), pp. 90–100.
12. *Answers to Your Questions . . .*, p. 30.
13. Ibid., pp. 23–5.
14. Striner, p. 299.
15. Ibid., p. 300.
16. Ibid., p. 300.
17. Ibid., p. 301.
18. Henry W. Hough, *Development of Indian Resources* (Denver: World Press, Inc., 1967), p. xiv.
19. Brophy and Aberle, pp. 20–2.
20. Striner, p. 293.
21. Ibid., p. 294.
22. Brophy and Aberle, p. 118.
23. Striner, pp. 301–2.
24. Bureau of Indian Affairs, *Indian Affairs, 1967* (Washington, D.C.: Government Printing Office, 1967), pp. 4–6.
25. Ibid., p. 15.
26. *Answers to Your Questions . . .*, p. 19.
27. Striner, p. 308.
28. Hough, pp. 189–206.
29. United States Department of Labor, *Manpower Report of the President, 1968* (Washington, D.C.: Government Printing Office, 1968), pp. 68–9.
30. Data were supplied by Ed Huizingh, Program Officer, Indian Desk, Economic Development Administration.
31. Striner, p. 309. See also Alan L. Sorkin, "American Indians Industrialize to Combat Poverty," *Monthly Labor Review,* Vol. 92, No. 3 (March, 1969), pp. 19–25.
32. Striner, pp. 309–20.

33. Unless otherwise indicated, this section is based on materials supplied to the author by the Bureau of Indian Affairs and on conversations with Bureau officials.

34. *Retraining and Migration as Factors in Regional Economic Development* (Madison, Wis.: University of Wisconsin Industrial Relations Research Institute, 1966), p. 12.

35. "A Followup Study of 1963 Recipients of the Services of the Employment Assistance Program, Bureau of Indian Affairs," Washington, D.C.: Bureau of Indian Affairs, 1966.

36. United States Department of the Interior, "Indians, Job Training and Placement Studies," Issue Support Paper No. 70–1, October 17, 1968, pp. 1–29.

37. Ibid., p. 75.

38. Ibid., p. 80.

39. Ibid., p. 81.

40. John A. Price, "The Migration and Adaptation of American Indians to Los Angeles," *Human Organization,* Vol. 27, No. 2 (Summer, 1968), p. 169.

41. Ibid., p. 170.

42. Ibid., p. 173.

Chapter 8

1. Celia S. Heller, *Mexican American Youth: Forgotten Youth at the Crossroads* (New York: Random House, 1966), p. 9.

2. Leo Grebler, *Mexican Immigration to the United States: The Record and Its Implications* (Los Angeles: U.C.L.A. Graduate School of Business Administration, Mexican-American Study Project, Advance Report No. 2, January, 1966), p. vii.

3. Ibid.

4. Joan W. Moore, *Mexican-Americans: Problems and Prospects* (Madison, Wis.: Institute for Research on Poverty, University of Wisconsin, 1967), p. 31.

5. *Manpower Report of the President, 1968* (Washington, D.C.: Government Printing Office, 1968), p. 66.

6. Ibid.

7. Walter Fogel, *Mexican Americans in Southwest Labor Markets* (Los Angeles: U.C.L.A. Graduate School of Business Administration, Mexican-American Study Project, Advance Report No. 10, October, 1967), pp. 19–20.

8. Moore, p. 35.

9. Fogel, pp. 98–9.

10. Robert F. Smith, "Employment and Economic Growth: Southwest," *Monthly Labor Review,* Vol. 91, No. 3 (March, 1968), p. 28.

11. Miguel Montes, "Need to Use HEW Funds to Secure Equal Educational Opportunity for the Mexican American," in *The Mexican American,* Testimony Presented at the Cabinet Committee Hearings on Mexican American Affairs, El Paso, Texas, October 26–28, 1967 (Washington, D.C.: Government Printing Office, 1968), p. 109.

12. Moore, p. 14.

13. Heller, pp. 39–41.

14. Moore, pp. 23, 26.

15. Smith, p. 28.

16. Moore, p. 29.

17. Fogel, pp. 32–3.

18. Elaine M. Krass, Claire Peterson, and Lyle W. Shannon, "Mexican-Americans and Negroes in a Northern Industrial Community," *Southwestern Social Science Quarterly,* Vol. 47, No. 3 (December, 1966), p. 244.

19. Walter Fogel, "The Effect of Low Educational Attainment on Incomes: A Comparative Study of Selected Ethnic Groups," *Journal of Human Resources,* Vol. 1, No. 2 (Fall, 1966), pp. 22–40.

20. Fogel, *Mexican Americans in Southwest Labor Markets,* p. 191.

21. Ibid., pp. 140, 192.

22. William Madsen, *The Mexican-Americans of South Texas* (New York: Holt, Rinehart and Winston, 1964), p. 13.

23. Grebler, p. 1.

24. Fogel, *Mexican Americans in Southwest Labor Markets,* p. 49.

25. Henry Munoz, Jr., "Labor Relations: The View of Organized Labor," in *The Mexican American,* p. 70.

26. Grebler, p. 63.

27. Ibid., pp. 63–4.

28. Ibid., pp. 93–5.

29. Ibid., p. 65.

30. Ibid., pp. 65–6.

31. Robert Sanchez, "Work Problems of the Mexican American," in *The Mexican American,* p. 92.

32. Grebler, p. 99.

33. Ernesto Galarza, "Rural Community Development," in *The Mexican American,* p. 3.

34. *The People Left Behind* (Washington, D.C.: Government Printing Office, 1967), p. 37.

35. Galarza, p. 2.

36. *Manpower Report of the President, 1968,* p. 209.

37. Fogel, *Mexican Americans in Southwest Labor Markets*, p. 107.

38. Ibid., p. 108.

39. Ibid., pp. 111–3.

40. Moore, p. 56.

41. Fogel, *Mexican Americans in Southwest Labor Markets*, p. 114.

42. Moore, p. 1.

43. Ibid., pp. 44–5.

44. Frank G. Mittelbach, Joan W. Moore, and Ronald McDaniel, *Intermarriage of Mexican-Americans* (Los Angeles: U.C.L.A. Graduate School of Business Administration, Mexican-American Study Project, Advance Report No. 6, November, 1966), p. 46.

45. Nancie L. Gonzalez, *The Spanish Americans of New Mexico: A Distinctive Heritage* (Los Angeles: U.C.L.A. Graduate School of Business Administration, Mexican-American Study Project, Advance Report No. 9, September, 1967), p. 122.

46. Madsen, p. 109.

47. Maclovio R. Barraza, "Labor Standards," in *The Mexican American*, p. 42.

48. Moore, p. 41.

49. George Roybal, "Manpower Programming and the Mexican American," in *The Mexican American*, p. 53.

50. *Manpower Report of the President, 1967*, p. 65.

51. Ibid.

52. For further institutional details concerning this project, see J. B. Andrasko, "Modular Training Concepts," in *The Mexican American*, pp. 65–7.

53. These data were supplied to the author by the Department of Labor and the Texas Employment Commission.

54. Andrasko, p. 66.

55. Data on participants were supplied by Professor David C. Ruesink of Texas A & M University. Data on rejected applicants were compiled by Mr. Honald N. Maidt in McAllen, Texas, at the request of the author.

56. Fogel, "The Effect of Low Educational Attainment on Incomes," p. 40.

Chapter 9

1. *Manpower Report of the President, 1968* (Washington, D.C.: Government Printing Office, 1968), p. 128.

2. Ibid., p. 139.

3. U.S. Department of Agriculture, *Communities of Tomorrow,*

Agriculture 2000 (Washington, D.C.: Government Printing Office, 1968).

4. Ibid., p. 5.

5. Ibid.

6. See Niles M. Hansen, *French Regional Planning* (Bloomington: Indiana University Press, 1968), pp. 16–7 and Chapter 2; and "The Structure and Determinants of Local Public Investment Expenditures," *Review of Economics and Statistics,* Vol. XLVII, No. 2 (May, 1965), pp. 150–62.

7. *Communities of Tomorrow,* p. 5.

8. Ibid.

9. Ibid., p. 7.

10. Ibid., p. 17.

11. Ibid.

12. Gene Laber, "Unemployment Classification of Major Labor Areas, 1950–65: A Comment," *Journal of Human Resources,* Vol. 3, No. 4 (Fall, 1968), p. 519.

13. William H. Nicholls, *Southern Tradition and Regional Progress* (Chapel Hill: University of North Carolina Press, 1960), pp. 13–4.

14. *The People Left Behind* (Washington, D.C.: Government Printing Office, 1967).

15. Ibid., p. 19.

16. Ibid.

17. Ibid., p. xiii. Emphasis supplied.

18. Ibid., p. 23.

19. Ibid., p. ix.

20. Ibid., p. 115.

21. Ibid., pp. 113–4.

22. Ibid.

23. Ibid., pp. 115–6.

24. Hansen, *French Regional Planning,* pp. 62–71.

25. These values are based on provisional data in Projet de loi de finances pour 1968, annexe, *Statistiques et indicateurs des régions françaises* (Paris: Imprimerie Nationale, 1968), p. 70.

26. Gustav Schachter, *The Italian South* (New York: Random House, 1965), p. 193.

27. Benjamin Higgins, *Economic Development,* revised edition, (New York: W. W. Norton and Co., 1968), p. 788.

28. Ibid., pp. 788–9.

29. Ibid., p. 789.

30. See, for example, H. Krier, *Rural Manpower and Industrial Development* (Paris: Organization for Economic Cooperation and De-

velopment, 1961), p. 82; and Jonathan Lindley, James W. Walker, and William J. Dircks, "Changes in Location of Employment and Opportunity: Implications for National Policy," Paper given at the conference on The Rural to Urban Population Shift—A National Problem, Oklahoma State University, Stillwater, Oklahoma, May 17, 1968, p. 17.

31. Victor Fuchs, *The Growing Importance of the Service Industries* (New York: National Bureau of Economic Research Occasional Paper No. 96, 1965); and *Changes in the Location of Manufacturing in the United States Since 1929* (New Haven: Yale University Press, 1962). See also Erling Olsen, "Erhvervslivets Lokalisering," *Nationaløkonomisk Tidsskrift* [Denmark] (Nos. 1–2, 1965), pp. 18–30.

32. Wilbur R. Thompson, "Internal and External Factors in the Development of Urban Economies," in Harvey S. Perloff and Lowden Wingo, Jr., *Issues in Urban Economics* (Baltimore: The Johns Hopkins Press, 1968), p. 53.

33. John E. Parker and Lois B. Shaw, "Labor Force Participation Within Metropolitan Areas," *Southern Economic Journal,* Vol. 34, No. 4 (April, 1968), pp. 538–47.

34. George H. Borts, "The Equalization of Returns and Regional Economic Growth," *American Economic Review,* Vol. 50, No. 2 (June, 1960), pp. 319–45.

35. Philippe Aydalot, "Note sur les économies externes et quelques notions connexes," *Revue économique* (November, 1965), pp. 962–8.

36. Fuchs, *The Growing Importance . . . ,* pp. 1–2, 17–9.

37. Raymond Vernon, *The Changing Economic Function of the Central City* (New York: Committee for Economic Development, 1959), p. 35.

38. Jean Gottmann, "The Rising Demand for Urban Amenities," in S. B. Warner, Jr., ed., *Planning for a Nation of Cities* (Cambridge: The M.I.T. Press, 1966), p. 168.

39. Ibid., p. 170.

40. Joseph J. Spengler, "Some Determinants of the Manpower Prospect, 1966–1985," in Irving H. Siegal, ed., *Manpower Tomorrow: Prospects and Priorities* (New York: Augustus M. Kelley, 1967), p. 91. See also J. Beaujeu-Garnier and G. Chabot, *Urban Geography* (New York: John Wiley and Sons, 1967), p. 162.

41. Edgar M. Hoover, "Some Old and New Issues in Regional Development," University of Pittsburgh Center for Regional Economic Studies Occasional Paper No. 5, 1967, pp. 12–3.

42. John Friedmann, *Regional Development Policy: A Case Study of Venezuela* (Cambridge: The M.I.T. Press, 1966), p. 28.

43. Economic Development Administration, *Industrial Location as a Factor in Regional Economic Development* (Washington, D.C.: Government Printing Office, 1967), pp. 23–4.

44. Harvey S. Perloff, with Vera Dodds, *How a Region Grows* (New York: Committee for Economic Development, 1963), p. 24.

45. *The People Left Behind,* p. 103.

46. Ibid.

47. Perloff, *How a Region Grows,* pp. 137–8.

48. These data were sent to the author by Peter M. Stern, Director of Regional Studies, Tennessee Valley Authority, Knoxville, Tennessee.

49. *The People Left Behind,* p. 114.

50. Ibid., p. 22.

Chapter 10

1. Jean Gottmann, "A Vision of the Future of the Urban Environment," *Papers and Proceedings of the International Symposium on Regional Development* (Hakone, Japan: Japan Center for Area Development Research, 1967), p. 53.

2. Hans Blumenfeld, "The Modern Metropolis," in *Cities* (New York, Alfred Knopf, 1965), pp. 48–9.

3. Subcommittee on Urban Affairs of the Joint Economic Committee, *Urban America: Goals and Problems,* 90th Congress, 1st Session (Washington, D.C.: Government Printing Office, 1967), p. 9.

4. David F. Darwent, *Growth Pole and Growth Center Concepts: A Review, Evaluation and Bibliography,* University of California (Berkeley) Center for Planning and Development Research Working Paper No. 89, October, 1968, pp. 44–5.

5. William Alonso, "Urban and Regional Imbalances in Economic Development," *Economic Development and Cultural Change,* Vol. 17, No. 1 (October, 1968), pp. 1–14.

6. Edgar M. Hoover, "The Evolving Form and Organization of the Metropolis," in Harvey S. Perloff and Lowden Wingo, Jr., *Issues in Urban Economics* (Baltimore: The Johns Hopkins Press, 1968), p. 268. See also Kevin Lynch, "The City as Environment," in *Cities,* pp. 192–201.

7. Edgar M. Hoover, *Some Old and New Issues in Regional Development,* University of Pittsburgh Center for Regional Economic Studies Occasional Paper No. 5, 1967, p. 6.

8. René Dubos, "Promises and Hazards of Man's Adaptability," in

Henry Jarrett, ed., *Environmental Quality in a Growing Economy* (Baltimore: The Johns Hopkins Press, 1966), pp. 27–9, 38.

9. See Edward Higbee, *The Squeeze: Cities Without Space* (New York: William Morrow, 1960), pp. 9–10.

10. "Stress Is Called Population Curb," *New York Times,* September 22, 1963, p. 79.

11. Kingsley Davis, "The Urbanization of Human Population," in *Cities,* p. 23.

12. See Niles M. Hansen, *French Regional Planning* (Bloomington: Indiana University Press, 1968), Chapter 1.

13. G. M. Neutze, *Economic Policy and the Size of Cities* (New York: Augustus M. Kelley, 1967), pp. 109–10.

14. See Hansen, pp. 34-7.

15. Alain Girard and Henri Bastide, "Les problèmes démographiques devant l'opinion," *Population,* Vol. 15 (April–May, 1960), p. 287.

16. Robert L. Wilson, "Livability of the City: Attitudes and Urban Development," in F. Stuart Chapin, Jr., and Shirley F. Weiss, eds., *Urban Growth Dynamics* (New York: John Wiley and Sons, 1962), pp. 359–99.

17. Ibid., p. 398.

18. John Gulick, Charles E. Bowerman, and Kurt W. Back, "Newcomer Enculturation in the City: Attitudes and Participation," in Chapin and Weiss, eds., *Urban Growth Dynamics,* pp. 356–7.

19. Cited in a speech by Secretary of Agriculture Orville Freeman before the Conference on Rural-Oriented Industry, Washington, D.C., May 13, 1968.

20. *Wall Street Journal,* March 24, 1969, p. 1.

21. Ibid.

22. Neutze, p. 27.

23. Davis, p. 23. An extended discussion of the economic and social impact of urbanization trends is found in Advisory Commission on Intergovernmental Relations, *Urban and Rural America: Policies for Future Growth* (Washington, D.C.: Government Printing Office, 1968), pp. XV, 54–61.

24. See *Economic Report of the President* (Washington, D.C.: Government Printing Office, 1969), p. 178.

25. Brian J. L. Berry, "A Summary—Spatial Organization and Levels of Welfare: Degree of Metropolitan Labor Market Participation as a Variable in Economic Development," *Research Review* (July, 1968), pp. 1–6.

26. Wilbur R. Thompson, *A Preface to Urban Economics* (Baltimore: The Johns Hopkins Press, 1965), p. 24.

27. Neutze, pp. 103, 109–18.

28. Ibid., pp. 117–8.

29. Werner Z. Hirsch, "The Supply of Urban Public Services," in Perloff and Wingo, eds., pp. 509–11.

30. Jonathan Lindley, "The Economic Environment and Urban Development," A paper presented to the Eighth Annual Conference, Center for Economic Projections, National Planning Association, April 28, 1967, p. 17.

31. Benjamin Higgins, *Economic Development*, revised edition (New York: W. W. Norton and Co., 1968), p. 468.

32. F. Stuart Chapin, Jr., "Policy Implications of Research Findings," in Chapin and Weiss, eds., *Urban Growth Dynamics*, p. 472.

33. John Lansing and Eva Mueller, *The Geographic Mobility of Labor* (Ann Arbor, Mich.: University of Michigan Survey Research Center, 1967), p. 24.

34. Ibid., pp. 72, 77, 312–3.

35. Ibid., p. 322.

36. Ibid., p. 345.

37. Ibid., p. 300.

38. Dale E. Hathaway and Brian E. Perkins, "Occupational Mobility and Migration From Agriculture," in *Rural Poverty in the United States*, a Report by the President's National Advisory Commission on Rural Poverty (Washington, D.C.: Government Printing Office, 1968), pp. 185–237.

39. Ibid., p. 212.

40. Ibid.

41. Ibid., pp. 212–3.

42. Theodore W. Schultz, "National Employment, Skills, and Earnings of Farm Labor," in C. E. Bishop, ed., *Farm Labor in the United States* (New York: Columbia University Press, 1967), p. 56.

43. Garth L. Mangum, *Reorienting Vocational Education*, University of Michigan and Wayne State University Institute of Labor and Industrial Relations, Policy Papers in Human Resources and Industrial Relations No. 7, 1968, p. 11.

44. Marion Clawson, *Policy Directions For U.S. Agriculture* (Baltimore: The Johns Hopkins Press, 1968), p. 47.

45. Peter M. Blau and Otis Dudley Duncan, *The American Occupational Structure* (New York: John Wiley and Sons, 1967), p. 410.

46. Harvey S. Perloff, with Vera Dodds, *How a Region Grows* (New York: Committee for Economic Development, 1963), pp. 137–41.

47. Ibid., pp. 140–1.

48. John B. Parr, "Outmigration and the Depressed Area Problem," *Land Economics*, Vol. 42, No. 2 (May, 1966), pp. 149–59.

49. Lowell E. Gallaway, "Labor Mobility, Resource Allocation, and Structural Unemployment," *American Economic Review*, Vol. 53, No. 4 (September, 1963), p. 713.

50. Wilbur R. Thompson, "Urban Economics," in H. Wentworth Eldridge, *Taming Megalopolis*, Vol. 1 (Garden City, N.Y.: Doubleday Anchor Books, 1967), p. 170.

51. Gerald G. Somers, "The Returns to Geographic Mobility: A Symposium," *Journal of Human Resources*, Vol. 2, No. 4 (Fall, 1967), pp. 428–9.

52. Blau and Duncan, pp. 409–10.

53. John F. Kain, "Postwar Changes in Land Use in the American City," Harvard University Program on Regional and Urban Economics Discussion Paper No. 24 (November, 1967), pp. 10–1.

54. Dorothy K. Newman, "The Negro's Journey to the City—Part II," *Monthly Labor Review*, Vol. 88, No. 6 (June, 1965), pp. 644–9.

55. John F. Kain, "Housing Segregation, Negro Employment, and Metropolitan Decentralization," *Quarterly Journal of Economics*, Vol. 82, No. 2 (May, 1968), pp. 175–97.

56. John F. Kain and Joseph J. Persky, "Alternatives to the Gilded Ghetto," Harvard University Program on Regional and Urban Economics Discussion Paper No. 21 (February, 1968), p. 4–5.

57. Ibid., pp. 18–9.

58. Ibid., pp. 19–25.

59. Eli Ginzberg, *The Development of Human Resources* (New York: McGraw-Hill, 1966), p. 237. See also Theodore W. Schultz, p. 62.

60. This position is also taken in Kain and Persky, "Alternatives to the Gilded Ghetto," pp. 25–32.

61. Emory F. Via, "Discrimination, Integration, and Job Equality," *Monthly Labor Review*, Vol. 91, No. 3 (March, 1968), p. 83.

62. Ibid., p. 84.

63. Bureau of the Census, *Population Characteristics, Negro Population, March, 1964*, Series P–20, No. 142, October 11, 1965, Table 1.

64. Bureau of the Census, *Population Characteristics, Negro Population, March 1967*, Series P–20, No. 175, October 23, 1968, Table 4.

Chapter 11

1. R. A. Gordon, "Introduction," in Robert Aaron Gordon, ed.,

Toward a Manpower Policy (New York: John Wiley and Sons, 1967), p. 7.

2. Arthur M. Ross, "Conclusions," in Arthur M. Ross, ed., *Unemployment and the American Economy* (New York: John Wiley and Sons, 1964), p. 207.

3. C. E. Bishop, "The Need for Improved Mobility Policy," in Joint Economic Committee, *Federal Programs for the Development of Human Resources,* 90th Congress, 2nd Session (Washington, D.C.: Government Printing Office, 1968), p. 223.

4. President's National Advisory Commission on Rural Poverty, *The People Left Behind* (Washington, D. C.: Government Printing Office, 1967), pp. 35–6.

5. Ibid., p. 39.

6. Wilbur R. Thompson, *A Preface to Urban Economics* (Baltimore: The Johns Hopkins Press, 1965), pp. 189–90.

7. Ibid., p. 213.

8. Ibid., p. 217.

9. Ibid., p. 216.

10. See Bernhard Scher, "The War on Poverty in West Virginia: National Program and Regional Realities," in Rosa Wessel, ed., *Journal of Social Work Processes,* Vol. 16 (Philadelphia: University of Pennsylvania Press, 1967), pp. 53–68.

11. *International Differences in Factors Affecting Labour Mobility* (Geneva, Switzerland: International Labour Office, 1965).

12. Jack Steiber, "Discussion," in Robert Aaron Gordon, ed., p. 38.

13. *Programs for Relocating Workers Used by Governments of Selected Countries,* Joint Economic Committee, Congress of the United States (Washington, D.C.: Government Printing Office, 1966), pp. 75–6.

14. Sol Swerdloff, "Sweden's Manpower Programs," *Monthly Labor Review,* Vol. 89, No. 1 (January, 1966), pp. 1–2.

15. Ibid., p. 2.

16. Ibid.

17. Carl G. Uhr, "Recent Swedish Labor Market Policies," in Garth L. Mangum, ed., *The Manpower Revolution* (Garden City, N.Y.: Doubleday Anchor Books, 1966), p. 377.

18. Swerdloff, pp. 5–6.

19. Uhr, p. 377.

20. Unless otherwise indicated, this section is based on information in *Moving To Work* (Washington, D.C.: Labor Mobility Services Unit, United States Employment Service, 1968).

21. Audrey Freedman, "Labor Mobility Projects for the Unemployed," *Monthly Labor Review*, Vol. 91, No. 6 (June, 1968), pp. 61–2.

22. Freedman's more reliable analysis of fiscal year 1967 shows that financial assistance for all projects amounted to $383 per family relocated. Ibid., p. 59.

23. Ibid., p. 61.

24. *The AFL-CIO Platform Proposals* (Washington, D.C.: AFL-CIO, 1968), pp. 8–9.

25. Ibid., p. 9.

26. Frank H. Cassell, *The Public Employment Service: Organization in Change* (Ann Arbor, Mich.: Academic Publications, 1968), p. 149.

27. Melvin Lurie and Elton Rayack, "Racial Differences in Migration and Job Search: A Case Study," *Southern Economic Journal*, Vol. 23, No. 1 (July, 1966), p. 93.

28. Arnold L. Nemore and Garth L. Mangum, *Reorienting the Federal-State Employment Service*, Policy Papers in Human Resources and Industrial Relations, No. 8 (Ann Arbor, Mich.: Institute of Labor and Industrial Relations, May, 1968), p. 66.

29. Ibid., p. 67.

30. *Job Vacancy Statistics,* Hearings Before the Subcommittee on Economic Statistics of the Joint Economic Committee, Congress of the United States, 89th Congress, 2nd Session (Washington, D.C.: Government Printing Office, 1966), pp. 8–9.

31. John T. Dunlop, "Job Vacancy Measures and Economic Analysis," in *The Measurement and Interpretation of Job Vacancies,* A Conference Report of the National Bureau of Economic Research (New York: Columbia University Press, 1966), p. 45.

32. Ibid., p. 47.

33. Cassell, pp. 153–4.

34. Freedman, p. 57.

35. Ibid., p. 62.

Chapter 12

1. For a review of French efforts along these lines see Niles M. Hansen, *French Regional Planning* (Bloomington: Indiana University Press, 1968).

2. A regional commission could be established for each of the largest SMSA's, since they include lagging areas (the ghettos) and rapidly developing areas (the suburbs). Some of these commissions would be multistate in nature while others would not.

Index of Names

349

Index of Subjects